WORKLESS

WORKLESS

WORKLESS
An Exploration of the Social Contract Between Society and the Worker

DENNIS MARSDEN

Revised and enlarged edition

CROOM HELM   LONDON

© 1982 Dennis Marsden
Croom Helm Ltd, 2-10 St John's Road, London SW11.

British Library Cataloguing in Publication Data

Marsden, Dennis
    Workless. - Rev. and enlarged ed.
    1. Unemployed - Great Britain - Cases
    I. Title
    331.13'7941   HD5767

ISBN 0-7099-1723-6

Printed and bound in Great Britain by
Biddles Ltd, Guildford and King's Lynn

Contents

For my father, Arnold Marsden

Preface to the Second Edition

This edition of *Workless* contains all our original interviews with the unemployed, although unfortunately rising costs have prevented reprinting of the photographs taken by Euan Duff which appeared in the first edition. However, his contribution has been lasting, from his first conception of the book, through the many discussions we had about unemployment and the workless people we met.

The opportunity of republication has been used to bring up to date the discussion of Britain's unemployment crisis, and here I gratefully acknowledge an increasing debt to Adrian Sinfield and Peter Townsend. This general discussion now appears as the last section of the book, and some readers may wish to begin there; although we ourselves did not start from an elaborate framework of questions and the book is really an exploration of issues which emerged from what the workless told us.

Dennis Marsden
Wivenhoe

'When I first saw unemployed men at close quarters, the thing that horrified and amazed me was to find that many of them were *ashamed* of being unemployed. I was very ignorant, but not so ignorant as to imagine that when the loss of foreign markets pushes two million men out of work, those two million are any more to blame than the people who draw blanks in the Calcutta Sweep. But at that time nobody cared to admit that unemployment was inevitable, because that meant that it would probably continue. The middle classes were still talking about "lazy idle loafers on the dole" and saying that "these men could all find work if they wanted to", and naturally these opinions percolated to the working class themselves. I remember the shock of astonishment it gave me, when I first mingled with tramps and beggars, to find that a fair proportion, perhaps a quarter of these beings whom I had been taught to regard as cynical parasites, were decent young miners and cotton workers gazing at their destiny with the same sort of dumb amazement as an animal in a trap. They simply could not understand what was happening to them. They had been brought up to work and behold! it seemed as if they were never going to have the chance of working again. In their circumstances it was inevitable, at first, that they should be haunted by a feeling of personal degradation. That was the attitude towards unemployment in those days: it was a disaster which happened to *you* as an individual and for which you were to blame.'

- George Orwell, *The Road to Wigan Pier*, 1937

1 Introduction: an Exploration of the Social Contract in Work

This is a revised version of a book originally written in response to the shock of the news that unemployment had risen above one million. Now there are two and a half million workless people, one in ten of the workforce, with predictions of three million unemployed by the winter of 1981/2, and even five million during the present decade. So our original questions have become all the more urgent. What are the burdens, the social costs of unemployment? What is it like to be workless today, compared with the experiences described by Orwell in the 1930s?

We talked to a range of unemployed people (mostly men but including some women) who had had contrasting work histories and who lived in widely separated parts of the country. Most of them were married with children, and they spoke about the work they had lost, their marriages and family life, their relationships in the community and with official agencies, and their daily routines and activities. We also visited workers on two programmes where work was subsidized by the State; teenagers on one of the early job creation projects and disabled workers in a sheltered workshop.

People who are 'workless' spend their days in very different ways. Some continue with activities very like the work they have lost; some men do a housewife's job, looking after the children while their wives work; others use the time to fulfil their individual creativity, perhaps in making pictures or writing; and still others satisfy their idealism by carrying out unpaid community work. A few do nothing. At first glance a number of the families seem to have enough money to manage on, and relationships appear cosy; but there are also couples who fight like cat and dog, quarrelling openly over money. The workless may lead isolated and lonely lives, or alternatively they may spend much of their time in the company of friends who are also unemployed. Some search cheerfully and hopefully for work; others chafe bitterly and angrily at the constraints of unemployment; others work illegally at small jobs which seem to act as a kind of safety valve for their energies and the various pressures they experience. There are a few who seem to welcome the chance to remain out of work. But there are also those who despair.

What can we hope to learn from a closer look at the lives of workless individuals? Clearly we will discover no grand economic recipes for curing unemployment; although our book is about the values and motives which underly economic policy. It seems obvious that if we want to find out about the meaning and importance of unemployment and work in society we should talk to those who have lost their jobs, yet surprisingly this has seldom been done. Our aim, therefore, is to give some of the workless themselves a voice in the discussions and arguments which affect them so closely and threaten their welfare. We seek to show that in any attempt to solve the economic problems of society as a whole, the burden of the social costs which weigh on the workless minority must be a major concern.

Since 1975, when we first published this book, there has been more evidence about the plight of the unemployed, for social change has cast behind itself the shadow of research.[1] But rises in the numbers and financial cost of the unemployed, and the threatened closures of British Leyland and British Steel, and the actual shut-down of plants such as the Consett steel works and the Linwood car factory, have not brought a unified policy or pressures to restore full employment. In comparison with the 1930s, right up to the sudden onset of the city-centre riots in 1981, the workless and the public have remained remarkably quiet and undemanding. And indeed there has been a growing sense that work for all is an unattainable goal.

WORTHLESS?

A kind of public 'schizophrenia' has developed where, as concern mounts with rising levels of unemployment, there is strong criticism of the workless as individuals: the workless tend to be viewed as worthless. This is because, in a society founded on the Protestant work ethic, work is seen as a moral duty, and we tend to value people who work and look down on those who do not. It is suggested that many of the unemployed are not genuine; they are too well-supported by the State so that they do not look hard enough for work; they should be prepared to take the jobs on offer, to accept lower wages, or to move to find work. Of all the myths of the Welfare State, stories of the 'work-shy' and 'scroungers' have been the least well-founded on evidence, yet they have proved the most persistent.

The workless are seen as expendable and, as a result, it is now confidently argued that government intervention to lower the level of unemployment is neither possible nor desirable. Society must accept a future where unemployment levels are higher, at a 'natural' level determined solely by the operation of the profit motive in a 'free' market. Unemployment, if not an act of God, has come to be seen as the act of the god in the economic machine.

What is now at issue is the right to work, and this raises deeper questions about the role of work in holding together the very fabric of society. We need to know what part work does and should play in the moral 'social contract' which binds individuals to the community in which they live. To what extent can and must work be regarded as a duty and a service, performed by the worker for society and made secure for the worker by the State, with subsidies if necessary? For if those who are workless lose status, esteem and

2

their own self-respect, is it enough to provide merely financial compensation for unemployment? Don't the unemployed really need work itself?

Through our interviews we have tried to explore the attitudes of the workless towards finding work not simply as a search for cash, but as a quest for meaningful activity, for security, autonomy, a sense of worth and a satisfying social identity. We ask to what extent does the performance of work express a sense of duty to some entity wider than a particular firm, to society itself.

WORK LESS?

But perhaps people should be happy to work less. As unemployment has risen, another line of argument in favour of higher unemployment has become stronger. Why can't we see unemployment as valuable leisure, as opportunity; in Ivan Illich's phrases, as 'useful unemployment', as 'glad' rather than 'sad' idleness? [2] For it is obviously too idealistic to pretend that all work can be pleasurable, rewarding and genuinely productive. Rather than a fulfilling social duty, much work is badly-paid, unnecessary, even harmful, limiting, dirty, dangerous, monotonous, boring or lonely. The appearance of larger numbers of workless people has raised interesting questions about why many people work at the inferior jobs which are all that society affords them. What happens when these individuals are dislodged from menial work by unemployment?

In our interviews we have kept in mind the possibility that unemployment might offer a release, an opportunity to explore and expand areas of the personality and capacities not fulfilled in conventional work. What do people do when they are out of work? Do they exercise a choice? Are the voluntary activities of some 'workless' individuals an oblique comment on the priorities and values of our society, carrying perhaps pointers to the future? Are the unemployed really all 'workless', or are they only workless in so far as our society pays them to do 'nothing' and defines what they actually choose to do as not real work and not worthy of payment?

Presentation of the interviews is divided into four main parts. In Part One the workless remember their experiences of work, and talk about the search for new jobs. In Part Two they discuss the help they have received, in their search for work and with financial needs, from the State and from relatives and friends. They also describe the pressures which they felt pushing them back into work. In Part Three we look at the different ways in which they coped with their failure to find suitable or acceptable work. At the end of Part Three we provide a postscript on the individuals we interviewed who regained work during the period of this study; and alongside their experiences we include descriptions of work by teenagers working in subsidized community

3

service after they had experienced a spell of unemployment, and by disabled workers in a subsidized sheltered workshop, some of whom had the real option of not working if they wished to take it. In Part Four we discuss what the workless, and we ourselves, learn from their experiences of work and unemployment about the importance of work and the way that the social contract is expressed through working. We ask, on the basis of our interviews, who breaks the social contract between society and the worker?

Part Five has been freshly written to bring up to date the rapidly changing picture of Britain's unemployment crisis, and to analyze the retreat from full employment which is now such a tragic feature of economic policy. First we focus on the paradox which we have called public schizophrenia, the persistent tendency to blame the workless and to say they are work-shy or unemployable at a time when there is mass unemployment; and we give an estimate of the true scale of the unemployment problem which takes into account the social need for work. Next we show how these ideas about the workless are embedded in classical economics and the ideology of the 'free market', which are an integral part of the traditional policy orthodoxy in Britain. Classical economic policies have once again come to the fore because of their basic appeal to selfishness, in a society which is unequal and divided by the threat of a decline in living standards; and hostile attitudes towards the workless can persist because the heaviest burden of unemployment is borne by only a relatively small minority. Finally, we discuss the limits of the economic, social, political and moral vision of traditional free market policies, in relation to the deep historical and structural roots of Britain's unemployment crisis. We argue that Britain's economic fortunes can only be repaired by establishing a social contract in society through work.

FINDING THE WORKLESS: THE DESIGN OF THIS STUDY

Of course it is only through large-scale surveys that we can gain an overall picture of inequalities in society,[3] but we were looking for accounts of individual experiences to fill out the larger picture. We wanted a range of interviews which would offer a coherent if incomplete 'mental map' of situations and feelings which are shared by many of the workless.[4]

We chose to interview mainly men in the prime of their working lives with families, to explore changes of relationship within the family group. But we also talked to the wives who were both employed and unemployed. We believe that 'external' pressures to work are stronger for men than for women, although women themselves have increasingly shown their desire to work, and they now face a more complex problem of wanting to work in opposition to the view, which is growing in the present recession, that they should stay at home.[5] The situation of 'the man as housewife and mother' was further explored with a widowed father who was caring for his family.

Type of work and levels of social security benefits make a difference to responses to unemployment. So in the south-east, where unemployment was comparatively low, we interviewed redundant, never previously unemployed, skilled workers. We also interviewed a new graduate who was not yet securely established in work. As a contrast, we looked for the stereotype of the unemployed man, the less-skilled workers in the forgotten north-east, where unemployment was much higher. Broadly speaking, this polarity, which tends to emphasize differences by running together the contrasts of skill and region, is followed in the presentation throughout the book and epitomizes a major dimension of inequality in unemployment.

Our emphasis on the family means that the old and the young, who are now increasingly likely to suffer unemployment, are not as central to our study, although we did interview a chronically sick older man and some teenagers. In addition we visited two non-profit making organizations where work was explicitly seen as the provision of a service for the young, and for the physically and mentally handicapped. In one scheme unemployed teenagers were being set to work partly at the government's expense to decorate old people's houses, to dig gardens, and to do other work with a more or less unusual element of value to the community. In the other scheme, conventional factory work, some of it skilled but much of it repetitive and uninteresting, was provided in a sheltered, subsidized environment as an occupation and rehabilitation, and in a deliberate attempt to give working status to the handicapped. These workers, had they chosen, could have stayed at home and received an allowance, although this would usually have meant a lower income.

We obtained our main interviews from a number of sources which are described later as the individuals appear.[6] Only one person was previously known to us, and we were able to interview about four-fifths of the people we approached. We believe that our book reveals what a variety of changes of morale, flexibility and creativity can be found among quite a small random group of people.

We interviewed couples together and apart, as the opportunity afforded. Separately, individuals would confess to feelings which they might keep from their spouses, the most striking example being a man who would not let us meet his wife whom he was trying to protect from the impact of unemployment. On the other hand when couples were together the opinions or versions of events offered by one would provoke disagreement, discussion or conflict with the other which could be highly illuminating.

We were able to interview a few of the families at intervals over a period of time to see how their situation changed, and some people found work during the period of our study. Interestingly, then they were sometimes able to be more frank about fears they had tended to suppress while they were unemployed.

We tried to reassure the families of privacy: no recording was done until attention had been drawn to the tape recorder; the names in the text are false. Systematic lying would have been difficult to keep up in this type of interview, and we had some checks in evidence from spouses and from other people present at some of the interviews, as well as in the overall consistency of responses by individuals who did not know one another. Photographs were taken on a separate occasion, often beginning with a visit before breakfast and continuing through the day, and Euan Duff's visits provided interesting extra valuable checks and information, on daily routines (including fiddling) and informal official contacts, of a kind not usually available to an interviewer who tends to stay for a relatively shorter time in a more formal setting.

In our search for the less-skilled unemployed we experienced a curious and significant difficulty which revealed that we must be on the work side of a social and mental curtain between the workers and the workless. Who would suppose that with one million unemployed we should initially find it difficult to locate a handful of not too strictly defined families for interview, especially in a high unemployment area like the north-east? Yet people like the union officials whom we first approached said they knew of no genuinely unemployed men; 'You might find a few layabouts, not really unemployed men, men who don't want to work, if you go to such and such a pub, or over there at the other side of the estate.'

Being thrown out of work seemed to alter social relationships and to make people less accessible. As in the national debates, there was a sort of mental barrier which defined many of the unemployed as disreputable, and friends and neighbours, relatives and workmates, might be that bit reluctant to disclose to strangers the slightly shameful fact of an individual's unemployment.

In the end we entered the world of the less-skilled workers in the north-east in the most tenuous of ways. A personal friend told us of a meeting some time previously with the sister of a man who was unemployed. Through the sister we located the man who agreed to be interviewed but subsequently, very apologetically, said that he would not 'feel right' being photographed. But from this moment we found ourselves at the centre of an ever-expanding set of overlapping networks of unemployed men, where we could have obtained many more respondents than we could possibly interview. A further instance will underline the point. We entered another network, in a different place, by approaching a youth-club leader, who spoke to a vicar, who contacted a parishioner whose son was unemployed, and the son agreed to be interviewed (proving, in spite of our line of approach, to be among the more 'disreputable' of our informants). During the interview the son's friend, also unemployed, called in and after about ten minutes he trusted us enough to pass on information about the neighbours: 'There's Willy, there's me, there's Mary; I think Mr Jones is cut

off - there's loads of lads round here that have got their electric
cut off because they can't pay their bills. Everybody here's on
the dole. I'm on the dole, Tom's on the dole' (pointing to houses
now). 'She's got nae husband, she's got nae husband - by! it's
great round here! - there's Jimmy's on the dole, the man next
door's on the dole, there's two lasses over there, all young girls
on the dole. Mr Stratford's on the dole. Mr Harvey's permanent
sick, isn't he, he's on the dole. They're all on the dole round
here man.'

So, at a precise moment, after a somewhat frustrating and
baffling search, we experienced the sense of passing through a
curtain from work into the world of the workless. Through the
daily lives of the workless men and their wives which are
described in this book, we hope we can communicate to the
reader a similar experience.

NOTES

1 In the revised section of this book we have drawn heavily on
   the most comprehensive and up to date discussion and biblio-
   graphy in B. Showler and A. Sinfield (eds.), *The Workless
   State*, Martin Robertson, 1981; and A. Sinfield, *What Unemployment Means*, Martin Robertson, 1981.
2 I. Illich, *The Right to Useful Unemployment*, Boyars, 1978.
3 See, for example, P. Townsend, *Poverty in the United Kingdom*,
   Penguin, 1979; and, for the workless, W.W. Daniel, *A National
   Survey of the Unemployed*, P.E.P., 1974; and the D.H.S.S.
   Cohort study of 2,300 men unemployed in 1978, *Employment
   Gazette*, August 1980. See also the new 8,000 cohort study
   from the Policy Studies Institute, *Guardian*, 19 May 1981, to
   be published.
4 A rationale for such a study design is given in B.G. Glaser
   and A.L. Straus, *The Discovery of Grounded Theory*, Chicago,
   Adeline, 1967.
5 See, for example, Lynda Chalker M.P., *Guardian*, 16 October
   1978. We have excized as much as we could of the sexist
   exposition which now appears so blatant in the first edition
   of *Workless*. See also M. Campbell in *Guardian*, 19 May 1981.
6 We rejected approaches to people in benefit queues, or knocking
   on doors, as too official or haphazard, and instead we used
   trade unions, newspaper reports of closures, claimants'
   unions and the procedure outlined later in the Introduction.

Part One:
WORK LOST

2 Work Remembered

This chapter introduces the workless through their memories of the work they had lost, for to begin to understand the meaning of being workless we must first ask what was the meaning retained by work. There is space for only short versions of work histories which were sometimes very long and complex, and we can say little about the men's early lives or (in this chapter) about their home lives. Nevertheless, we hope we have included enough to show how the men had approached work, what they had tried to make of it, and how much they themselves had been moulded by their work experiences.

We adopt the sequence which we will try to follow throughout the book. The work histories begin with accounts by redundant skilled workers who had seemed more securely established in work with better contracts. We then move to more fluctuating careers where the lives of the less-skilled men, and their security and commitment, had been more subject to the vagaries of the economy and to personal conflict and misfortune. The sequence ends with those who seem to be 'dropping-out' of the world of work.

Mr Vickers, Mr Fellowes and Mr Haigh

We have here combined the experiences of three men who were all made redundant by the same firm. Their names were given to us by their union. All were alert, and seemed on the surface confident and thrusting men. All were ex-grammar-school boys who had become skilled workers with supervisory responsibilities. They had never previously been unemployed, but about five months before the first interview they had been made redundant. All three had migrated at the invitation of the company to the area in the south-east where they now lived in their own houses. Their incomes came from unemployment insurance, earnings-related supplement, a private redundancy arrangement from the firm, the residue of the lump sums of government and private redundancy pay, and tax rebates.

'I never planned any sort of job for longer than twelve months. I never bothered to think that far ahead until I came here, and then I thought I was settled for the next ten years. It looked good, a new factory that they'd spent £3 million on, some of it government money. And we were encouraged by the price of the houses, the special scheme. They must have known at that time there was some chance of redundancies, but there was not a word about it. Well, you wouldn't expect a brand-new factory to close down that's had £3¼ million spent on it.

'We were proud of that factory, the sort of working conditions we had there. I know some of the jobs I go for now, the bosses aren't pleased when I show them what I think of the conditions they have to work in. I used to look forward to work. I don't say I looked forward to Monday mornings, I don't think many people do. But when it came to Friday I hated it. You know how it is, when you're doing something that you haven't finished, and you don't like stopping.

'I think normally when you're working you tend to get in a rut, you take things for granted, the fact that you've got a job. I think it's really a case of "I'm all right Jack". You close your eyes to it, you don't say to yourself this could happen to you. You get complacent. I don't think you know, until you've lived through a redundancy, what it's like. It'll be difficult to get over in a book. The nearest thing I've seen was that T.V. programme they did. That hit me pretty hard at the time, watching that, because I knew it was going to happen then. Well, falling orders, and the Americans and their huge spare capacity. Just to keep going they were prepared to sell the stuff at a ridiculously low price and we couldn't compete. We went up to London and tried to get Davies to put a tariff on the goods coming in from abroad, but he said oh no, they couldn't do, bad for trade. Then next month Nixon slaps 10 per cent on! That's the way they are, the British, don't do the best for ourselves somehow.

'Industrial relations got very poor. When we first came from Thomsons' other works there were no unions, no staff unions anyway, and the attitudes were good. It was the redundancies that started it. We began to make a big noise. Well, you don't just sit back, it was a damned big upset for a lot of people. We wanted to negotiate so we formed a union eighteen months ago – what am I saying, eighteen months, you say eighteen but the months keep going on – but the management refused to talk. They said they didn't expect changes, there weren't going to be any redundancies. But let's face it, it was obvious to anybody. Then the first came, overnight, one hundred people were laid off.

'We were going to organize a factory occupation, but it didn't succeed because the factory threatened to sack the hourly-paid staff without redundancy pay. There was a lot of nasty words spoken, you know, in the last days anyway.'

Mr Weston

Mr Weston's name was provided by his union, and he also lived in the south-east. His manner was quiet, almost diffident, but there was about him a curiously contained air of self-sufficiency. His whole work experience proved difficult to size up and place. His elementary school education had been interrupted by the war, and under pressure from his family he had started work as a greengrocer's boy. Since then he had changed jobs more than a dozen times, once becoming self-employed. Sometimes he had attempted to improve his position or to avoid bad work conditions, but also he had sometimes been sacked. More recently, in a larger firm, he had begun to find his feet. He had moved with this firm to the new area where he now lived, although he had not bought a house. Here, however, he had been made redundant twice in the last three years (the two redundancies, which stem from the same drying up of work, are here collapsed together). In spite of his varied career, the present spell of six months was the first continuous unemployment he had had. Three months before our visit he had had his unemployment insurance suspended for refusing to take a job at a lower wage (a controversial decision which he describes later in the book), and he had lived off the remains of his redundancy pay and what he could make from odd jobs. Although he would have preferred to regard himself as 'self-employed', he said himself that, although he was not registered at the employment exchange, 'To all intents and purposes, I'm unemployed.'

'One time there was a job in the saw sharpeners' shop going. Anyway, all it is, it's one of these saws and you go "Bonk!" and "Zzzm!", and you've got to watch it all day long. You couldn't think about much else because if the thing goes round once too often it was spoiled. All right, I can put up with that. But there was a wall, been damaged during the war and all it had was tarpaulins up. Now he's coming round with the tea-trolley and I put down my tea-cup and within twenty minutes there was ice forming in the bottom of the cup. I was absolutely frozen. Well anyway, I went to the shop foreman, and I went up to him and – it's a job I got thrown out of, this is – I said, "This place here," I said, "who's the shop-steward?" He says, "What! We don't have a union here." I said, "There, look there, that must be against factory regulations," I said, "I've got ice cn my cup," He says, "So bloody what? You're a man, aren't you?" I says, "I'll soon show you whether I'm a man or not. I'll get the factory inspector down here." And there I was, slung out.

'I had ambitions, but unfortunately I picked bloody ragtime firms. After this I went to a place called Brush Furnishing, right? I went there and I told them I was a cramper – somebody said there was a cramping job, I never even knew what it meant. The thing is, when I got there they were doing door-frames, you know, kitchen cabinet door-frames, at thirty-two an hour. The first thing the bloke said to me, he said, "Thirty-two an hour, or otherwise you'll be left at the end of the day." This was the attitude. So I thought to myself, "I don't know how the bloody thing works," so I said to another feller there, "I wonder if you can have a look at my cramper, it seems to be sticking," and he came up and he set it straight away. It was so simple you couldn't go wrong. Well, what I've told you so far, it might be just me, but what I'm going to tell you now, I don't think it is just me. Anyway, after a while, after about a fortnight, I thought of a brainwave. I was going to do sixteen doors in one operation. Now it was no bother, putting them all together, packing wood so they wouldn't spring up in the air. Well, when these doors went up from thirty-two an hour to about 390, this is the sort of firm it was, the bloke didn't come up to me and say, "Look, you're making a packet, aren't you?" He just come up and he says, "These doors are now 200 an hour." He hasn't told me he's been timing me or anything. So straight away I went to the shop-steward, and the shop-steward says, "Ooh, I'm not having anything to do with this," and that was it. Anyway, I accepted this, like an idiot, but I was still making a good wage. I was married by this time.

'Well, during our doing these doors we'd have to wait for the wood-machinist to supply panels and rails, and the chargehand, he comes up to me and he says, "What you doing?" I says, "Cleaning me cramp down." He says, "Get on the effing broom." Now I don't mind being asked to do something. I mean, as I say, I'm not proud, I'll do anything. But when a person speaks to you like that, well, if you've got any grey matter, any spunk at all, your back goes up. Anyway, I took him at his word. I got on the broom – I stood on its head! Because I was so bloody wild. He come back. He says, "I thought I told you to get on the effing broom?" I said, "I am, I'm standing on it." There was no ... I mean I was out of the door quicker than that! They even sent me wages on.

'In 1953 I tried to start a furniture bureau. We were producing things very cheaply – glass display cabinets they was, under-cutting the cheapest that anybody else was making by about a third. Then we got a big order from this wholesaler, for a hundred cabinets. We got into debt to make up this order and then the bloke turns round, deliberately, and says he doesn't want 'em. He says, "Now I've broke you; serve you sodding well right!"'

'I went to another company, and I've stayed there ever since until I was made redundant down here in this place where we moved to. I started there as a straight wireman, wiring up circuits – a beautiful looking job – and from there I went to the model shop. I suppose then I knew there could be a promotion ladder, and I did gradually go up the ladder, from straight wiring to the model shop; that's where from an engineer's design you make models to see that everything fits. Anyway, in the model shop it came to pass that what I was doing was to put on the drawing the modifications I was doing. I was drawing it out, sort of reverse draftsman, from the model I was making. Well, anyway, the chap who was in charge of our shop, he put in a word for me. He said, "We've seen your little drawings, and you've definitely got an aptitude for drawing. We want you to come with the firm when we move, because you know the practical side so much that you'd be really handy with the drawing board." So I said, "Well, what's the money then?" Of course it was more than to go on doing what I was doing. In actual fact, when I became a draftsman I exactly doubled my wages for a shorter working week, for a start. So being human, what alternative did I have?

'I'm not boring you am I? Now, I come down to this place – now I got to do a bit of boasting here to put you in the picture – I started anyway, I got in there and there was a dirty great printed circuit. Cor! I couldn't get it on the drawing board. Anyway, I took this over from a bloke that had just gone on holiday, and I'm a conscientious bloke when I'm working, so I got stuck into this, and a bloke come to me and said, "Here! You ain't done that already, have you?" And in that first morning, he reckoned I'd done more in that first morning than the other bloke had done in the fortnight previously. No, this is true this is, it's not just bulling, because I thought I must do a good job for these people. And this bloke was absolutely astounded. I was working with two engineers, because these two blokes never wanted to know any other draftsman. They used to say, "You've got it on your fingertips, Dave." Now this was it, this is no bull. Well, when you've finished something like that you think, "Cor! I done that," and two or three years ago you'd never have thought you could do it.

'Only thing, I used to have remarks made, by the other lads, about "crawl-arse", when I used to keep working, you know, on a Saturday when there was no-one there to tell you off. But from the point of view of being paid to do a job, you do a job. This is my maxim, I mean this: "A fair day's work for a fair day's pay."

'Eventually, what I was doing was running the office, the whole work was going through me. The section leaders was coming to ask me how it was done. I was on this job and they were getting all the profit really, through my person. Right, I done all this. Well, it's no more than, "Look after the firm and it looks after you." Right, now, I thought I was going places. Because all these people were chasing me. You could become chief draftsman, four or five thousand a year, project leader, design draftsman.

'Then I got made redundant. This is what happened. The Americans come over and all their big bods, and they done the Americani-

16

zation of this firm. There was all effing and blinding on the notice-boards from the work people. It was terrible, it was really, because they made such a drastic cutback after the promises that there'd be five years' work, no need to worry for five years at least. I mean they conned us into moving down here really.

'But this is what made me really bitter. With the experience I've had, you're supposed to be one of the best blokes and you're made redundant. I was always told at that firm, "When the redundancies come, you'll be the first to go", but anyway, it hadn't occurred to me about redundancies. I goes round to the personnel, and I says, "Does this mean I've worked meself out of a job by working hard?" He says, "Well, unfortunately you're one of the last in. We must streamline the firm by cutting down excess, and although we think a lot of you, you're one of the last in, and the unions will have 'last in, first out'." So I said, "Where can you streamline a firm like that?" I said, "If you think I'm that good, it would be worth having trouble with the unions." I mean the union bloke was there, and he says, "Yeah, that's right, last in, first out."

'If more people with my opinions became active, the unions wouldn't go above what the unions was meant for. A union is to make sure a man isn't exploited, but in lots of cases they're making men to be exploited. I mean I was exploited by getting slung out of that firm in that context. I mean unions are a must! I mean let's have no doubt about this, I've served on a union committee. Because employers have never given us a good standard of living: the unions have got it. But even so you mustn't go too far one way or the other, with the power.

'So where do persons like me go to? Because to look at 'em both, they're both right. The point is, it's all right for the union and the employer, but the bloke who's a conscientious bloke is out on the street.'

Mr Odell

While unemployed Mr Odell had become an active member of a claimants' union in the south-east, and it was via this union that we contacted him. Softly-spoken, his accent was at times difficult to make out and his manner was more priestly than revolutionary. He was a skilled worker, a bus driver; four months before our visit he had been given the sack when he was caught stopping for a cup of tea while on duty. However, matters had been arranged so that he could keep his unemployment insurance, and he also had a tax rebate. He was buying a small, old house. Somewhat surprisingly, in view of his political stance, on his bookshelves were the biographies of power politicians and military leaders.

'I started off training in a monastery in Ireland, specializing as a chef. I thought it was a fine thing to have thirty or forty people out there, and me making a meal for them, doing something for them.

'After I came over to England, I've done a factory job, twice, for a period of about twelve months and about eighteen months, and at Christmas I was on for about eight weeks and I didn't like it. I just left. My first job was packing, and then I was sort of transferred, I was moved over to the trimming section. A lot of that work was done by a press, cutting off excess on castings from the foundry. The only satisfaction was to get good money, but in order to get good money you get frustrated because you had to produce more for them. Most factories are on some sort of piece-work, and there's competition and jealousies among the people that are actually working together. Relationships don't *appear* to be unpleasant, but they can be because people are jealous of one another. It's the sort of relationship that's pushed on to you by capitalism.

'I left to work on the buses. I just like driving. I'd never driven before, but the first time I liked it. I do like driving a lot, especially in summer. I don't think I can describe it. I just, sort of, like driving buses. I wouldn't mind being a bus driver for the rest of my life. I don't know just what it is. The only thing I don't like is that bus-stops are too close, I don't like that. I didn't like having to stop. I like to drive a bus fast, if you had a good bus. It was very frustrating if you had a bad bus, which you had most of the time down there. I think I'm a good driver. I used to drive fast but I think I was safe. I used to drive for the conductor, not the passengers, and I didn't like being overtaken by cars. A woman once reported me for giving her a fast ride, but I don't think I was dangerous. It's true what they say: busmen hate the public and the public hate busmen. But it's not their fault. It's the system.

'I like driving and I liked the union activity, organizing people to try and make the job better. My friends now say I'm not revolutionary enough, but I can't hate anybody. When I'm out of work I miss working with the union. And we had a scheme going, to make the buses free. They'd ban cars from the town centre and only let the buses in, and that way we'd get a better service to the public and a better town centre. We didn't only talk about it; we had it all worked out in detail, with the services and the time-tables and everything. And we had our own bus magazine.

'I don't want to be an inspector; if I did put in for promotion it would be a joke! The buses were in really dangerous condition.* The trouble is that the people down there are frightened to lose their jobs, so if one man refuses to take the bus out the inspectors can always turn round and say, "Well, so-and-so took it out and there was nothing wrong with it." They don't stick together. When they can't get men the company will take anybody on, no matter what they do, and you can get away with murder, but in times like these when there's high unemployment, the least little thing and they'll get rid of you, and they always pick on the ones who make trouble for them. One of them was awfully annoyed when a small hard core of us wouldn't accept the things that management wanted us to accept, and he was very annoyed, and he was heard to mutter, "I can see a lot of people are going to get the sack here!"

'It could have been worse. I could have been suspended from dole for six weeks, but the boss said he'd make it easy for me. He'd put "unsuitable for buswork" on the cards so I didn't lose money at the labour exchange. The only thing is that that means I can't get a job round here with any of the bus companies.'

Mr John

Mr John was a West Indian whom we contacted via another claimants' union in the south-east. Physically large and strong-looking, he had a voice to match; the interview was a harangue, difficult to interrupt or guide, and repetitive in its stress on colour discrimination. He reluctantly refused to be photographed for fear of official

* Some time later there was a scandal about this in the local paper.

19

prejudice. He was a skilled worker with an I.Q. of 125 (attested in a letter we saw from a College of Technology) and a number of A level and City and Guild certificates in his craft. However, he had not completed an apprenticeship.* His work career had consisted of a number of moves, some of which he had initiated, some where he had got the sack. He had remained on short contract jobs without permanent security, although one of these had involved moving with the firm to an area where he now lived in a council house, a move which he made partly to get the house itself to better his living conditions. Unfortunately, he had subsequently been injured in a road accident, and he still had difficulty in lifting heavy equipment and metal, which he needed to do for his job. When we saw him a year after the accident he was again officially registered as fit for work, and was drawing supplementary benefit at the employment exchange.

'My father is a vicar of the church. You see, I was well brought up, you see what I mean, so therefore it's helped me today for the home life that I have and teaching, and adopt the right way of life as my father has taught me. Not like in this country, my father do not rely on the church members to support him, he's self-supporting. But I cannot be a Christian in this country for the fact that I see too many problems that arises on me in this country for me to be, to follow the Christianship. Oh man! I have done terrible work, and I suffered other damn hardship. I tell you, my experience in this country, it's more than I can explain. Because the fact that if I goes out and simple problem arises like looking for a job, and in working, and I find that I have been treated somewhat unfairly, and in all that aspect of living in England I find that I have been treated unfairly in the point of getting a good job, and to be paid equal wages with the rest of the other white fellers.

'Well I was ambitious! I know from leaving school I must be something. I must do something constructive, whether it will be practical or theoretical work, but I must do something. I know defi-

* In this sense Mr John is typical of older immigrant workers who in their work careers encounter the barrier between unskilled and skilled workers which also blocks the careers of unskilled white workers. Although this is not to say that Mr John's accusations of colour discrimination were altogether misguided.

nitely that I'm not going to sweep the road, or just lay about; or having to be someone who any ... you go to a firm and you know nothing and they just says to you, "do this" or "do that", and just having to be using you like a damn fool, and using you like that. I know that I wasn't going to be, because I'm not a fool. I'm going to be in the position in which I can have something to sell and the highest bidder come along, I will be able to tell him and he knows if he is going to buy a person by interviewing me and testing me out, he will know if I have anything good to offer.

'The apprenticeship in this country, they have far better privilege. When I come here in 1961 I saw people, fellers here and young people, walking the street and just laying about, and it was disgusting to us who have, who is ambitious and have a lot of self-principle and pride. To me it was disgusting because the fact that if I could travel many thousands and thousands of miles from Jamaica to here, and ambitious enough, come here with a lot of ambition that I could try myself to do further education here into the College of Art and Technology, if I could have ambition to go there, I sure know that many of the English boys that I have seen that born and bred in this country, walking the streets, if they did get ambitious enough to think of themselves and the future of themselves, they will go and do a part-time studies just like what I did.

'I enjoy welding because it is something I have studied technically in. I know how to approach a job and the problems that I can overcome. There are many welders today who, really, they know nothing. They never make it a point of getting to know technically what's happening in welding and to learn the topic and to study the welding technology, as far as taking A levels, which I have, say, three. I do hope to be a manager very much, but I haven't been given that opportunity, has never arise yet. I wanted to do teaching. From the moment of starting studies, when I go to College, I want to be technical instructor or technical adviser in welding and cetera, or welding research, and I try several times. There is several firms which I have tried. If, as I said, people wouldn't know what I could do, the majority of them, until they give me such opportunity, that's all I'm begging for. Which is not too much in life to ask, is the opportunity to prove what I can do.

'I tried first at the Ministry of Labour to get a job and they would not entertain the idea of offering me a job as a welder, and I was, you know, I could see the resentment in these people because they think like all people like our colour is goddam stupid and to me it's the wrong attitude ...

'I went down there to another scrapyard, and I saw a big Irish bloke who is foreman there, very big and, you know, it remind me of – I wasn't born in the slavery days, but hearing about the slavery – it was like slavery come back down there with this big Irish bloke. Well, anyway, I work at that job for a while, and at the time I was at Tech, and one of the instructor who was instructing me in College, and we is getting quite well-know to each other by our surname, and we get along pretty fine, and he seen his son and he tell his son about me, and his son, he's got me a job. That was the first firm which entertained me as a welder in this country. And when I went for the interview and fill up the form, I had to take a practical trade test, and oh! the trade test went very nicely, just like that, and they accept it and it was firm. It was not easy stuff because it was thin stuff they give me to weld by electric arc, and then oxy-acetylene, because they were proving that you know if you can weld the thin gauge then they know fairly well that you are able to weld things like up to a quarter of an inch and over, but when they gives you something like a sixteenth and ten gauge to weld by arc ...

'I went to the firm to do oxy-acetylene welding for aluminium. I went on to work, and this firm, when I discovered that they was paying me less money than what they was paying the other fellers, and after a while I decided I want the money made up, and well, the management, of course, don't really want to do that, because they see us, coloured people, and they think, "We're going to use you bastards to our advantage to cheap labour." The fact is it wasn't nothing to do with me not having papers to prove I was skilled. The fact is, if I can do the job it's all that matters by them, that is satisfactory to them, but it wasn't satisfactory to me, because I know that I was victimized by them, and being discriminating against, not paying me my fair share of money what I am earning when I'm turning out the work better than the other feller, better than them as well.

'I start to have discussion with the man in charge, the foreman, and they giving me a lot of rubbish, story. Anyway, it turned out one day that I finished welding the aluminium and there wasn't much work left to be done. So this bloke who was in charge, he thinks to himself, very kinky, he came up to me, he says to me I had to get a pile – he didn't request, he come up to me and give me a direct order – I *has* to get a pile and start piling up some of those frames because welding, he haven't got any more frames for welding, and so on. So I said, "Look. I came here as a welder and that is what I am working *as*, that is what I employ *as*, and I won't be doing your piling. You going to give it to the people who doing your piling, and I won't be doing that job." He said, "Well, you got to do it." I said, "No. There's not such thing that you *got* to." I said, "There's not such rule as you got to, man." I said, "You are forgetting who you are talking to. You must try to remember now. You see this colour of skin is different from yours, but don't try to think that you can block me into doing something against my principle or my ambition." I say, "I won't be doing piling, and I won't be doing general labouring for you. I'm a welder, and that is what I am working as, a skilled man." He said, "Well, you got to do it, otherwise you must go." I said, "Well, I will go." And I did, I did!

'Once I work for another firm, and that firm it was a very good firm, that was. The management very, very nice. I think they are one of the best in England up to now that I have experienced, very fair and helpful as much as possible. They wanted at that time an argon arc welder, a man who is experienced in argon arc to weld chrome nickel steels, and therefore the welder must know his job and the work must be top standard. It must be good, because everything has to be welded and then polished. There mustn't be any cracks and crevices and defects at all. And I have one of the big bosses and another of the bosses, the shop-floor shift man, and another one that work in the office. I greet them bravely, as usual, and explain to them theoretically how this process works. There was three section there of the argon process, and I explain it to them how the process works, and what the purpose each one for in argon arc welding. And after telling them, I then give them a practical demonstration. And they couldn't believe that it was possible for a man normally to stood there and just to explain something so briefly and give them the basic facts so sharp, and convince them and they were all satisfied, three of them. And at that time I have the opportunity to have a word with the boss and I have a word with him and I let him know that I'm here for the highest bidder that's willing to pay me, I'll work in.

'I find the personnel manager there to me, he is a gentleman, and he's a fair nice man, who is willing to assist and to help and to see that the firm helps one who is honest in himself and trustworthy, and who is ambitious and want to get on. That firm, they give me the opportunity to apply for a job in their office, off the shop floor they give me the opportunity, because they know that I have, they can see that I have potential and that's the reason why they want to invest in me and back me up. But I didn't stay to do so. I would have done had I stayed there, but I didn't like travelling on my motor cycle, because I start coming off because of the conditions of the weather.'

Mr Spain

Perhaps this is a suitable point to introduce as a contrast the other West Indian whom we interviewed. Mr Spain, the widowed father of eight children, was contacted through a claimants' union in the south-east. He spoke slowly, movingly, philosophically, with a relaxation bordering on resignation, but shot through with concern for his children and with sudden humour. Although shy of publicity, he agreed to be interviewed because, 'There's a lotta drama in a man's life. You can't stand back and say, no, I don't want to know, or nobody else know the drama there is in a man's life.' His wife had died shortly after the birth of his youngest child, during a sterilization operation, and he had been living on supplementary benefit for a year while he looked after his children.

'Well, I used to have my own boat, like, back in West Indies. Well, I used to do a lot of fishing and that, like, and lumber, I used to carry lumber. I never used to sleep at night when I was back home, and when I come up here it was hard, really, to adapt the system to go to bed at night. Well, most of the time I'm at sea, innit? And my job at sea, I used to be a round-the-clock man. But in the days I always relaxed, you know, and sleep. Well, it's a nice habit, really, it's bloody good, because look, going to sea, the type o' mineral that you get from the air keep you going, make you feel fit.

You never feel no pain in your body, and you just feel young, because look, although I go to sea for seven or eight or nine years now, I just feel like I'm about fourteen, fifteen years now, in my body. Before my wife died I was going to go back to my boat again.

'Oh, I come to England, it was disgusting really, because I couldn't find nothing to my suit. But I just gradually get in the system like. Well, I used to work in a plastic place, I used to work on a table, like cut the stuff up. It was a bit rough, like, because you're not used to that type o' life. Then I leave, I got on this bloody place, I spend a coupla month there and I pack it in like. It was too dirty, it was nearly like human muck.

'Then I got on to a brake drum firm. It was a bit dirty, but it wasn't too bad, that type o' job; nobody round your neck, you know. Working in industry really don't do your body no good, because you have a lot of fume and different things, carbon dioxide. But that job wasn't too bad. I used to work on a plant, like, clean drums, you know, nobody never used to round your neck, because you know what you're doing, and you just do it the proper way and that's it. You try to do the job the best way you can. After you get used to that, well, I never skipped my time at work really, I'm a bloke that like to live independent like, really.

'Tell you something, at work here, really, the type o' work that you get, specially industrial factories, they are boring. Well, it depends on the type o' job that you doing. If people don't crawl round your neck, you enjoy it; once you can do your job properly, you don't feel it. But it's when you really trying to do a job properly and a bloke crawl round your neck every minute, and say, oh, take you off of that one and put you on that one, it become boring. You don't want to know nothing about work, you know! Well, if, you know, you get into a system and that's your job and you keep doing it until it becomes an habit to you, it's interesting to do it.'

Mr McBain

The scene now shifts to the north-east. Mr McBain was one of the men whom we contacted casually there. Burly and rugged-looking, his manner was a wry, sometimes outraged but often also amused recollection of the enormity of the obstacles which he now felt he had faced from his early upbringing and during his working life. He seemed to have run the whole gamut of the insecure and dangerous jobs in the district, and he had had more labouring jobs than he could recall, interspersed with a number of spells of unemployment, some of up to two years in length. (We describe these later in the book, although in a sense they are an integral part of the work career). During his most recent spell, which had lasted about a year, there had been a recurrence of the tuberculosis which he had originally suffered briefly in his teens. Now he had been pronounced fit again by the doctors and was classified as unemployed and living on supplementary benefit. He lived on a council estate.

'When I was at school and I went for the examinations, they called me down from the seniors to the juniors and they wanted to know the reason why I didn't pass it, because I was pretty good, you know, I really was, in the juniors. But going up from the juniors into the seniors something just happened, like that!' (He snapped his fingers.) 'You know, and I just lost bloody interest. Well, I know why I didn't pass it; because I didn't even try to pass it. I lost interest in school altogether.

'I could have got a job in the shipyard serving me time from school, they got me that job, have you got me? They said, "We've got you a job at the plumber's, apprentice ship's plumber." Me father wouldn't let me go. It was the money, like. Oh, I was mad over that. I said, "It's the only chance I'll ever have of doing anything," you know, "I'm going to end up a labourer like you." And I was right! Yes. He said, "Looka son," he said, "You don't realize what it's like. It's got a bad accident rate." But I would only have got about twenty-four bob a week there.

'At that particular time, I don't think I was as advanced as I should have been at me age, do you know what I mean? I mean, when I see kids now at fourteen years old, I realize how much of a bloody disadvantage I was at fourteen. I hadn't a chance, I hadn't a clue, compared to what the kids are now. They'd look at that sort of job today, and they'd say, "I'm not going to do that! You must be joking!" They don't care. My first job was in Jacks's, twisting and shearing. It was making angle iron for the building trade, you know, for the morticing. You ought to have seen them, with their hands split and twisted, you know. I was there about five months, and I was getting only 25s., and in there there was all sorts of bloody red lead, and all sorts. They had to be dipped, you know, some sort of oil, they dipped steel into it after it's been done. Bloody awful smells.

'Well, I finished there in 1947, there was a big redundancy at that place. Aw, bloody hell! It's an incredible feeling, what it was then to me; fourteen and made redundant. I tell you what. It's had an effect on my life, I know that. It's had a bad effect an' all. I don't know, I think, you know, when I was, when I got finished out of Jacks's, it was a bit of a smack in the eye to you, because, you know, a kid like you are, I wanted to go out to work, you know what I mean? I wasn't doing any good at school. I thought, "Oh, I'll go out to work and get meself a job." I was always thought well of, you know, wherever I've worked an' all. And I got that job and I got bloody knocked back, you know, redundant. To a man: "Oh it's work's finished," like, but I mean, to a kid he doesn't think like that. I was thinking to meself, "They've finished me because I'm not good enough," you know what I mean? There was bloody hundreds got finished, but it's just the way it takes you.

'I went straight from there and I got a job at a place where my father always said, "You're not going to go!" The props! The thing was, it was good money. When I first started on the props I was getting £2 14s. Mind you, it was bloody harder, you know what I mean? But in actual fact, for me, for a lad going out, it was a better job than the expansion, the metal works, in actual fact, healthwise, because you were out in the open, see. They worked in the rain and everything, and it was bloody hard work an' all. The men used to come home with all skin off their shoulders through carrying the props, running backwards and forwards, grabbing them up and running up bloody plankways and gangways and stacking them on to stacks, you know, they'd be running like hell. But you get used to it. There was a lad killed next to me, with the waggons, between the buffers. Then I went on the bench, pulling off the props when they were sawing them. And when I was only fifteen, on the saw-bench, there was a kid arguing, you know – the kids used to like to get on the bench because it was better than getting mucked about by every-body else – I said, "Away, get off!" He said, "No, I'm on it now," and he started going like this in front of the saw, and he chopped three fingers off. He didn't think what he was doing, see; just starts sweeping the sawdust away from the table in front of him just like that. I've got a few marks on me thumbs at times, you know. You know the set on the saw, one tooth goes that way and one goes that way. You get two nicks in your thumb without cutting it, like two scratches. You say, "By! You've got a good set on there!" Ha, Ha!

'Oh, I was there till I was about seventeen and a half, going for the army. They finished you about six months before your time – well, there was plenty of kids knocking about the town at that time, and I was getting about, what, about £4 under a man's wage, you know what I mean, a grown up's like. Well, they could have brought another lad in and give him about £3, something like that. I signed on for the Air Force because there was a scheme, and then again it was better money if you signed on. I passed, I was like a bull, I was perfect then. Working on the sticks, I had bloody arms like that, I tell you.

'But before I went for the R.A.F. I was walking about for about six months, looking for a job, walking about in bloody shoes with holes in them. I went back to ask them for a job, doing anything, you know, until I got in the Air Force proper. No chance, I was walking around for ages, see, six or nine months, and the bloody bobby, every time he seen me in the street, used to pull me up. He thought I was dodging, you know. I *had* to go looking for a job! I had to get a bloody job. My father couldn't keep us, he'd have put us out, he'd say, "Out!" He couldn't, there was so many of us, you see. Of course, the old girl was feeding us as well as she could, like, me mother, but it wasn't, not so much. Well, you couldn't expect it. She wasn't getting a lot off me father, you know. He was always a bit greedy with money, you know, me father like. He used to come home slogged, you know what I mean, fall down on a chair absolutely buggered many a time. To tell you the truth, when he dropped down dead, I think that was one of the reasons for it, through the bloody life he'd led working on the sticks.

'Well, you know, winter time, and I had big holes in me shoes, and I got to Bedford for the Air Force, and they said, "You're losing weight." I lost about something like a stone. Anyway, they sent me home again. They wouldn't have me. I'd got silent pneumonia. It left a little shadow. Well, I came round, the doctor gave us a course, and I was, like, another six months.

'How I finally got a job that time, I'd been running about for ages, and I'd been down to a firm and I'd *tortured* them, absolutely bloody tortured them I had. I got a bit of help over that, come to think of it. I had a mate working there, and he said to me, "Go down and see Scotty and tell him you're a mate of mine, you know, and you might get a kick in," he said, "Because he thinks a bit about me." I got the job, and I had an old feller called Randall in charge of me, you know. We got on fabulous. He thought the world of me. We had a crew, him and me and me two mates. I got me two mates, started through me starting. I was only there about six months, and old Randall, he used to say, "By! That's my lad!" like, you know, because I was digging in like, "I wish I had a few more like you." And I used to say to him, "I've got two bloody mates out of work. Why don't you start them?" And after a while he said, "Well, fetch them down." I brought them down, like, and there was us three together. We were emptying wagons, and where previous it used to take a shift, two or three men to empty a wagon, we'd empty one inside an hour. We used to drive into it, and heave the lot out at one go, and we'd be finished then for what, an hour, an hour and a half, and we'd go and have a cup of tea with old Randall and have a chat. We were finished before every bugger else. By that time I'd started to pile flesh on, you know. When I was working and handed me money over, me mother used to feed me like a horse, and I could eat like a horse an' all, you know what I mean.

'Well, the foreman, Scotty started interfering with me, and I told him to see Randall. I said, "Look, we're doing our work. Why should you interfere with us? What's the matter? Are you narked because we've got the bloody wagons emptied, and we can go to the cab and have a cup of tea, and you yourself have to stand there, still working?" I said. "We can't help that, if we're better than you. We work twice as hard as what you fellers are doing." There was blokes who'd been working there for years who were terrified of a bit of work. They were messing about like this, where somebody with a bit of strength in them used to dive in.

'I was there till I got married. I finished the week I was married! I had a row. I went to see Scotty and I said, "Can I have a week off?

I'm getting married." He said, "No chance! All the holidays are arranged. If you take a week off, you're finished." I went back after a week, to go back to work, like – I knew I was finished, like – he said, "You have no chance. Go on, beat it!" Old Randall got finished that week an' all, like, the whole gang got clocked off. So Scotty was getting bloody shot of the lot of us.

'Aw, I felt bloody awful. You see, the attitude they had was, if you didn't do what you were told, you weren't wanted. You had *no right* at all to go against anything they did. You had no right, you weren't able to think. They used to think you were a horse or something like that! Suppose you'd get whipped, and feed you, and maybe give you a few quid each week to pay you for your trouble. But to talk back to them, or to argue against any of their conditions – no chance!

'Well, I've never liked being a manual worker. I've worked on the buildings for a length of time, and I've worked right up to a ganger. I can read drawings and everything, and use a theodolite, just by learning meself when they were doing that sort of thing. The first job I ever had on the buildings, they put me on digging this hole, and I just stopped and I thought to myself, "What the bloody hell am I doing in here, digging this. Is this your capabilities here, just digging this bloody hole here, just digging a hole out of the ground. Is that all you're capable of?" You see, I'd been out of work a while, and to get back into work you've got to take anything, and when you do start to work, you realize that you've been stampeded into something that you should never have taken on, you know what I mean? I suddenly seen a vision of meself in about twenty bloody years' time, digging the hole out, like, and I didn't like that at all. I thought, "Bugger this!" Got out of the hole and threw the spade down. I got out of the hole, chucked the spade away, and the boss of the whole firm happened to be there. He said, "What's the matter, son?" I said, "Do you think I'm going to stick down there until I'm about forty-odd?" I said, "I'm only a young feller," I said, "that's not for me. Let's have me cards." And he said, "I tell you what I'll do," he said. "I'll give you some extra money to do a charge-hand's job. You don't have to touch a shovel. You tell'em what to do." I went to Redcar and all over for him. I finished up paving.

'Anyway, the same thing happened there. I had a row on there with his son. It was the nearest I ever come, where a man put his own son out of work and kept me on. And he used to send for us to go back. And one job he gave us a reference. Me mam said she'd never known a labourer to get a reference.

'Well, hold on, after a few jobs I was out of work and then I went in the shipyard, through me brother, he was painting in the shipyard. 7½d. a square yard! Would you like to do that job? On the side of a ship. 2d. for red lead, twopence for flat white, and 1½d. for gloss, a square yard. I fell off. They have these little cradles, swingers, and I fell off, left me boots in the dock. When this tug went down the river it went too fast and it sent up a big wash. Have you never seen that? The boat goes up in the air like a horse, and the bloody thing's rearing right up in the air. The bows'll go up first, and the bloody ropes go tight like that, you can hear them wanging and cracking! You know, and then it comes down and the bloody stern goes up, and it's going this way and that way. You want to see it. If I'd have fell off in the water I'd have been bloody flattened; if I hadn't been drownded, I'd have been bloody flattened. I was hanging on. My brother said, if I hadn't have been so strong I'd have been dead. They thought I was drownded. I lost my boots. The bloody wire marks were in me hands, you know, where I'd been holding. The old feller who I worked with, who was looking after us, he was crying on the dockside. He said, "Oh, he's gone, he's gone!" They were all along the dockside and they couldn't see me you know; they were all shouting and screaming, and I was laid along the bloody board, with me toes wrapped round the board and me hands round the wire, and they couldn't see me. And the poor old feller was crying his eyes out. He said, "He's dead, he's dead." He was looking in the water. "I can't see him." I said, "I'm here!" And then I come home – oh no, that was another time, when I was wearing a cap and they took me to hospital and I'd split the top of me head right open, right across the top. Ha, ha!

'I finally got into steel erecting, through a lie. I got twisted like. Right, I'd been inquiring down to the steel erectors' union, and they said, "If you get a billet to say you've been working for a construction firm, you've been erecting and that, we'll give you a card." I said, "Righto. I wonder where I can bum a billet off, because it's going to be a lie anyway." I wasn't even bloody working at the time. Have you got me? So, oh, me brother comes up and he says, "Hey, there's a job up there at Garford Construction." I thought, "*Construction*". But you should have seen it when I started, pipe laying it was. Middle of our morning's work, ten o'clock comes round, like, we had tea. We went into a little cavern. It was about that wide, about from here to that table, and there was about six of us in, me brother and these four Irishmen. You should have seen them. They had bloody stockings round their feet and all sorts, and all they had on the floor for heating was one of them bloody primus stoves, you know, like that. By! It was bitter, it was like crawling into a bloody ice-box when you went in there. They were all sat there with their feet on top of each other like this. I thought, "Aw, I'm not sticking this." So anyway, I went over to the agent in the caravan and asked him, and he said, "I don't know whether we've ever employed riggers before," but anyway he give us a billet and I took it down, and bob's your uncle! They give me a bloody union card, and I got a job straight away.

'I was at Tees-side Construction for three months and I got pretty involved, with me brother being militant. He's the most militant man around this area, and he can't get a bloody job anywhere. They gave me a shop-steward's job. I shouldn't have got involved, but the builders, who'd been there for years, didn't want to know, so they roped me in on it. And I got threw out. The boss said, "These fellers is using you." I believe in working men sticking together, but they don't, like. It's never happened to me anyway. Anyway, I got finished from there – they said it was redundancy, like, but it was over trouble.

'I started work on me own, putting these fireplaces and boilers into council houses. I had me own wagons and everything. I worked with me brother-in-law and a plumber and we got £50 a week each before overheads. But mind this was grafting. Scrap was worth £4 a day an' all. But my mate got into trouble with a court order and we had to sell the lot. It would have been worth about eight hundred quid.

'I was off work about eighteen months after that, then steel erecting again at Ellesmere Port. By! we were militant down there. We were so militant that they closed the job down, sacked the lot of us. I was home a week, and I got a job at Heysham, steel erecting, for only a week or two. It was a place where there was a lot of dust, you know, all over the place. The sort of job where, when you come home, you were still spitting dust out, and when you coughed it was on your lungs. And when I was there I kept getting these bits of pains in me back, you know. I thought, "What the hell is it?" I thought, "Have I pulled a muscle or something?" And anyway it went away, that, and I came away. Since then I've been off work nearly a year.'

Mr Lucas

Mr Lucas was a close friend, sometime workmate and clubmate of Mr McBain's, who also lived on the same estate. He had shared some of the latter's early labouring experiences, for example at Jacks's where he had got the sack for reading comics while minding a machine, and on the 'props'. He had had almost two years of unemployment, and now lived on supplementary benefits.

'When I got the push from Jacks's I was about sixteen then. I thought, well, that's my limitation in work, like. I joined a gang and got into trouble, bother. I had about six years' solid police bother, like – not for stealing, like, fighting; breach of the peace, drunk and disorderly.

'Me uncle wanted us to be a bricklayer. He was a master builder, and he would have took us to live with him, but I wouldn't go. I said, "No, I've been at school up to fifteen, I want to get into the money." My mother was a widow and she'd always worked to bring us up. As soon as I could I worked on the pit props until I was seventeen, that was two and a half years. The props paid £11 a week, and £11 for a sixteen-year-old kid was good money. But now I might have been a bricklayer, you know what I mean, and I might never have hit unemployment, I might have had me own business. So for that few extra quid I jumped into the money job.

'I got married. She was only seventeen and I put her wrong like, you know, and we got married like, and I had no more bother. We had a good life. I was married at twenty-one, and from then on there was no bother between then and 1969, just a peaceful coexistence. Going to work eight till five, £40 a week coming home. That married life, she seemed to be working, and I seemed to be working, and we had a little, you can call it luck if you want. We never hit any right bad patches. We weren't well-off, like, but when we got the kids to, like, school, she got a little job and I had a job and it was the top of the world, like.

'I was in a steelworks. It was a job, like, that nobody wanted, poorly paid, hard work and poorly paid, but when I got married I had to take some sort of a job. I was only down as a general labourer, then I was a sheeter, then I made a scrap burner. I had about £33 then, double shifts. I was working doublers and treblers, grabbing, you know, what they call grabbing. That was when I bought me furniture, because I bought all this furniture here cash, like, and fitted carpets in the house down there, like, where we used to live. And that's how we worked it. I got the first going to school, and she got a job, and I still had that job scrap burning, and things got to be that good when I had that few extra bob.

'But when the lads were coming home from the contractors' like, £70 and £80 ... but they don't last, you see what I mean. Our lass was saying, "Stop here at thirty, where you're getting thirty. That'll do us. We'll manage." I said, "You what! And there's so-and-so getting seventy-five!" I chucked it and I went to the construction. Hell of a job for eighteen months. I was getting seventies, sixties, all kinds, you know what I mean? I was a mate, an instrument fitter's mate, carrying a little tiny bag about that size, because he's no tools bigger than that. I carried that about and made his tea. Great! Great! I never banked the money. I always had about seventy to eighty on me hip. It was a great feeling. I went down to the top shop in the town, and I said, "I want that telly." At the time it was rental, you had to put so much down, it was £40. He said, "It's £40." I said, "Aw, give us it." It's a great feeling, like, you know what I mean?

'I come off there, well the job was running down, you see. There were pay-offs every week. I went to work at the chemical works. That was 1969, my wife died. I left the house and I got a job that finished, and since then I've had no really what you'd call luck.'

Mr Paton

Mr Paton was another 'unskilled' worker in the north-east. Cheerful, bouncy, expansive, talkative and plausible, he had been out of work about four months and lived on supplementary benefit.

'I was a welder when I was a kid like. I was working in the pits, making gaskets. I packed it in, I got sick of it. You see, I'm a lad that likes a change, like. I cannot stick in one job, you know. Mind I can do anything, anything on a building site, I can do it, apart from driving, although I'm classed as a labourer at the exchange, unless I get a job on a building site and I'm classed as a handy man. I was a ganger, that's because I could do everything; burning, welding, scrap welding, finishing, rubbing up. I've even used explosives.

'There's no better grafter than me like. When I was on painting, I was getting £40 a week. I was a rough painter, you see. I've been all over, concreting and that. Like, I was shot-blasting in the shipyard. I was getting forty-five every week, buying my own house, like. You can go and ask me wife this. When I started for the foundry I was killing meself. Mind you, I was getting £38 a week, but I was killing meself for it, you know. You see, everything you done was a bonus job, you know. He'd say to you, "I want eight barrels of sand." You'd say, "How much?" If he said a pound, you'd bargain for it, "Oh no, five bob a barrel," and that's the way you'd get your money, you know. And I used to have to go in and dig red hot moulds, you know, where the moulds had been like, and I had to dig it red hot. And I've went to work with pleurisy. The doctor put me on a sick note for a fortnight, and I strapped myself up with a kaolin poultice and I went to work next day, just because it was nearly Christmas and I didn't want to drop me money, see, and I was working till nine o'clock at night.

'I've seen me work three days and three nights off the dot, without any sleep, you know, just to get good money. What I used to do, the foreman he'd say, "Will you come back at five o'clock?" I'd get meself home at four, back for five, see. I used to come home, get a quick meal and get meself a wash, like, wake meself up a bit. Back to work, work all night, and he used to say, "Will you work all day today again?" Then I used to work. Mind, you used to get the money like, but then you kill yourself. But I always find a labouring man always does kill hisself at work. Whereas the tradesman's sitting about, getting good money where he shouldn't be getting it, and the labourer's doing all the graft. I've always found that out.

'Well, I packed in. You get sick of the job, like. Well, what reason I finished, there was nine of us finished like, it was when a ship went through the Tyne to the big dry dock there. It's where they blow her, see, and they'd been on good money, £60 a week, and they left us all in the yard just on nae overtime, just on flat rate, so we all packed in, like. See, you've got to go where the money is, like. But I was earning good money when I worked there, like, but now they've stopped all that, you can't make a good wage.'

Mr Miller

Mr Miller was another of this group contacted casually in the north-east. A fast talker, presenting a 'fly' image with his trendy clothes and long hair, he was nervy, guarded, and not too keen to talk at length. He also worked on steel erecting contracts which took him away from home. In the last eighteen months he had had only two jobs of four months' and three months' duration. He now lived on supplementary benefit.

'We've had a bad time for the last eighteen months. In that eighteen months it's been lean for me. Before then I've always worked. I've had two year on one job, I've been straight out of one job and into another. When I'm working, a steady two year I had, I used to pay £380 tax a year, so I mean I don't feel as though I'm taking anything I'm not entitled to now. When I was working and I was getting good money, I was smoking forty and fifty a day. I was going to work on a Monday morning – I could have been out every night since the Thursday – and I was going to work on a Monday morning with £10 in my pocket still.

'If I have to come off, like, it's a very lean time round here. I mean the lads have never known it so bad, to be off so long, honestly, I've never. You're usually in and out with jobs. I mean at one time here you could tell the gaffer to . . . and go to another job and get another start, but things have really tightened up round here now, like, you know what I mean. But in the last eighteen months I've had two jobs. One lasted four months and one lasted three months. I was never out of work before the last eighteen months.'

Mr Ryan and Mr Nottingly

Mr Ryan and Mr Nottingly were the last of the men whom we saw in the north-east, who lived on council estates supported by supplementary benefit. Neither was very articulate about work, although they seemed to have had the same sorts of jobs and job changes as the others.

Mr Ryan was relaxed and untroubled by being interviewed – he had just got back from the pub. But there was evidence from his wife and his mother who were present for part of the time that, to say the least, he tended to present an idealized picture of his behaviour as a worker and husband. There was some doubt about how long he had been out of work: he said about a year, but Mr Lucas estimated that he had not worked regularly during the last four years. He, too, talked about his high earnings and prowess in work.

Mr Nottingly was an ex-apprentice who had left to get more money on contract work, but who had returned to his trade and finished his time so that he was a skilled tradesman. Since then he had had a number of small contracts. Of all the men we saw, he appeared the most hangdog. He had currently been unemployed for about nine months.

Teenagers

This is an appropriate place to introduce the experiences of some teenagers, also from the north-east, whom we met through a community work organization. The early pattern of their work seemed to begin to repeat the experience of the older workers. All had recently been unemployed for spells of over six months and even a year. While not working they had drawn supplementary benefit. Making allowance for the awkwardness of the interview situation (they were interviewed while working) what still struck us most was how guarded, even cowed, some of the teenagers seemed – how very little they had to say about work.

'Warehouseboy, £3.92. I packed it in after a week.'

'I had a job with a milk round, £7 odd. I got paid off. They give you the work for six months and then you come off before you get more money, you know. They paid us off before we can get our award.'

'I was at the oil refinery, £7 to £8 a week, that was all. You were lucky if you come out with six, like. I had me boarding money to pay me mam, so much club money, and then me fares. Well, I went for a smoke and we were away for an hour and a half, sitting on a wall, getting sunburnt, like. And he come and he says, "Aw, where you been?" like. I says, "I've just been for a smoke." He says, "Aw, it's the sack." I says, "Fair enough," like. Just put me coat on and walked out.'

'I used to work at the steelworks, apprentice sheet metal. I got the sack. They said I wasn't brainy enough to do things like.'

'Sawmill. Packed that in, for cause the wage was poor, £3.65 a week. Others used to work for about a week, and then they'd pack it in. Stuck it for eight months. Went as a milkman. Packed that up, £6 odd, three weeks. I couldn't get up of a morning, and I didn't like the running about; you see I had a big round. Then I went to a slaters. Why, the wage varied like. See, if you were working out of town you got paid extra travelling time. Oh, about £10. I stayed about six months and then I've been out of work ever since. I got paid off. Bad timekeeping, oversleeping. You see it was the work I had to do, and I got sick of that job.'

'I was working in a furniture shop, but I got fed up with that because I was only getting £4 2s. 6d. for a five and a half day week, and I got fed up of that. And I got a so-called apprenticeship as a plastics worker. After three weeks I got finished there, and when I told them at the dole they knew the bloke. He does the same trick all the time.'

Jimmy Weaver's family

We also talked to three teenagers whose names were given to us by the Youth Employment Officer. None of them had worked during the year since leaving school. Two of them had modestly comfortable backgrounds with parents in steady work. However the third, Jimmy Weaver, had already had four years of experience of supplementary benefits before even he left school. His father, a miner,* had been five years off work and had only just returned to work although he was not well. His hands, which hung abjectly and uselessly, were huge and scaly with peeling nails and skin which cracked each time he attempted to wash – they looked like the imitation monsters' hands which can be bought in 'joke' shops. His wife, small and thin like Jimmy, with bird-like eyes and a deferential manner, described the father's work and the resulting illness which had been such a powerful daily presence in Jimmy's life for the last five years.

'He's down the pit. We know there's a lot of collieries on the way out, but this one'll be the last to close, because there's thousands of pounds been spent in the last ten years, and if he'd kept his health he was in a good job. He was a drift man, what they call a drift man, machinery, of course, again. Like he used to cut the stone with it for the men to get coal.

'He's just been to work this last few weeks. He's been off five years, skin trouble. I mean, really, let's face it, he's no better. He won't last. They've got it down as drug allergy. You see he was on a drug for his chest, and they kept him on. Mind, he was really bad with his chest. Well, I don't dare mention it, the doctor at the infirmary will think I'm daft, but you see he'd been on this drug quite a long time before it got its hold, and as it happened he was doing so well with his chest

---

* Mr Weaver was one of the considerable proportion of elderly and physically disabled men whom the labours of the younger miners in the coal industry used to carry in better times. Now – in the drive for greater productivity – such men are being retired prematurely from work at the age of fifty-five onwards, although the redundancy payments in lieu of lost wages will not carry them through until sixty-five. Ironically, Mr Weaver, in a profitable pit, could not get the option to retire, and must work on.

that they didn't get him to strip each time, otherwise they would have seen it. They said he'd just have to live with it.

'He's been in and out of hospital, in and out. I mean we moved to here thinking, because we had no bathroom, we moved here thinking that the bath would be better for him, see. But he comes in at two o'clock for his dinner, and I'm not kidding, he goes mad! With the water, when he's washing, it gets in the cracks in his skin. He sits there scratching and scratching. He's been back about eight weeks. He had to go back or they said he'd lose his pension rights, and he's got no compensation. I didn't think he'd have lasted that long, but he cannot put one foot before the other. It's terrible. It's a light job, but you see that's not the point. He's still down practically near the coal face. He cannot get the dust off his skin.'

Mr Coxon

We now return to the south-east for the remainder of these work histories. Mr Coxon was an older man, an ex-lorry driver, disabled by a heart condition, whom we contacted via the Child Poverty Action Group. He needed no encouragement to talk about work almost obsessionally, seeing the scenes in his mind's eye in the minutest detail as he described them to us. He had not worked full time in the past ten years, during nine of which his supplementary benefit had been reduced by a wage stop.* Just recently he had been given the status of permanently sick so that – unless he still wished to – he need no longer register himself as available for work.

'That must be the cause of all my illness, you know, when I was young and that. I've been in bad health since I was a kid. I can't read, you see, because I never went to school. I was always in hospital with something wrong wi' me. I didn't go to school see. I can make out printing, but I can't writing, not like some of them do it.

'The first of all, when I was eight years of age, I used to go out and forage for wood and coal, and clear the place up, scrub the bare boards. My sisters and all, and on Saturdays we used to get up at

* In this he was typical – two thirds of those affected by the wage stop are disabled.

40

four o'clock in the morning and go down the Marylebone High Street. My mother used to give us a shilling. We used to take an army kitbag with us. We used to go down the Marylebone High Street, and we used to get three pennorth of stale bread, three or four loaves, go in the butchers to get three pennorth of pieces, what's been cut up, the trimmings, six or seven pounds. Go in the bacon shop and get all the bits and pieces of bacon, sometimes good rashers. And then we used to go to the cake shop and get three pennorth of cakes, stale cakes. Then we used to cart that home. And after that we used to have a cup of tea, and a lump of bread with a lump of margarine on it, and that was your breakfast.

'You see my father didn't get much wage, and he didn't work, he couldn't get a job. If you were two minutes late your job was gone. And my father, well, I admit he liked his drink. He had his drink, you know, especially of a Sunday, he liked a pint with his bit of dinner, and my mother wouldn't give him tuppence for to have half a pint of beer with his dinner, so he never used to eat no dinner. And that's how, when he did start work and get a few bob, he used to get drunk and to come home and smash the home up. But I liked my father. My father was a good man, but my mother was a bad woman. She was a miser. After all that, she died leaving hundreds of pounds hoarded away.

'The best job I ever really had is driving. I can't work indoors, I like working out of doors. I been a coalman. I used to carry two hundredweights of coal when I was fifteen, sixteen. Used to get up at four in the morning and me and another chap, we used to unload a fifty-ton wagon of coal in three hours, start at four and not finish till seven, a fifty-ton truck. That's work. I started on a brick lorry. We used to do 2,400 bricks a load, that's four loads a day. Well, you handle them bricks twice, that's 10,000 bricks a day, and you handle 'em twice.

'We used to go up to Cambridge, and one time we were a bit late coming home. He was a bit tired an' all. And he said to me, "D'you reckon you can handle this?" So I said, "Well, I dunno, I'll have a go." That what I always used to say, "If you say it's all right." He said, "I think you can because you've watched me a lot," he said, "I know you're gonna be a driver." So he pulls over, so he says, "You know what to do." So I could see what gears he was putting in.

He left the engine running, because if that stopped we'd have to crank it, see. He says, "You know the gears," he said. "If you look down there, you'll see a big brass bar down there; it's got the gears, the numbers of the gears are on there, see." He said, "It's a slow gear, very slow." I said, "I know." He said, "The clutch is very hard to push out," because it had a very short drive shaft, see. So anyway, I got in, and put the clutch there, and you had to slam it in, see. You just can't ... And I took the handbrakes off, two big handbrakes, just knocked 'em off and started off. And after that he told me when to change gear. You see we had no meter to tell what speed in them days, in 1928, and he said, "Right, double clutch it," and I double clutched it – because I was only little then I had to stand up when I put the gears in. Put it in third, came right down, you know, right up to top gear, and away we went. I had me foot on the clutch. He said, "Pull up the clutch," he said. I said, "Right!" I had about ten miles o' that. He said – we came to a hill – he said, "Change down. Watch your speed, don't get that too low. Change down into first gear." So I done that. He said, "Blimey!" he said, "You should be a bloody good driver when you do get a licence out."

'I never got a licence out when I was seventeen, mainly because I couldn't read, see. Till I was about thirty, and then I got me driving licence out. Me wife said she'd help me with the reading if I'd get the licence.

'I went for one job at the Post Office and a bloke took me out on test. So he says "Right, away we go. Follow me in the garage." There's all these mail vans lined up, you know. He said, "Right oh," he said, "Go and start that one up, would you. Drive it out a bit, on your own." And I just open the door, and just touched the whatsername, the gear – see if the handbrake was on – went round the front, started it up. Choom! Up it come. He's watching all the time, he's watching all the time. He said, "Right. Drive it out." Drove it out. "Away you go out the garage." I said, "Where d'you want me to go?" He says, "I'll tell you where to go." Went all round the city, all round the city. All back turnings, get the van up there. You turn in them off the main road, you see, you had no indicators. He had to put his hand out, only had one mirror. You had to turn in there to see if your wheels touched the kerb or not. Done all that. You see, they'd whitewashed the wheels. They'd put whitewash on the back wheels to see if you touched the kerb when you got back. And they take you down the big post office, there, and get two vans, shoved close together, and get you to back in there, see if you can get in there. Well, I just did the lot. That's easy, back in there. And you go up to the garage, back to the garage again. Now while we're out, they've got one of the fitters to close the vans more, so that where I got this one out of, that won't go in no more, to see if I will try to get it in there, see. They know I can't, but they think I'll try to take it back in there. So when I got back there, they said, "Right, put it back where you found it." I looked, I thought, "It looks a bit narrow to me." I said, "I can't get it back in there." He said, "Why not?" "That ain't wide enough. The vans have been shifted."

'There was only one bloke in that office that knew I couldn't read, that gives the services out. I told him. He said, "Right," he said. "I'll look after you, see." I went back next morning to be sworn in like, and the bloke gives me a card. He says, "Here, read that." I says, "Yeah." I didn't tell him I couldn't read, or they wouldn't have started me, but I had an idea I understood it, but yet I couldn't read it. It was like in the police courts. Some of the other chaps used to help me at first but after the first few times I could do it blindfolded. The south-east, that's the parcel depot, and the south-west, that's the letter part. There's Victoria, that's letters and parcels. Then there's the northern, that's at the Angel. Then there's Mornington Crescent, Camden Town, they're the biggest.

'The last big job I had, I got a job working sometimes twenty hours a day for £8 a week.' (His wife said, 'He liked working for the boss. He was friendly, very friendly. I used to say to my husband, "Slow down, take it steady. In years to come they won't think anything of you if you can't go to work." ')

'You see that's the part about me. When I start a job, I like the job. If I like a job, I get on with it. I'll work all night and all day. I like doing a job and I like helping people. And I'm a man for time. I don't like to be late, and I don't like to be early. I'd go off all day, and I'd tell her the time I'd be home, and then I'd be home at that time. She'd hear the lorry come round the corner, changing gears, and she'd be out the street door, waiting.

'I used to polish that lorry up and treat it like a baby, never had no accident, never any trouble with the police, all that time I was driving. Here, look at these licences, all clean. I like lorries. I like the fun of it, because we used to go on it, pull up half way, to get a cup of tea and that, and you'd meet the other lorry drivers there, and you'd get to be friends, you know. And in them days, another lorry driver's in trouble, another driver comes along, pull up and ask are you in trouble, something like that, try and help you if you can. But these days, whew! that's all they think about. You'll see the old uns in these cafes all muck in together, but the young ones, you won't see them mucking in together.

'When I used to go up to these factories, even the guvnors up there all liked me. All the work people, "Wotcher!" Everybody was pleasant with me. If I could help 'em I'd do it. Go in the office and a cup of tea with the guvnors. Oh, it was good it was, and I used to like it.

'But it got me down and I had to turn it in. It would have killed me. Five-ton lorries. I had to load it myself, and all that mileage. Well, what it was, I knew there was something wrong with me, because sometimes I got a bit naughty, getting up in the morning. D'you know, I used to start feeling like not going to work, I was so tired and I wanted to sleep. And you see in them days, if you had a couple of days off on a job, your job was done. They got another driver. It's not like today: you have a week off and your job's still there. That was it, you see. I had a week off and they took on another driver. Then after that I began to get worse, I didn't want to get up in a morning.'

(Mrs Coxon said, 'He was too ill to go back on to work. He used to keep going round to the doctor, and he'd say, "No, you stay out a little bit longer." But you see in them days, if you was out of work a certain length of time, and then you went to get a job, they used to ask where you'd been. And if you'd been sick, if they used to see that your card hadn't been stamped, they used to think you'd been in prison or something like that. Well, of course, you found it hard to get a job then, see. People wouldn't start you until you'd been at work. But anyway, eventually he got another job.' Then a quick decline through shorter, poorer jobs into unemployment.)

Mr Dover

We contacted Mr Dover through a claimants' union in the south-east. He was a good talker and manifestly enjoyed the interview, which he treated as something of a joke. He had been unemployed over the winter months, drawing supplementary benefit. (He was separated, but lived with Miss Hebb, whose story appears next.)

'Actually, I've never had a regular job. Just a few weeks to get the money together. The longest I've ever worked is about sixteen weeks, I think, that was on a fruit farm. Usually it's a couple of months, say on a building site or something, you know. The idea of getting a job is because you want to get some money to do something with really, you know, and once you get the money together, you've no more reason to work.

'You know how you've always got something to blame for the way you are? I always say the reason why I've never been able to save up any money is because my father broke into my moneybox when I was a kid. We moved around quite a bit. The last school I went to, I enjoyed quite a lot, the last eighteen months, it was quite bearable, you know. But there were no G.C.E.s at my school. I don't know whether I'd have taken them or not, but looking back I wish I had got some O levels and some A levels when I was younger because, well, although it's easier, perhaps to adapt to learning now when you get a bit older, it's a bit of a drag. I left school at fifteen and I left home at fifteen. It was a bit of a bad scene. Like, my parents have since, you know, split up and married again. And my sister got married to get away from home. My father used to get into debt for money. He was mostly in the building trade. He is, in fact, a master builder, you know, or anything in the building trade; bricklaying, carpentering, tiling. You see, I used to do it at weekends for him. I've never served an apprenticeship, but I can lay bricks and tile.

'Yeah, it was good to work, because you, er, some of it was hard work, but it was, like, good to feel your muscles working, you know. Also, you got a different occupation all through the day. Construction work, I did tunnel work, sometimes I'd go on bridges. You have to be fit for it. In those days there was quite a lot of machinery on the site, and most of the concrete had to be mixed not by hand but shovelled into the machine. Tiling was a nice job. Modern tiles, I could teach you to do it in two minutes, but the old tiles, you know, it's quite sort of skilled. Sometimes, if I worked on an old house that was in a terrible state, putting new tiles on, and I used to think I'd made a good job, I was satisfied with it. Only on the old work though. On the new work, if I could have stayed with it, it's just like any other, it's just the money, you know. We always had a good social life; a lot of your social life does lead, in fact, from your work. On a building site there's a terrific social life with these guys. You've got quite a bit of money to spend, you know. You'd get to a new town, new job, you know. Find somewhere, and before you used to get fed up with the town, you're on the move again.

'You went up and down quite quickly. One day you'd be living quite highly. You'd have a hundred pounds in your pocket, and you didn't even think about it. You just had a good time till the money was gone. Oh, I used to nip over to Paris for a couple of weeks or something, pick up a dolly somewhere. I'd go all over. I think I've been in every European country, plus Scandinavia, Libya, Egypt, right across Asia. I've been as far as Thailand, Java. I don't know, it seems like once you get to know people, and you've been together a couple of months and you get to know the way they think, you start having the same conversations. You just get boring, and you've got to move on.

'At one time I cultivated a cockney accent, when I was a teddy boy that was. I sometimes used to think I'd like to get into the creative side, and I used to write a bit, you know, and I mixed with a very arty crowd. I had a lot of money in those days and I remember one job, tunnelling, I was on eighty quid a week, and I used to have a tobacco tin stuffed full of £5 notes, and I used to get on with these blokes because I'd got so much money. I used to get into places like the Royal Oak, and when I came up to the bar the crowd would part. Nobody would want to talk to me, and the barman would wonder whether to serve me. But then I'd get out my tin of £5 notes, and everybody would come back and start talking to me – I'd get served all right!

'The best job I ever had was shot-blasting. It didn't look much of a job when I went along, but when I got there it was a new firm just starting up, and the manager was only a young bloke, and after I'd been there only a short time he said to me, "Why don't you take a couple of A levels? Get on a course, and we'll make you a manager here." And I thought, "Christ! Manager! I don't want that manager bit." So I collected my money together and split.

'I'm talking very nostalgically about the old days. I suppose I do look back, I think I do. I think I miss the lack of responsibility, and just sort of chasing the chicks, you know. Now, with the times, it seems to sort of involve more. That is, I used to be able to live like that, until I got my dicky back, you know. The difficulty is now, I can't do labouring work because I've had a bad back for the last few years. I was doing a bit of work, self-employed tiler, and I fell off a scaffold, and I had a couple of loose discs and things, you know, and I've been back and forward to hospital ever since. People say, "Ha, ha! Another one!" But it's since I've done this back that it's been very difficult.

'Since I've done this back in, I mean what sort of job can I get? At one time I was at the cinema in the morning cleaning for four hours, and the afternoons off. That was for seven days a week. Then I used to work in the bakehouse occasionally, just to make ends meet, but that was more, sort of, steady work which lasted, oh, for three months, something like that. But you know, after a while, you imagine doing the same damn thing every day of the week, making the same journey every morning. I used to think of different ways to get there, so I didn't have to go the same way. It used to take me *hours* to get there. I used to have to be catching one bus down this way for a few miles, it used to cost me a fortune, just so I didn't use to have to go up that same bit of road. A bus used to arrive outside my door which would have dropped me at work but after that first journey ...

'I used to like working with people, but I liked working on my own initiative. Like, I'd hate being told what to do. I usually, you know, point out what's wrong. I'd get it worked out properly, and then they'd give me the sack! You know, down at the fruit farm when I was there in '69, they'd treat their students like shit down there. But I'd been there a while, and they just couldn't get the beanery – they called it in the jargon – working efficiently, and so, you know, I did little things and got it working, and the foreman pulled out and left me to do it. And I even got the people working and gave them smoke-breaks and so on. But they won't employ me any more. I think they got a bit frightened of losing their jobs, the foremen.

'One way that I'm different from other people, you know at factories, like, when you all line up at the end of the week for your pay packet, some of the people, they'll say, "thank you" for their pay packet, but I don't, I just take it. And one or two of the guys who've handed it out to me asked me why I didn't say thank you, so I told them. Why should I thank them? I've worked hard for that money. *They're* privileged to have me working for them on a boring job like that.

'It's surprising how you change, how your attitudes change. When I was younger, I had a job in a linoleum factory, and there were some West Indians there, and these West Indians, they'd work like the fuck all morning, and then by lunchtime they'd done enough work, they reckoned, to last them for the rest of the day, so they'd just laze about for the rest of the afternoon. And everybody else would be talking and they'd say, "Look at those lazy sods over there, bone idle!" And I'd be the same, I used to say the same kind of things. But now I've got round to the same way of thinking as them. Why should you do the work? Why should you do more than is absolutely necessary?

'The trouble is it's starting to change. They're not employing casual labour any more, and they're getting more machinery. And they're training, they've started training pigeons to pick peas off a belt. I've been done out of a job by a pigeon!'

Miss Hebb

Miss Hebb lived with Mr Dover in a furnished house. Although she volunteered to be interviewed, she seemed to find the situation embarrassing, and her story was punctuated by pauses, nervous laughs, and uneasy shuffling in her chair. She had been living on supplementary benefit for the past eight months.

'I've always done what I was told at school. I suppose I've always been a conformist. I suppose it does make a difference, not having a father, not having anybody to fall back on, like, you know. I always used to lie about it. I used to say I had got a father, so the other kids wouldn't know. But I think that's got a lot to do with it, not having anyone to turn to at school.

'I did maths and science because I was good at it. I went to university to study maths, because it was the expected thing, with my mother being a teacher. She didn't push me a lot; she didn't show a lot of interest. She's a good teacher, but she's quiet and conventional. In fact, she's said since that in some ways she admires me, the way I live now. She's always done one thing all her life.

'When I was at university it was as though I'd got nobody behind me, nobody to help me any more. That threw me and I've never been able to pull myself together. The place I went to was a kind of C.A.T. then, and it was the kind of course where you spend six months in an office, and I was so bored. It was just adding figures up all day. And the people there! I went in the first day and I was all happy, laughing, talking and nobody said a thing. I wondered what was wrong with them. But after a few days I got to be the same as them, and I got frightened because I didn't want to be like that. And there was a girl who was on the same course as me and she was just finishing and she was just like them. I took a day off from that job. It was a nice day and I wanted to go down to the river, and I told them I was sick or something, and I went down to the river. But when I went back next day they were all bitching away, because I'd had a day off; but I thought to myself, well, why didn't *they* have a day off!

'At university I couldn't seem to work somehow, and after I dropped out, I took a job on the farm for summer, and I really loved that. I loved everything about it, milking the cows, and I really wanted to be a dairymaid for life. But my mother talked me into going back into a different job, and they sent me to see the vocational guidance people. At that time I fancied doing something creative, I fancied something like that.

'I was conned really, it was a con trick, the way they presented it, the managerial side, it sounded as though I'd be doing something creative, but when I got there it was just a catering course, and the people there were just as bad as the other place. I don't want to be snobby about intellect, but the people there, I used to get on better with the students. It was a sort of private university catering manager's job – but I wasn't allowed, you weren't supposed to fraternize with the students. I just didn't fit in, I couldn't stand it, couldn't stand it. They told me when I left the course that I'd done very well, but I'd wasted my time really because I wasn't a suitable person for what I'd trained for, the whole set of industrial catering. I was head cook, I had a lot of people under me. It went all right, but I got the sack. No specific reason, except just unsuitable, I was unsuitable, just the sort of mentality, I think. I could do the work O.K., but most of the time you live in, and if you're not quite the same sort of person as them, you just don't fit in there as well. They didn't like me having a messy room, and having junk everywhere, and just, you know, going out late at night, and things like that. They were just *very* ordinary people.

'When I got the sack I was shattered, I was absolutely shattered. I just couldn't seem to get over it. I couldn't pull myself together. I thought I'd try something else, and you know, try and sort myself out a bit, and go and live on a kibbutz, because I really fancied the way of life, you know. I was on the kibbutz for a long time, I didn't want to come back. I was going to stay there, but I had jaundice. After that I was in Birmingham, I was helping at the play centre, but that wasn't a paid job or anything, just helping out, a couple of months. The last job I had, I was a secretary, for a couple of weeks, but I didn't like that. I was getting less at that than I could on the S.S.'

Mr Calvert

The last of the people we interviewed in the south-east, Mr Calvert, is the only one chosen specifically on account of the little we had heard about his response to unemployment. An unemployed graduate, he was also a would-be writer. Since receiving the sack from his last fill-in job in an office he had been unemployed for four months and he lived with his wife, who was also unemployed, in a rented flat, drawing supplementary benefits. He spoke thoughtfully, almost over-seriously, but with flashes of cheeky amusement. He apparently enjoyed the chance to talk about his writing, but was wary in case he should seem to claim too much for it.

'I'd always sort of written sporadically, from being a kid, odds and ends, when I was about twelve or so. In class there were two of us that wrote sort of things, and you'd just arrive at school with a new verse to a sort of joint four or five of us. These things would last for 135 verses. We had a lot of poems about Rockers, Elvis Presley, and developed a lot of cult objects, like a particular make of car. I didn't write for the school magazine because I didn't like the idea of a school magazine, really; it was just "school, school, school".

'It was a segregated grammar school with great pretensions. You know, it was very formal, assembly in the mornings. As far as school was concerned, I didn't get on very well with many people at all, on the staff. I don't think anybody understood me. I don't think anybody made any effort. I mean, the contacts with the staff at school were so meaningless that it more or less came about that I didn't do what I was supposed to do, and this came about that it looked like, you know, a planned refusal.

'Well, I used to go to school in the morning, and I used to hear perhaps four or five things in the day, you know. I mean I was just not present, but I usually managed to do enough at the end of term to counterbalance a terrible term position by a reasonable exam position.

'At the school, you know, so few careers seemed to open out. I didn't think of anything else apart from going to university. I took economics because, well, half way through the last year in the upper fifth, the economics teacher came in – who'd kept aloof from the junior school completely – he sort of appeared as the figure of the new adult treatment for schoolboys in the sixth form. Well, he made a few jokes that were on a more equal and intelligent basis than the normal staff, and it was, you know, it would have seemed transpicuous today, but he seemed really unique, because he was a mysterious personality for a start – he used to park his car in the headmaster's private spot, you know! I got into a university, really, because of the special pleading of the economics master in the reference he gave me, not on the head's report.

'As far as the university course was concerned the work was merely a repetition of what we'd done in the sixth form, and anyone who'd done economics, you know, just used to go to about one lecture a week. At the end of the year I didn't do too badly in the exam. Sort of got between upper and lower seconds. My very unsympathetic supervisor took the attitude, "Well, you'd better pull your socks up next year", you know. I always found him a very odd person. I couldn't relate to guys who were interested in economics at all. I mean it must be very interesting to be able to discuss the effectiveness of Stalin's successive five-years plans, but you know I really don't think anything much is there apart from the act of talking in a room to a teacher who is saying, "Yes, you've obviously read the book." By the second year it became a comic classic really. It had just degenerated into learned papers in American journals that were just a mass of, you know, mathematical symbols after an introductory paragraph.

'I began to feel very insecure, obviously coming out of a small region like the north-east with its set type of jobs. And I began to meet people; well, I met one person who had read a great deal more than I had, you know. And more or less over the first year I came to terms with the fact that, you know, any finished writing product that I'd be satisfied with now would be something that would come at the end of perhaps two years' really hard sort of reading and stuff, thinking. It wouldn't be something that would come automatically any more.

'Well, I felt the degree creeping up. And I didn't want to adopt the attitude, "Well, if I don't get a degree I'll be just like everybody else" – that was the attitude that was being pushed at home, and this was an attitude that was sort of creeping in, you know. It was another ticket to a privileged position, and stuff. But at that time I didn't want that, because university had been a more or less divisive experience. I mean I realized I was now cut off from people I knew and could accept. At one stage at school I used to knock around with people who were, you know, sort of apprentice teddy boys, but at university I was cut off from them, you know. That was another clash.

'But in the end, you know, I just started to do the work and stuff, and fortunately I hit a sort of insomniac streak and it just, you know, came on. I got a lower second. It's average, you know. In the last two months I was thinking, you know, of just packing it in, you know, because I had so much to do. But in the end I just got as much grasp as possible, and there were other people who did the same thing, and I think it's generally recognized that that's the sort of degree that one gets when that happens, when you do that.

'After that I got into Queen Mary College to do a master's degree in economics, and I did a fortnight there. I'd got in at the eleventh hour. Well, I wasn't disenchanted with the idea of recouping my losses at this stage. I didn't regard them as losses. I just thought that economics was too diffuse a subject and that it was an unworthy master in that sense. One should be able to confine it to a compartment, and not dedicate one's life to it. However, my local authority didn't come through, and I got a sort of illiterate letter. I've got the letter still to this day, and I can't understand what it says.

'First I had a sort of fill-in job for a market research firm. I worked at writing just as steadily when I was working in an office. I used to get into trouble for writing things down at work. The briefest notes people took objection to, you know, and if you brought a book in, a book when there was no work around, everybody, you know, went beetle-browed. Well, I mean everybody would be sitting eating an apple and looking out of the window, and yawning, and then you'd get a book out, really, I mean arguments used to start from that point, because I used to say, "Don't worry, it won't hurt you." Or pass it over and try and get them to touch it! Huh! Because they were all discontented with the education system. They'd all dropped out at some time or other, you know, and books were like a hideous apparition to them; they didn't want to be reminded.

'It was about that stage when I started thinking seriously about getting a job and things. Because to me it was always something in the future before that. I'd felt that my attitude to writing was realistic, and I wasn't just using it as a sort of cop-out. It always seemed to me that soon I'd be sufficiently together with writing to be able to work a job with it at the same time. Well, I suppose I thought I could teach in college because, not because, um, you know, I didn't fancy any other walks of life, but because, um, you know, I was generally more interested in explaining the realm of ideas and suchlike. At the time industry just seemed another cop-out. I mean I had remarkably few ideas to rub together about jobs, surprisingly, and later they got fewer.

'The first job that came up, though, was a job on research in teaching methods, for two years. Well, you know, it wasn't bad. I met some reasonable people. I mean I was interested in educational methods and things. But you know, I would be absent for a while, and in the end my attendance was very poor, because, you know, you get really cheesed off with, um, you know, doing the same thing on and off. Me and the boss just about managed to finish the course between us. What I was thinking about, really, was the personal position of my life, which was very tangled up to that time. The boss there was very tolerant, and he realized that research assistant jobs were jobs, you know, where people go to get themselves together really. Increasingly the job was something that barely got noticed. I just used to turn up.

'After that I had some bits and pieces of part-time teaching, liberal studies to building workers, to keep going. It was quite nice really, like having to teach, as opposed to having a given audience who wanted to pass exams.

'I went back into research part-time, just to have enough money to go on writing, you know. It was just working in an office, you know, a computer, converting survey data on to punch cards and tabulating. But I thought it was desperate. It was like being in hell, just relating to the people there. I mean people would bring about a quarter of themselves to work. I mean you get *taught* by work to leave most of yourself at home, you know. You can't indulge yourself fully, and most places, offices, I don't like very much because awareness is taken to be synonymous with the ability to do nothing in particular. Both of my jobs in offices were terminated by my employers, very emphatically. I just didn't fit in at all. I've always resented people, who, in the end, I couldn't make myself understood to, and who wouldn't try to make themselves understood to me.

'I think office work tends to bring about the absolute worst in men for a start. I think – I don't know whether you're interested in Jung at all? – well, I think it tends to encourage men to live almost entirely by identifying with the anima, which is the sort of female component of their personality. You know, they tend to nag. And blokes come up to you and tell you that their shoe-laces have snapped or something, so often. I suppose, on balance, I was going to keep the job as long as it took me to find somewhere else, but I was getting more and more disgruntled with it, and I suppose it was just becoming more and more evident. Things like I'd sleep in in the morning, repeatedly, the alarm wouldn't wake me up. And the mornings I did get up I missed the bus. You know, there were little squabbles about all sorts of things like discipline. When this was all over the boss would say,

"You know, this is no good," and I tended to get into work on time. This happened with everybody who worked in the office, regularly or otherwise. But I think it was felt with me that profoundly and over a prolonged period I'd proved unsuitable for the work.

'I think the actual manual working class are much more gainfully occupied than the office workers, you know. I think they've got much more psychological capital riding on their work. I think they feel able, while digging a ditch, to talk to one another, while getting exercise and fresh air. They can go to the pub at lunch time. They can go to the betting shop, if there happens to be one near the building site. I'm not presenting a caricature of the working class or anything – this is how it always was for me, this was how it revolved when I've worked on building sites.

'In the end it was just not being suitable for the work in that office. It was genuinely felt by the people there – there seemed to be no personal animosity – they felt it was just genes or something! I really, you know, it was really something that I couldn't defeat. It wasn't an environment that I could settle down in. You know, I think it was a genuine case absolutely. It wasn't just a case of throwing up the work and deciding to go on the dole, you know. I actually lost the last job because of the tension between the two things. It's not as if I've got objections to conventional jobs. It's just really how much my work, my writing, at this stage is compromised by almost every other type of job!'

3 The Search for New Jobs

In this chapter the workless describe how they set about looking for new jobs. There were of course limits to the numbers and sorts of jobs available for individuals with their particular skills. But, to some extent independently of these constraints, the workless themselves set other limits to the kinds of work they were looking for: they stipulated the level of wages they wanted, the sorts of skills they preferred, and the distances they were prepared to move.

Whether or not they found a job would depend on the thoroughness and enthusiasm of their search, and also upon its scope, and upon how they got their information about work. Obtaining work would also depend on how 'flexible' they were when they met with setbacks in the search, or when they encountered employers who offered them jobs and conditions of work which were different from the ones they wanted.

Starting wages

Most of the workers whom we saw tended to be more definite about their starting pay than about the sorts of skills they wanted, and they fixed their requirements at or above the level of pay in the job they had just left. The white-collar workers tended to look for a slightly higher wage. Mr Vickers said, 'I just want to ensure that I sort of maintain a standard of living and just sort of slightly improve all the time. It's a very, sort of, shallow ladder, because I think, human beings being what they are, they always want, they're most happy when they're going ... they're always looking for something better. So providing you can just keep things improving a little bit all the time; whereas if you're on a plateau you tend to take for granted what you've got and you tend to become a little bit discontented.'

Mrs Haigh said, 'You think if your husband starts a job and works hard at it, well, he should be – rewarded. As time goes on you'd think he'd get a better salary.'

The redundant workers, Mr Fellowes and Mr Weston, were especially bitter at the way they felt their firms had sometimes added insult to the injury of the initial breach of trust of redundancy by offering jobs like their old ones but at lower pay. Mr Weston said, 'Well, if they don't offer me a fair day's pay for a fair day's work, I won't go back, it's as simple as that. I mean this would be dead against my principles, to go back to the same job at a cut rate. I mean that's just, a man's definitely out to exploit a person, without any shadow of a doubt. Some of the blokes that they'd made redundant, they kept them off for a day or two and then asked them to come back at a cut rate. My boss, he's the sort of bloke, if he knew he could do this and get these blokes back at a cheaper rate he's laughing. He thinks they've got no spunk, that's the word he uses.'

The less-skilled manual workers of the north-east, who had had more fluctuating wages, tended to hope at first for the higher wages they had earned in the past. Mr Miller, for instance, was inclined to hope that what he regarded as his luck would turn and that better-paid work would come back to the north-east: 'I've always liked money when I get a job, I'm on about sixty or seventy a week. When it comes to the crunch, when I'm back on the job I pay a lot of me debts back, you see, who I borrow off now. I mean I owe now, I must owe her mother about a hundred. Where you get a job down here like, go on the buildings, get about £15 a week, you know what I mean, I've never been *used* to £15 a week. Well, when a man starts working I reckon his wife's worth about £25 a week for housekeeping, with prices like they are today. And I reckon the man, when he's going out working – especially if he's doing my type o' work, *deserves* about ten to twelve. Down on that building site travelling men are getting their sixties and seventies a week. It's only what I've been used to.' Mr Miller has only two children.

Mr Paton also said he intended to wait for a reasonable starting wage because of his family commitments: 'For my rent, with all my kids, you'd want £35 coming in to pay your debts off as well. Well I wouldn't start for no job unless I was getting £28 to fetch home, I wouldn't take me coat off for no less because I couldn't manage on less. I work as much overtime as I can get, me like, you know what I mean, because I like to get money, pocket-money.'

However, not all the workless put so much stress on their starting wage. There were some who stressed also the skill they wanted. And there were others, like Miss Hebb and Mr Dover, who seemed to have no clear impression of the sort of money they would need, or even the sort of job they would like to do.

Skill requirements

Perhaps surprisingly, in view of the fact that they had the more interesting jobs, the skilled workers put less stress on getting a job where they would continue to exercise their particular skills. In choosing a job it seemed almost as though, if they wanted to maintain a given salary, they felt *constrained* to keep on with the same job they had been doing. Mr Haigh said. 'You specialize, and then within that specialism you specialize, so by the time you've been doing a particular job for a few years, other employers look at you and say they don't want you. You're *too* specialized. Take me. I've been in this line all my working life. Now if I switch to engineering, say, I won't know any more than a new graduate. But because of my age I'll be getting more money, so why should a firm employ me? That's the reason I stay in this line. You can't change.'

Mr Calvert, the economics graduate, had put little stress on money, but he also described how restricted he felt his choice of job had become through the narrowness of his specialized education: 'I thought I'd start teaching, definitely, because, you know, I talked to the careers person at the labour exchange and explained to him genuinely that it was the only job that I'd been prepared by my academic history for, you know. It wasn't a question of having a predilection for teaching.' For him, job choice seemed to have narrowed down to this one occupation, and even so he would not be prepared to give it all his energies: 'My writing would only have to compromise timewise with a job. It wouldn't stop or anything, even if I got a full-time job.'

It was those skilled workers in the south-east for whom a return to their old occupation was not assured who seemed most to stress their desire for a job with a particular skill as well as cash. Mr John, still suffering the after-effects of his accident, was still determined to get a welding job paid at white man's rates. Mr Coxon after he became ill had clung for years to the idea of getting another driving job. Mr Odell, who was now officially categorized as 'unsuitable for buses', also wanted to get back into driving, but not just any driving: 'One of the reasons, one of the larger reasons for why I want to work again, is to become actively engaged in the unions.' His ideal job was therefore a driving job with large vehicles and enough men to have a union.

For the other, less-skilled workers, the requirement of a particular starting wage could put a limit on the jobs they were initially prepared to consider. Mr Miller clearly associated his high pay with his dangerous and insecure occupation, 'See me, I'm an erector; I wouldn't go looking for another job.' Mr Paton said, 'I don't think I could stick a closed-in job for the rest of me life, like. I couldn't stick inside a building, I like outside, like.' And the combined effect of this requirement for an outside job with his need for high pay meant that he must get a labouring job where there were no restrictions on earning from contract or piece-work imposed by unions. He explained, 'Now say I say, "I'll work tonight and I'll work till eleven o'clock," they'll say, "Oh no, you can't." "Well, how's that, like?" "Union rules." You're only allowed to work so many hours a day.' Others among the less-skilled also preferred to be 'outside workers'.

Finally among those with clearer job preferences there was the disabled miner's son, Jimmy Weaver, who passionately wanted to be a fisherman. He said, 'First job I wanted to do, I always wanted to go to sea, like, right from I was fifteen, from about eight or nine years old. I've been on the boats since I was about eight or nine. There's a harbour down there where all the boats and all the blokes are. You just sit around and have a cup of tea with them like, hang around like.'

Locality – mobile couples

A number of the more-skilled workers had already moved to their present work, and broadly speaking the more specialized an individual had become, the more resigned he was to the prospect of moving. Also they knew that they would receive some help towards interview and removal expenses. If Mr Haigh was to continue with what he had been doing there were only nine firms in the country to whom he could apply, none of them very near. He said, 'You've *got* to move where the job is, when you're in that sort of job.' The other technicians were also prepared to move.

Without passing any judgement on the quality of their relationships, it was clear that in the skilled workers' families the spouses were closer at least to the extent that they had discussed together the problems raised by moving. And correspondingly they seemed to have links with relatives which were more flexible, and to have fewer local friendships which would tie them to the area where they lived at present. An example of a couple who had moved after work and who had since formed fewer contacts with the surrounding locality were Mr and Mrs Vickers. Mrs Vickers said, 'We've never had many friends. It's all relatives really. When I first came here I was very friendly with a Scottish woman, and I used to have her in for coffee, but it got a bit too much of a good thing. She was coming and staying until my husband came home, so he got a bit cross about that, and I made up my mind when she went that I wouldn't have any more to do with people.'

The technicians had even briefly considered emigration. Mr Fellowes said, 'I'd dearly love to go abroad. I've got a yearning to emigrate. The opportunities in this country are so restricted somehow.' Mr Haigh felt the same way: 'I don't know how it is but in England the salaries are getting higher, but somehow they're not high enough to pay for the standard of living, you know what I mean? Other countries, they're not much better off, but they have the purchasing power.'

However, for the moment the idea of emigration had been shelved. Mr Haigh said. 'We're attached to England.' And there seemed to be strong ties between the wives and their relatives. Mrs Vickers said, 'My sister's always telling us that she won't let us move away.' Mr Vickers said, 'In my case I like to see my parents if they're close enough, but I don't rate that very high on my list of priorities. In my wife's case she would not emigrate. She would not even consider it. I just briefly talked about what I could do, but she wouldn't even consider it.'

Although these technicians were more prepared to move about England, this does not mean that any of them really wanted a change at first. They liked their homes, and it was very evident that they had put a great deal of effort into furnishing and decorating them to their taste. Mr Vickers felt he had got his home just right, and 'You never really get back what you've put into a house.' There was the further difficulty that some of them had bought houses from the council under a scheme which meant that they were not allowed to sell within five years of purchase, yet two years of this period had still to run. Mrs Vickers was reluctant to move because 'I wouldn't like to let my house. I wouldn't fancy the idea of anybody else using my things and furniture.'

Another skilled worker, Mr John, who had moved once to better his accommodation, was not prepared to uproot his family again unless there was the prospect of improving his wage and buying his own house: 'To move from one council house to another is not much progress.' Mr Odell, who had originally come to England to join his relatives and find work, considered getting a government resettlement grant to enable him to move to another town to work on the buses there. But his wife did not want to leave her relatives who lived locally or the house they had recently bought – 'I'm not bloody moving!' And in any case Mr Odell was not the kind of key worker for whom the grants were intended.

Travelling men

In contrast, when the less-skilled workers of the north-east considered moving their homes it was more as a last resort. Mr Miller said, 'It's no good talking of moving. Things aren't that bad yet, they'd really have to get bad. Well, say, give it another few months and I'm still not working. That'll be bad, because I shall be exhausted with debt, and I shall be beyond it, and then I will get people calling me a bum – that's when you can't pay things back, then you're a bum.'

These men did not find it easy to describe what it was that made them want to stay in the north. Suggestions that they might move caused some irritation, as an interference with their freedom. Mr Miller said, 'Like Prince Philip said, to one bloke in Sunderland, he said, "Why don't you go to Australia?" Him, a Greek! "Why don't you go back to Greece?" That's what I'd have said to him!' There were diffuse bonds with the place where they had been born, and the men said simply that they 'liked the place'. Jimmy Weaver said, 'Well, I've just been bred and born here, that's all. I just don't want to leave it. It's a canny area, like, really. I like the football team.' (He had, in fact, refused an offer of a job on a sea-going yacht, and the chance of a place in a training school in the south.) Mr Lucas was more explicit: 'I like the people here. Honestly, I don't think I would move. *I'd* go: I'd go to work, send money home, right? But I don't think I could drag her away. I don't know what there is about the place, like. If you was from anywhere else I don't suppose you'd come here to live, like, you know. But same as, the like of Charlie (Mr McBain) and people, you get to know people. You get roots.'

It was noticeable that these less mobile workers stressed the relationships which they and their wives had formed *separately* in the surrounding locality, as if there were two wholly different sets of ties to be considered in moving, and as if the issues would be quite different for themselves and their wives. Also, ties with the locality and relatives seemed much less flexible than for the more mobile workers. Even though the emphasis on the greater strength of the wives' feeling for relatives was the same, there was more insistence on staying in the immediate area of the north-east, rather than staying just in England.

The less mobile workers described the problems they would have faced, had they tried to move to other areas. Since all these families lived in council houses there were the practical difficulties of moving house. Mr Ryan said, 'Where you going to get a house at? You know, if you work for a firm and you're, like, a tradesman, they find a house for you, but when you're a labourer they'll say, "We're not going to, like, get him a house and give him a job to bring his family there." ' The only transfer scheme they knew of was that run by the Coal Board, and was for more-skilled workers to go to Nottingham colliery jobs where working conditions were rumoured to be very unpleasant and unhealthy.

In fact, the less-skilled men felt that the only chance of moving that was open to them was the invitation, to the man only, to become a 'travelling man' on a temporary contract, living in a camp for migrant workers. Mr Miller had been away before and he said, 'I'd be willing to travel away if I could get the money.'

However, for those men who had travelled away, experience of the south had not encouraged them to think of moving their homes away entirely. Mr Ryan's impression had been that the south was exclusive and exploiting: 'Sometimes they're bum jobs – might get about £30 a week and have two homes to keep. I was in Cambridge, I was paying £10 a week for digs in a boozer about seven miles outside Cambridge, £10 odd a week! We were on twelve-hour nights, we were, five of us, all in the same room, five of us. Tried all over, couldn't get in anywhere, with the students see, Cambridge.' Mr McBain had found that the south had few jobs 'for the likes of us'. As migrant workers they had remained outside the everyday life of the south, enclosed within the work group, and they had scarcely made any contacts and had put down no roots.

Gaining information about jobs

Bound up inextricably with the sort of work they wanted and with their willingness and ability to move, was the way individuals set about finding information about jobs. For the more-skilled workers the problem of looking for work was very much an individual and somewhat impersonal task of searching through adverts, checking qualifications and sending letters. For example, Mr Vickers got a little information, but very little, from friends over the 'grape vine', and he said, 'I don't have any relatives who could help. None of my relatives really know what I do for a living, to know what sort of job would be useful to me anyway.' There was almost a sense that he would reject help from relatives and others as a sign of dependency and weakness. He estimated that only 5 per cent of the search for work was luck, and the rest would depend on his efforts in searching the job columns and sending in applications by letter.

In contrast the less-skilled workers relied very much more on personal approaches. Mr Nottingly said, 'You don't get many jobs in the papers, they get filled up right away.' Mr Paton's method was, 'I just go to the building site and look at the notices, and if it's got

"Bricklayers wanted", well naturally they want a labourer. You just follow the tradesmen, that's all.' If they were in luck, Mr McBain said, 'Any of the lads that's got a car, we'll get in the car and have a run round.'

In times of shortage it was not enough for the less-skilled to be willing and to search hard. Employers did not need to advertise jobs, and the workless were dependent on their friends in work to help them with information, and with that information there came also the personal influence which might get them the job. Mr Lucas said, 'You know when I was working in Sparrows and there was lads unemployed asking, "Can you get us a kick in?" You try to get them a kick in, you know what I mean? That's how you get jobs, your mate gets yer a kick in. Now if Charlie starts tomorrow and there's jobs going, if he can get me a kick in he'll get me a kick in, and vice versa.'

The local working men's club was a kind of informal employment exchange, and Mr McBain's wife said, 'Even now, if he went into the club today one of his mates might say to him, "Hey Charlie, they want men up at so-and-so", or "The Forth Construction want men", or "so-and-so want men", and he goes down.'

This highly personalized system of getting information and jobs was a further reason why these less-skilled men would find it difficult to move south. Mr McBain described his efforts to find work in Chester when he was working on a contract near by: 'I made inquiries like, but I think when you first go to an area like that, if you don't know the area at all, which I didn't and it's pretty widespread. Do you know Chester? Well, it's nothing where they're outside, you know, work that'd suit me, d'you get me? Well, it took all the day I was working, and I couldn't very well afford to take the time off while I looked for a job.' And even had Mr McBain found work he would have lacked the personal influence which came from friends already working with the firm. He had gone so far as to make an arrangement whereby friends he had made in different parts of the country while on construction work would try to get him jobs and notify him of available work. 'There's a couple o'lads there, say if there's anything doing they'll let me know like, they've got me address. And a couple of scaffolders from Scunthorpe, they phone the club up, you know, if there's owt going through there. He's phoned through a couple of jobs, but when we've went up they've been full up, you know. If you have good contacts, you know, you need never be out of work.'

Keeping up contacts sometimes meant drinking in the club or in local pubs. It also meant keeping in with other men who were working. Mr McBain continued, 'I had a fight the other night in the club. These fellers were picking on me the whole evening about my brother Jimmy, they set upon me two or three times. I don't know how it is, he's got a reputation for being militant, and they don't like it, and it rubs off on me I suppose. Anyway, we got outside the club and they started again. I told them to give up. I held out my hand and said good night, gave them a chance and walked away, but they still kept on. So I went back and planted them. But there you are, you see. If a job comes into that club now, and them fellers hear about it, that's one job that I won't get, because they won't tell me.'

Because of the importance of personal influence in getting jobs, Mr McBain resented what he saw as the increasing impersonality of the process of applying for work with firms. He complained, 'It's all form work. Now they've put fences round everything, you go to the gate house, you see, they've got a gate man. He gives you a pink bill, like that. You have to put the last three jobs on, how old you are, some forms your religion, some forms your political beliefs and all shines! It's unbelievable, you know what I mean. They fold it up, shove it in a drawer and close the drawer, and if you've got nobody on that site – if you're unskilled, put it that way – opening their mouth for you with a bit of, like, pull behind you, you have no chance. You haven't that much chance.'

Encounters with employers

The way individuals searched for work, the way they conducted their interviews when they encountered employers, and their reaction to the failure to get work, all revealed further how important it was for them to get work of a particular kind.

Mr Haigh, who was the most specialized of the technicians and who was looking further afield, described the repeated cycles of build-up and rejection over a number of days or even weeks, which were a feature of the impersonal search for white-collar jobs by means of letter applications. 'You send off for a job and you start making plans and wondering about buying a house, and you say, "Well, it wouldn't be so bad living there" and you get built up. But then the rejection comes and you're right down. So then you send off another application and you start building up again and thinking, "What will it be like living in this other place?" and then – down again.'

Mr Calvert expressed both a lack of enthusiasm for looking for work and a sense of devaluation in the stress he laid on the way he felt he was having his job defined for him by the process of job finding. 'I've found in London that the chief thing is the amount of time it takes you to get a job. I mean you need a mental constitution of absolute, you know, adamance, I mean actually to keep at it, when you're trying for a job in a field you know nothing about. I mean at least with teaching I feel reasonably at home, because I've seen the heaps of publications that come for jobs, and see the half-hearted procedure of sorting them out and having somebody type out your curriculum vitae. I mean, as I say, with my sort of background and history a departure into anything other than teaching would be a very short one. I'd feel at a disadvantage.'

Mr Vickers had developed a filing system for checking advertisements and grading and processing his applications and the firm's responses. 'I just wanted to get an idea whether I was applying for more engineering type jobs than I was managerial/supervisory type jobs. This column is my first letter, dated. The second column is whether I've filled in an application form; and these are "no replies" after that stage or refusals at that stage. So far I've had seven interviews out of forty-two jobs, and out of the last fortnight I've had four.' He usually sent with his application form a duplicated copy of his curriculum vitae, in which he set out challengingly a description of what he felt he had to offer as a worker.

SUMMARY OF EXPERIENCE AND CAPABILITIES
Have experience of constructing, testing and servicing electronic equipment using valves, particularly audio and video amplifiers ... Very skilled with hand tools of very wide variety. Experienced at supervising a section with a strength of 120 female operators and six male supervisory. [This is a considerably shortened version.]

Mr Vickers's criticism of interviews was that they were not searching enough or taxing enough of his talents, and his reaction seems to have been characteristically pugnacious and calculatedly off-hand. On one occasion, he said, 'The manager's only, sort of, assessment of me was to ask me what size drill you would use for tapping O.B.A.s and what have you, and I said, "I can't remember at the moment, but I'd soon look at the chart and decide that, you know, that's simple enough." And he accepted that, and he said, "Can you set a micrometer?" I said yes, and he fished one out of his drawer and said, "Here, can you set that at nine sixteenths or something?" I said, "Well, what's nine-sixteenths as a decimal? I can't remember that as well, either!"'

From his carefully worded applications, Mr Vickers sometimes obtained an interview, but often he received no answer at all, or perhaps only a curtly worded note. He said disappointedly of one recent interview, '"Well," the chap said, "I'll probably offer you the job, sort of thing, and you can decide whether you want to take it or not." Funny thing to say really, when in fact I got a letter from the personnel saying I wasn't on the short-list. There's a big difference I would think.' At another firm, 'I just got a very prompt reply, "Sorry no vacancies." I think it must have been handled by a little girl in the office and I suppose she sent some pretyped letter.' He showed us a letter, 'Look at this one; at least it is hand-signed. They annoy me some of these firms. That tends to be the way: no reply, no acknowledgement. And it takes a lot of time, I spend about an hour writing a letter. There's the standard thing, but there's always some special question you've got to devote more time to.'

Mr Fellowes, too, described his sense of devaluation and being under personal attack in the interview situation. 'Sometimes you feel pretty grotty when you go for a job. There was one job, a progress clerk, I was there all day. They've got a long complicated process of interviewing, and I got to the last man and he said, "We'll employ you." So I said, "All right, perhaps now we can talk about the money", and the wage was £22.90! You see the employers, knowing the pool of unemployed, they weren't prepared to pay any more. But I needed £25 a week to manage on. At that wage I was doing no better than the D.E.P. and I'd be sinking. I wouldn't take less than £25 a week on principle. When they offered me the money, you'd have thought he was doing me a favour, but I tell you, in two minutes

I was out of that place and I walked for three miles before I stopped just to cool off. It was a difficult job as well was that, a job that none of their own men wanted because it was too difficult.'

According to Mrs Odell, her husband put on his best front when he went for jobs. 'I don't see why he shouldn't get that job. He put a suit on and a nice clean white shirt. He even had his hair trimmed a bit. The trouble is that sometimes they think people are too old. Even he's been told he's too old. Some of these employers, they want younger men. Any job that's a bit more interesting, they won't look at men over twenty-five.' Mr Odell said with irritation, 'They thought I was applying for a job below what I should have been doing and it really annoys me. I just dressed as I normally dress, when I went up there. I put a suit on, collar and tie. I went for a similar one once before, a factory job, and the guy said I should try for a job collecting rents! I suppose it was because I was too well-dressed. I just couldn't figure out what way to get round it, because I've always worn pretty good suits and that's why I get annoyed. I don't think it ought to matter.' Mr Odell was apt to respond to these attempts to up-grade him, or to denigrate the job for which he was applying, by becoming politically argumentative.

The West Indian welder, Mr John, could also be touchy and un-compromising in interviews. Describing a recent occasion he said, 'I passed this brazing test, trade test, and he really then interviewed me, and asked me about the equipment. He says to me the first time when I came it shows to him, it appears to him that I was preju-diced, that I have some chip on my shoulder. I said, "What chip are you referring to?" I said, "Would you mind explaining yourself when you's talking about chip?" I said, "If you talking about fish and chip, or some other kind of chip, but you must be more ex-plicit," I said. (Ha, ha, ha! That time I was trying just to be awkward with him, because I know what chip he's talking about, but I like to get people when he's trying to be funny, you know.) So I said, "Look. I'm fed up with this so when you talking about chip I have a chip on my shoulder not against the colour but against unfair treatment, victimization of getting opportunity of getting into a better position and being paid the right money as what you are paying your other fellers, them that are the colour of you that working here for you." When he's wrote and offered me the job, he had the audacity to put in it that he will employ me as brazing and general welding. He have the *bloody audacity* to do that! And I said, "You can take that and you can ... know what to do with it, because I will not allow my bloody self, although I'm in the situation I'm in, I will not allow myself to be used by them any more.'

For less-skilled manual workers, whose chances of employment depended more on locating work and using personal influence rather than performance in an interview, the search could be equally depressing. Mrs Miller described her husband's return from looking for work: 'Well, they seem to come in bad-tempered and depressed. I can't really ... you'd have to be here to see it, you know, because you think, "Will they get work?" Because you're on tenterhooks wondering, "Will they get a job?" And when there's still nothing doing, well, you can tell by their face when they're coming up the road and they haven't got a job.' Mr Ryan said, 'You're walking around all over the shop. One day, hey, where'd I go one day? I was out five hours, Middlesbrough wasn't it? I walked from here till Middlesbrough on the road and I asked fourteen different people for jobs.' His wife added, 'And he come back and he had a hole in his boots.'

Flexibility of job choice

The workless had usually begun their spell of unemployment with fairly conservative requirements for their next job, but when they encountered setbacks in the search they showed a degree of flexibility and preparedness to change their requirements and to think of other work. Individuals shifted their ground on cash, skill and locality in different ways.

The more-skilled, more-mobile men began to extend the range of their search beyond their immediate locality, perhaps by taking newspapers with a wider coverage, and they became more resigned to travelling further afield. Mr Haigh, for example, considered living away during the week and returning home only at weekends. Mr Vickers began to look at jobs with up to an hour's driving each way. Mr Fellowes said, 'Thank God we're so near London. I come from Durham, and when I was a kid my father was more out of work than in, but at least you can always get some kind of work in

London.' The issue of emigration might become once again a live topic of discussion between husband and wife.

Mr Odell was torn between going to a smaller firm with buses but no union or a larger firm with a union but no buses. He tried the post office but met with his old trouble: 'Some of the questions were, "Why do you want to become a postman?" Some ridiculous questions! One guy says to me, "I should have thought you'd go for a better job than a postman" – this was a postman who'd been promoted, and he didn't have to wear a uniform – and this annoyed me very much, and I said, "I don't understand. Do you not think a postman's a good job then?" And it became very critical. One of them made subtle remarks about my hair being very long. Another said something about, "I thought you might be more interested in the arts." That must have been something to do with me having long hair. I told him I didn't know anything about the arts, that I didn't know exactly what he was on about.'

The less skilled became more likely to consider working away as travelling men, or failing that, lowering their sights to accept less wages. Mr Miller said, 'I'm starting to get a bit fed up, you know, a bit like getting in somewhere like a permanent rigger or something, just go for a steady wage, maybe a maintenance rigger.' He was beginning to lose faith in his luck and to look for a job where the supply of work was more assured.

The emergence of 'ideal' jobs

Still further setbacks in the job-search provoked the workless to think more adventurously. Self-employment seemed attractive to individuals at all levels of skill. Mr Haigh said, 'To make any money you've got to work for yourself.' It turned out that in the past he had wanted to build up his own stamp company, trading through school clubs on approval, and during the first good patch of work when he had been working overtime, 'My ordinary salary covered our everyday needs and the overtime was going into the business. But when the overtime ended all that stopped and the business had to hang fire.' But he still thought about opportunities for self-employment. Mr Fellowes told us of a number of men who had completely changed their field upon becoming redundant from jobs similar to his, one for instance, going into the wine retail trade.

Characteristically, self-employment seemed to appeal particularly to those among the workless who had felt most acutely that their energies in work were restrained by employers and unions, or by the nature of the work they were doing. Two of these men, Mr Weston and Mr McBain, had already tried to go self-employed on previous occasions, only to suffer setbacks which had contributed to their feelings of frustration. Mr Weston said, 'I've always had this feeling, looking round the other personnel, no disrespect or anything, you think to yourself, "Cor, the amount of work these other blokes are turning out, I'm making somebody a big fat profit. Why shouldn't I do it for myself?" ' (Mrs Weston had her own dream of getting away from urban industrial living: 'You know, I'd like to go away on a farm, work on a farm.')

In fact, unemployment had given Mr Weston a stimulus (of a sort) to try to attain his ideal. 'The initial thing's a bit of a shock, but afterwards you start thinking to yourself, what bloody point is there in putting yourself out for somebody else, when if you fully exploit your own talents ... I'd been around and I hadn't even got further than the gates in most places. They weren't even bothering to let you in to have an interview or anything; there was no point if there was no jobs. We went all over London trying to pick up odds and ends, we was about five hours and we picked up nothing except a cold. Well, in that time I'd already felt that if there was no job coming up I was going to work for myself on contract work. Anyway, this bloke had an old place that he'd been using as a warehouse. He said, "If you'd like to decorate it up you can have it." So that's what we done while I was unemployed, we redecorated this. A lot of my redundancy money went on this.' At this point his insurance benefit was stopped when he refused to take a job at below union rates, 'So I said, "Right, I'll take the chance to become self-employed wholly." Well, we had a few jobs to do, and we'd actually got quite a big job in, but we got slung out of the office. This bloke wanted to expand, so he slung us out of the office, so there again I was exploited.' (Mrs Weston began to look in earnest at the country newspaper sent by her sister, to see if there were any adverts for farm helpers.)

Another of the workless, Mr Paton, had a dream of opening a pet shop, and he criticized the local pet shop's policies with some insight and imagination. He had also thought about a gardening business, or handyman's firm, 'Concreting, like, there's a lot of people in that game. Grass cutters; if I had a pair of grass cutters you could make a bomb like, as I say, and you had transport. Then you'd need money for a van, tax and insurance; then your machines are about £40 apiece, and you'd need something to start yer off, because you'd need a couple of machines, you'd want two working. You could do it, but, you know, you've got to get up and go, like. You've got to say, "I'll work late just to get the extra little bit of money." But I'm like so many, I'm bad in saving up, you know. I canna save. I get me money, I like to spend it on me house. I've got a canny home, like, it's not too bad, like, but whatever I get I spend on me home. But if I had the capital I think I could start me own business.' Mr Nottingly also thought of self-employment. Mr Spain, prior to his wife's death, had been intending to return to the West Indies and get another boat, a dream which continued unfulfilled.

Apart from self-employment there were some who thought of jobs requiring greater, or other, skills than the ones they already possessed. Mr Vickers toyed with the idea of becoming a lecturer in a College of Technology, and also, 'I'm thinking of doing a correspondence course. I've always wanted to get more into electronics. And I used to let my eyes stray into the old representative area, the idea of sales engineer type jobs, with there being a bit of a recession in the industry people look more towards their sales so that's an area where there are more jobs.' Mr John, too, wanted to be a teacher, and had done ever since he encountered the teachers of welding at the college where he had taken his certificates. Now he began to badger the employment exchange to put him on an instructor's course, for which he claimed there were places and he was eligible.

Mr Dover, who had moved backwards and forwards between labouring and travelling, had come into contact with students and had grown to feel that he would like to do something socially useful, like youth club leadership. However, this would require a course, and to get on a course he had to have educational qualifications, of which he had only one, an O level taken some years earlier. 'I know educational qualifications are a conventional line, in a way, and I've met all these people who say, "Well, I've got all these bits of paper and they're not worth a damn", you know. And I say, "Yes, but you've got them there." I mean, if I'd got a degree now, I'd just have to shave off my beard and smarten myself up a bit and I'd be able to get a job as a teacher. It's very easy to say qualifications are no use when you've got them. I mean what else is there to do. I don't want to become a tailor or something, one of these rehabilitation courses.'

In this chapter the workless have described how they saw their requirements for work and the directions along which they were initially prepared to be flexible. Together with memories of work these descriptions have provided indications of the importance of different aspects of work in individuals' lives, and about how far they had come to see themselves as particular kinds of workers with clear work identities. In Parts Two and Three of this book we will be exploring further this legacy from work by looking at the way different individuals react to their experiences of social security and their changed relationships with the surrounding community and their wives.

Part Two:
SUPPORT FOR THE WORKLESS, AND THE
PUSH BACK INTO WORK

4 Finding Work through the Employment Exchanges

In this chapter the workless describe their experiences of the employment exchanges and the social security offices through which came support and pressure from the State. Both the Department of Employment and the Supplementary Benefits Commission run services concerned with job-finding and training; but whether these services are guidance and help, or direction and compulsion, depends on how welcome they are to the workless and how far they are backed up and imposed by sanctions.

We should stress here that the people we chose for interview were probably the least well served by the exchanges, which were in any case functioning at this time at their lowest efficiency. Apart from the sheer pressure of work on officials, the exchanges were not notified of all available jobs. For more-skilled workers there were private advertising services (although the Department of Employment has a special Professional and Executive Register). While in times of high unemployment when they had men calling at their gates, employers with less-skilled work had no need to notify the exchanges of vacancies except for those which were more difficult to fill, often because they were poorly paid, or unpleasant to perform.

Job finding and occupational guidance for the skilled

On the whole the technicians and skilled workers had fewer complaints about the employment exchanges, and Mr Vickers was typical in saying that he felt as far as he was concerned that the officials gave him a 'quick and efficient' service, although in fact he had had only one in eight of his possible jobs through the Professional and Executive Register. Apparently he did not expect the exchange to produce work.

The only exception among the more-skilled men was Mr John.

At the time when he first came to England without credentials he regarded his work experience in the West Indies as an adequate training, and he failed to appreciate the lack of power of the exchange officials to provide him with skilled work. 'I axed them for a job as a welder, and one of the employment officers says to me, "I'm sorry but I cannot give you a job as a welder." I says, "Why?" I said, "Man, you are talking rubbish! I am entitled to get a job through your organization here. This is the appropriate place. Is the employment agency of the country, which is a public place where you control the employment system in this country?" He said, "Yes." I said, "Well are you going to tell me now that you can't give me a job?" I said, "*Whom* the hell give you such provision of such right to make such a decision?" I said. When I go here and I discover that these people try to mess me about, they gall me, they gall me. The situation in which I'm in, and don't try in any way to help me, employment and thing. They're going to try and ignore me, to know that I'm a human being and an individual person, have more ability and qualification, and they're trying to give me a lot of rubbish, you know, which I'm finding down here.' Over ten years later we found Mr John again engaged in an argument with the exchange about what he alleged was their reluctance to put him on an instructor training course.

Lacking vacancies for skilled jobs on their books, the exchanges offered occupational guidance to individuals who already had particular skills, so that they might acquire other skills. But the advice was not pressed hard at first where the workless were well-qualified. This lack of pressure was clearest where the individual had educational credentials. Mr Calvert said that since he had gained his degree, 'They're very understanding, which they never were before when I was a student. Before they used to say things like, "You've got four weeks to get a job," which was just four weeks of being worried. But this time when I explained to the vocational guidance person about teaching being the only thing that my past training had suited me for he was very sympathetic. The way I look at it, there must be lots of legitimate people who're looking for jobs in fields where, if I get a job I'll take up their space, squeeze them out. I mean the employment place must be sensitive to that point of view, you know.' Mr Calvert was not alone in feeling that there was almost a hint of generosity in someone who was less interested in work standing aside and leaving more room for those who were more eager to work.

Miss Hebb had already been for a 'vocational guidance' interview. 'They've never offered me any job at all. They made me uncomfortable at first, but now I get on very well with them. I just go and have a chat. Oh, at first she kept saying, you know, "You've got so many qualifications, you can get a job," and then when I say, "Well, I've only got A levels in maths and physics and things," they say, "Surely you can get a job in this." And then, well, I've been to see the Employment Officer, um, and sort of registered as a clerk, but she couldn't offer me any clerks' jobs because – and this is what she said – "You can't have a job like that because you're too qualified, and if you have that job you're doing somebody else who's not as qualified as you out of a job." I couldn't believe it when she said it, but that's what she said. When I go up there now, she just says, "Oh no, nothing for you this week." Huh! I've got an understanding that she won't put me in for any more professional jobs, because of my bad records with that. Well, I was on the Professional and Executive Register for a while, but cards got lost and things, so I'm not on the Register now, so they can't offer me that kind of job. They can't offer me something sort of menial, you know, because I'm overqualified, so I'm in a position where . . . huh, huh!'

Skilled manual workers, also, had experienced at first little pressure to change their idea of themselves as workers and to change their skills or accept lower pay, although they too had been offered occupational guidance. But Mr Odell was keen only to be a driver, and when alternative training was suggested to him his ideological objections to any specialization were aroused: 'I believe we should all have a lot of different skills, and move around from one job to another.' Mr Miller said, 'I specify what type of worker I am. I'm a steel erector and we have to travel away. I'm down as that at the labour exchange. They've never tried to change me to a labourer. There's not much work of that type; they know it wouldn't suit me anyhow.' On the other hand, he said, 'They asked, "Why don't you go to see the careers officer, to see if there's a chance of getting on the dock? D'you know what I mean? Huh! No chance! I'd like to be a welder, but you just can't. You can do a welder's course, and then when you're done you can't get a job, through your unions.'

Only one skilled man whom we met had had his grading changed by the officials. Mr Nottingly said, 'They sent for us not so long ago for to change, for to scratch us out as a painter. Well, they asked us to do it. You could, like, please yourself.' To Mr Nottingly there seemed to be so little work about of any kind that the question of his grading at the exchange was irrelevant.

Signing on at the exchange

Although skilled workers had rather little expectation of getting work through the exchange, they were still required to 'sign on' there once a week, as an indication that they were available for work and willing to accept the exchange's instructions, which is the condition of receiving social security benefits. Although initially they experienced little pressure from the exchange officials, this does not necessarily mean that signing on was free of discomfort. Mrs Weston said to her husband, 'You don't like the labour money, do you?' Mr Weston replied, 'Oh, I like it, but if you can get away without doing it, then why go on it? I mean what's the point of sitting back and saying, "Oh, they're keeping me." Well, it makes you feel a bit guilty. If you're an able-bodied man, you're just leeching, aren't you? Poncing, or whatever you like to call it, on society.'

For Mr Vickers the experience of signing on was mixed. On the one hand the queue there could be supportive, and he said, 'I saw one lad there this morning. He commented he'd been out of work six months and he'd still not got a job. I didn't even know he was out of work.' But the feeling that others were in the same boat was tempered: 'I do have some bad moments. Sometimes, deep down, it's desperate. Well, when I've been talking to some of the other fellers down at the D.E.P. it brings it home to me, when they tell me the sort of experiences they've had. I'm still fairly confident, but my confidence does get knocked. When I'm talking to some of the chaps I think maybe I'll never get a job. Another thing upsets me. While they're unemployed, I don't feel so bad, but as each one gets a job I'm left out more and more.' He added uneasily, 'The only thing I don't like is that you're down there and along with the genuine ones you've got some others who don't really care whether they work or not. There is a certain type, particularly the buildings worker. Well, I look at some of them and I think, well, they don't look as if they're particularly keen on work. There's one bloke there, patterns all across his forehead and arms. Oldish blokes I'd tend to put in a different category, since I know how difficult it is for an old man. But this young lad, he's about twenty-three, and he's just finished his apprenticeship, so he's still hot in other words, isn't he?'

Mr Calvert felt that the experience of signing on varied from exchange to exchange. He had been to two different exchanges since he graduated and, 'In the other place about six tenths of the people signing on seemed to be alcoholics. It was more unpleasant when you signed on at half past three in the afternoon. You just expected to get a lot of trouble. I mean if one of the officials asked you something and you said, "Sorry?" they'd really, sort of, repeat it *loud*, you know. Half of the officials there, they're just psychopaths, but they're psychopaths because they've met people who conform them to that mould, you know, they're just used to getting a lot of abuse and things. This exchange here, oh, it's very different. You just go up and sign and that's it. Nothing is said whatsoever. If you care to say, "Good morning", or "Cheerio", they say, "Good morning", or "Cheerio".'

Suspension of benefits

The less-skilled workers tended to be more resentful about the exchanges, and to see the job-finding services as, at best, irrelevant to their needs; with the difference that unlike the skilled they complained about this. Mr Ryan said disgustedly, 'I've got one month's job out o'there, the labour exchange. The rest I've found meself.' Mr Nottingly had been doing labouring work because he could not get a job at his trade, and he said, 'Well, if you know somebody, like, you stand a better chance. If you go from the dole office, you don't seem to. I've never had a job at the labour exchange in me life. All you've to go there for is to draw your money.'

Mr McBain still recalled an incident from the fifties. 'I've never had a job off the labour exchange in me life. They're a waste of time them beggars, just a complete waste of time. They give us one, a green card, £5 a week, and I was married!' (The green card referred to is the formal notification to a workless individual that he has been sent for a job, and he then takes the card to the employer concerned, who must report on the interview.) 'It was a tyre firm, they got me dole stopped, I hadn't been off that long. Anyway, took me green card down like, to the job, and the bloke looked at it. He said, "Are you married?" So I said, "Yes." He said, "What the bloody hell are they sending you up here for? I can't understand them," he said. "I told them it'd have to be somebody single. It's only £5 a week." Well, I was sickened again, you know. That's the sort of thing that sickens you. This tyre firm, they said, "You'll have to take it or we'll stop your dole," that was the exchange, like. I said, "Well, it's six and two threes. I get three pound off you here, and I have to work all week for £5 and I get me stamps off, whatever." I said, "It's a waste of time." So they stopped me dole.'

Mr McBain was still having trouble years later after he had got himself into the steel-erectors' union and so into semi-skilled work. 'You see, that's summat an' all that's wrong. I'm in a bob-hole. D'you know why? Because I started working on the props, I'm down, at the exchange, as a prop worker. They change it to suit theirselves. There's two jobs I've got me name down for. Now I got a job, like, steel-erecting, you know, for about two years. I went down there, signed on. He said, "We've got a job for you here on the buildings," he said. "Oh," I said, "no," I said, "that's finished now," I said. "Do you want me to take a retrograde step?" I said. "I've got a bloody semi-skilled job," you know what I mean; it's a bloody good job an' all, I was getting about thirty-odd quid a week, you know. I said, "You want me to go back on the buildings for about £11 a week," I said. "You're not on! I'm starting to go up over," I said, "and now you want me to go bloody back over again," I said, "no, I don't want to." He said, "Well, your dole's stopped." I said, "How's that?" I said. "I'm in the union," I said, "you can't make me take that job." He said, "Here. See that," he said, "timber worker and building worker'", it was on me books. He said, "You don't take the job we give you labouring," he said, "your dole's stopped." They did an' all, stopped me bloody dole again.'

Conflict with the exchange was not confined to the less-skilled, however, and the other individual we came across who had had trouble over his reluctance to accept a poorer job was, as we have already mentioned, Mr Weston. 'The employer and me were discussing things and he said, "Oh yes, you're just the man we want" and he looked at this that I'd filled in, salary required £1,780, "£1,780," he said, "and you're not prepared to accept £1,500?" It was never any case of haggling, him coming up and me coming down, it was absolute finish. "You turning down £30 a week and rather live on £17.25. You ought to be a-bloody-shamed o' yourself," that's what he told me. I said, "Well, if I took this I'd be more ashamed of meself, because I'm admitting defeat straight away." So I went up to the labour exchange, told them I wasn't accepting the job. I didn't argue. What's the point? I could have argued. I could have got the union involved as well, because the union minimum rate for my age, even down here, is £33.25 a week, and that comes to about £1,720. I don't see that there's any law in the land that can make a man take a job. Well, it was such a vast cut.'

Other individuals, by compromising or through negotiation with employers, managed to avoid jobs they did not want without having their dole suspended. Mr Lucas said, 'Well, I can tell you now, the only job I think in me life that they ever sent me for was for a side lad, side lad humping coal off the side of a wagon for about £12 a week, you know what I mean. And I just said, I asked the bloke, I said, "Will you put unsuitable? It's no good to me, like. I think I'm better than humping coal at £12 a week," I said, "I've humped wood, like. I'm not humping coal now." He said, "Fair enough, you're not suitable." I got me own job.'

Another way of circumventing pressures from the exchange was to behave 'unsuitably' in the interview. Mr Odell, who wanted a job with a large driving firm with a union, had been sent to a small family firm, 'So I stuck a copy of the *Socialist Worker* in my pocket and I asked if they'd any unions. He just looked at my hair and said the job was filled!'

Mr Dover had once pretended he had O levels, so that the exchange would put him down as a clerk, for which he knew there were no vacancies. But now his bearded appearance seemed sufficient protection from employment he did not want. 'They sent me down to the gasworks here, sub-contractors are pulling it down, you know. That means you've got to hump around big hammers, you know, and carry big weights around, and the guy just laughed at me, you know, "It's a waste of time sending you down here," you know. But there's nothing else to offer. I haven't been classified as disabled or semi-disabled, but I daresay I could get one if I wanted to. My back won't get better unless I have an operation, and there's a big long waiting-list, about three years.'

Sending men for jobs

The official policy of the Department of Employment is that it is sufficient proof of a man's willingness to work if he signs on at the exchange and presents himself for any work the exchange thinks suitable. The workless were no longer officially required to furnish evidence that they had been out seeking work as a condition of their being paid benefits.

However, men complained that when they were sent for jobs, they found that others had been sent too. Mr Nottingly said, 'Well, they sent me for a job, but there's always more than one goes and somebody else gets it; there's about seven goes.'

The Youth Employment Service

The teenagers were still more resentful about the shortcomings of the Youth Employment Service (which is part of the education services). Jimmy Weaver said, 'I think it's a waste of time going there, like. You've got to find your own. They try to give you jobs for about as much as what you're getting there, and they expect you to take them.'

They consistently claimed that large numbers of youths were sent for jobs they had no chance of getting. One teenager said, 'Well, you see, like last week, you see an advert in the steelworks, they wanted three apprentices. Well, the Youth Employment, they sent fifty-eight boys there. Well, it's not worth it, is it?' Another said, 'Well, I got sent for about four jobs while I was on here a year, and they used to send about another dozen lads for it.' His friends agreed, 'Aye, we had nae chance of getting a job. We used to gang to the office for a job, and there'd be about eight blokes sitting outside. It's a bit daft to my liking, like. They should only send about three or four, not a dozen, like.'

While admitting that it might not be all the Youth Employment Service's fault, Jimmy Weaver had nevertheless found the experience disappointing. 'Down at the dole they send you for them although when you get there they've been filled a month or two month, you know. They dinna tell them when the job's been filled. Well, it's just like that all the time like. You just accept it, it's one of them things, you know.' However, Jimmy still showed a curious suppressed resentment at the Youth Employment Officer himself. 'I'm neutral about him, like. If he's all right, he's all right, but if he gets funny with me, like, I'll lamp him, give him a dig. If you get cheeky, then they can stop your dole, but they can stop mine if they like. I mean I'll only go straight out of there and get it from the social security, like, just the same.'

Claiming supplementary benefit at the social security office

If their insurance was suspended, or if they were uninsured, the workless must apply for a supplementary benefit allowance at the social security office. These offices were said to have an atmosphere and procedures which were harsher and more stigmatizing than those of the employment exchanges.

Mr Calvert had had experience of both, his first visit to a social security office being during his undergraduate days, when he had thought about trying to get social security during his vacations while he looked for a job (this was in the days before students had taken to signing on in larger numbers). But, 'I was always discouraged by the experience of those places, because everybody was coughing away like mad, you know. Just the emotional impact discouraged me, of going along and being treated like a sort of semi-tramp. I mean even if a man is more or less basically of a sanguine disposition it can be shocking. And if you don't believe too much in the grace of God, you know, you're not too far away from the condition of the people there!' On that occasion he had left and continued looking for a job.

Some of the workless suggested that the delays in the office were a calculated deterrent to easy access, 'It's harder than working.' Mr McBain described the sequel to the earlier suspension of his insurance: 'I went down the bloody national assistance the following week. They said, "Why, you've no chance." I got threw out, like. I said, "I have to pay the rent." He said, "Well, you're married," he said, "your wife can keep you." I said, "Blimey, I'm not getting married for my wife to keep me." He said, "She'll have to. That's the law." I said, "Well, I want to save my marriage," and all this patter. No chance. He said, "I tell you what. Hang on." Went out the back and he come back about an hour later. I'd been sat there that time, I was fed up. Aw, it was pathetic at that time, you used to sit there for bloody ages – you still do really, but not ... then it was worse still, you know. It was like a big room and they hadn't any chairs, they had bench seats, and I thought, "Well, I've got summat anyway." Heh, heh! He said, "Will you sign here," so I signed, like. I said, "What's that?" He said, "What do you think it is?" a bit cheeky like. I said, "It's a bloody half-a-crown is that." He said, "That's what you're entitled to." I said, "Here! Give us hold of it!" He give us the half-a-crown, and I nearly took his head off with it, you know, threw it at him. We were in bad. I said, "I'll break your ... neck," I said. Anyway, he said, "I'll get a policeman." I said, "Aw, bugger it." And about two or three weeks later I was sat in the house and a knock comes on the door, like, and my wife said, "There's a feller to see you from the national assistance." And I thought, "Ah, they've changed their mind. They've looked further into it." They'd only brought the piece of paper up for the receipt for the half-a-crown! I went mad. I said, "Get out or I'll kill you." You know, that's the sort of thing that happens, bloody stupid really.'

Mr McBain's reception over the years by different supplementary benefit officials had led him to the view that, 'At the social security they've got special "stop men". They can't just be ordinary people, they must have been specially educated up to it. You go in and there's this feller, and you tell him what you've come for, and he'll say, "No chance! You're wasting your time. No chance, you might as well go home." I always ask to see the manager now. I don't bother with them blokes. Then they take your name and you have to wait about two hours. It's terrible. I've been waiting all day sometimes. What gets me is there's people in the same situation, they go in there and one of them will get £7 a week and the other will get nothing. I've seen this with me and my mates. They've come in and they've met these fellers on the counter and they've been turned away. They've been told they were wasting their time. And I've gone in, and I haven't been prepared to accept that, and I've asked to see the manager, and I've got something. And I've gone out and told them what I'd got and what they were entitled to and they've got the same as me. But they wouldn't have got it, that's where it is, they wouldn't have got it unless I'd asked to see the manager. Do you get me? Mind you, it's not just them on the front. They'll be acting on instructions from higher up.'

During the period when we followed the fortunes of the Westons, Mr Weston's bid to become self-employed had led to the family running out of money about eleven weeks after the suspension of his insurance, and although he had started a small job he was not due to receive any money for two weeks. Because he said he was tired, Mrs Weston in desperation had herself gone to the social security office to try to claim something. 'Well, first of all I went down there, and I had to line up an hour and a quarter just to be told where to go, and then after that I went upstairs and sat down and waited another hour, and then just told 'em all the details and how my husband had started work but we hadn't got any money for the next two weeks, whatsoever, to live on. Like last week we had £7, this week is the same, but no rent was paid. He said, "We can't help you at all. It's entirely up to your husband to support his family." I said, "Do you mean to say we've got to go without?" He just shrugged his shoulders. I said, "All we want is something just to tide us over for two weeks which we offer to pay back." He said, "We can't help you whatsoever." But he was so *nasty*, he just didn't want to know at all. You see I didn't think they'd give him anything for hisself, but I thought they'd give me and the children something. If they'd given us a couple of pounds that would have been something. Because we'd lived on our money for eleven weeks today, you know. We wouldn't have gone there unless we definitely had to. I mean I could have gone down there weeks ago, we could have kept our money in the bank. This is what annoys me so much. He was so nasty, he was really nasty about it, you know. I felt terrible, as I was walking out, I felt as though I'd done something really terrible by going. We didn't want him to give it us, we'd have been willing to pay it all back to them, but you see, you've got to be a sort of a layabout or ill before anyone wants to help. If you're willing to work and you just want to borrow some money, then they're not interested, that's what it seems to me.' (Mr Weston, as the head of the household, should have gone to claim himself, when, arguably, he would have been entitled to a 'sub' out of his coming wage, a standard practice with some casually employed workers.)

Mr Dover in particular had had frequent trouble with officials because he moved about frequently (and there was thus a danger that he might be claiming allowances from different offices at the same time). 'Sometimes everything goes smoothly for a few weeks. Then one week it'll be stopped. So you have to hustle and get a B.1 [the application form] see, and shoot up there, and they come out with all this load of crap, "Oh, we don't think you're living where you are any longer, and you were seen in Northcliff one night," they said, "And you give an address in Fenton, you know. We think you ought to be at the Northcliff office," you know. So, it was silly really, I'd just gone down to see a girlfriend. So, silly little things like this, they stopped my money, so I had to go through all this pratting about to get it switched on again, you know. It's crazy. I don't mind if they fuck me about at the social security. I can take it. Well, it's the way they treat you, somehow. It's the way the chairs are arranged. You go in and you sit on a chair and you find it's bolted down to the floor and you can't move it. And when you come up to the counter, if you want to speak to the guy you've got to sit right forward on the edge of your chair, and he's behind a little window, and he says, "Speak up". But I don't do that now, and if he wants to hear me, *he* has to come out of his window, pull the barrier aside, lean forward and talk to me. I don't mind them messing me about, but the trouble is there are some genu-ine claimants up there, and they get messed about as well.'

Yet Mr Dover allowed, "I don't think the S.S. men start off bad. I think a lot of them go into the job because they've got a genuine interest in people, but when they get into the job they turn sour. They've said to me sometimes, "You know, you're getting more than we are." ' And Miss Hebb agreed, 'Yes, one of these guys said to me, "I'm not like these others up here. I'm more like you. I often pick up a guitar and give it a strum when I'm on a visit." And he began telling me all his problems. Me!'

5 Standards of Living on Insurance and Means-tested Benefits

The eagerness of the workless to seek and find new work will depend to some extent on the financial pressures they experience while they are out of work; that is, on the difference between their usual standard of living and that afforded by the two state schemes of social security and by incomes from other sources. In this chapter the workless discuss the adequacy of the living standards provided by the State's income maintenance programmes, of insurance for those with a better work record, and means-tested supplementary benefits for those whose work record had been poorer. Broadly speaking, those who were now drawing insurance benefits only were the more skilled, while those who lived on means-tested supplementary benefits were the less skilled, although the students too, were means tested. Some of the less skilled had previously drawn insurance, but this had either now run out, or it had never taken them above supplementary benefit levels.

To look merely at the current weekly incomes of the families without a caution would be misleading, for to decide whether living standards are adequately protected we must suspend judgement until we have seen what happened over the whole period of time; from the period before unemployment when work fell off and earnings diminished, to the point when work equivalent to that lost is eventually regained.

Insurance benefits

Taking all incomes and lump sums into account, a redundant worker could *over a short period of time* draw more money than when he was working. For example, one of the redundant technicians had £7 earnings-related benefit to add to his unemployment insurance of £18 a week. The firm was making his income up to two thirds of his working salary by paying him £1.50 weekly until he should find another job. In a special redundancy agreement with the firm (at double the government's recommended level) he had received, with tax rebate, over £600, and in an emergency he could have drawn out his accumulated occupational pension of £400. For the moment this matched his commitments: 'I need to clear sufficient to pay my bills. I've got £58 a month going out on the mortgage and the car and the road fund, and I need £14 a week for the rest, groceries, petrol, beer, cigs and what have you. Altogether I need £28 a week. I should say we spend *more* now, if anything, than we did.' Spending had a slightly unreal quality about it, because the usual careful budgeting had been abandoned under the impact of the large lump sum.

Mr Weston, the first time he became redundant, had had a similar experience. With his £500 redundancy pay, 'I had three weeks' holiday, the best holiday I've ever had.' And during the early days of his second redundancy Mrs Weston said, 'We've not cut down on anything. In fact the children have had more – like, that was out of the redundancy money, mind you, a lot of that was – they've had clothes and that. We've not had to cut down on food.'

Without a large sum of redundancy pay, the day-to-day living standards of the family living on unemployment insurance benefits might be protected in other ways. Mr Odell, when asked whether he was economizing, said, 'Well, we would be only for Sandra's work. Dole wouldn't be sufficient because we'd only be getting £17, but because Sandra's working the money hasn't dropped that much since I've been unemployed.' Although his wife earned £11.50, only the amount for her support was stopped from the insurance, so the family had about £25 a week.

There was even evidence that the redundancy pay had given some of these families more cash than they felt they required for their immediate needs. One of the technicians, for instance had chanced his luck on finding a job and had bought a car out of his redundancy pay. Mr Odell was saving £8 a month to buy an old van.

However, not all the technicians had worked as long for the same firm, so they had less redundancy pay. Mr Fellowes seemed to be feeling the pinch, and he explained, 'This suburban estate here that we live in, we live by a set rule. Whatever you may say about it, there's a rule we live by, whether you agree or not, on this sort of estate. The kids have got to have various things. You've got to keep up with it, you've got to keep a face on. And we find we've definitely got to be more careful. My wife's always been keen on the kids, seeing that they were well turned out. She used to come home, say, with £7 left of her wages. Well, she used to spend that on the kids. But she can't do it now. We've got to the stage, if the boy wants a football – before if he wanted he'd only to come home and ask – but if he asked we can't get it now. My children don't have free school meals. It's a silly thing, I know, but, well, you don't want to send the kids off to get free meals, you know what I mean? You don't want them to be different. We wouldn't do that! If I had to go and work on a bloody building site to stop that, then I'd go and work on a bloody building site!'

After Mr Weston's insurance was suspended his family ran into difficulties. Mrs Weston said, 'You see, when he was made redundant he had the money and a few tax rebates and that, and we was able to – all the bills were paid, sort of thing. But now the phone bill's in, which should be paid this Friday. They read the meter for the underfloor, which should be about £24. I mean there are things – well, not the phone, that's a luxury, if you can't pay it they take the phone – but you must keep up, mustn't you?' Mr Weston had been intending to buy his house from the corporation, 'But becoming redundant put the tin hat on that.' This was just the time of the steep rise in house prices, and while he was redundant houses increased in value by something like £1,000.

Further signs that the families were not really happy about their financial position emerged in their feelings of insecurity and their reluctance to plan for the future. Mrs Odell showed us the alterations which she had intended to have done, but which were completed only when Mr Odell was back in work. And the Odells' children would now be separated by a wider age gap than had been intended: Mrs Odell said, 'I'd like to have had another one before now. The first one's just getting to that age when he gets fed up of being on his own, and they can help with the second, you know. But . . .'

Supplementary benefits

We now turn to the families who were on the means test. Although the incomes of families who had been granted a supplementary benefit allowance were subjected to a means test in various ways, the application of a single level to all claimants runs the risk of ignoring needs which are peculiar to minority groups or individuals. Accordingly, in its design the supplementary benefits scheme is intended to take account of variations between claimants, and officials are given discretionary powers to make lump sum grants for clothing, furniture, and a very wide range of other items of expenditure if they judge the claimant is in circumstances of 'exceptional need'. As far as is thought possible by those who administer the scheme, these circumstances are spelled out in rules of guidance for officials; these rules remain secret, but a digest of some of the rules is published in the *Handbook* which has been referred to in the Introduction. This handbook has to be bought, and no written indication of their assessment is given to claimants by the officials who judge their claims. Such claims may be dealt with in the office, if they are sufficiently pressing, or an official will call round at the claimant's home if an application is sent in; or alternatively the matter might be raised on the occasion when the official calls to check that the circumstances of the family have not changed.

The means test

The most important manifestation of the means test for most families was in the matter of earnings. Because they were only allowed to earn £2, a number of wives had been prevented from going out to work. However, we will postpone discussion of this earnings barrier until we look in a later chapter at the whole question of wives working.

The most stringent restriction was the wage stop, and the Coxons had been subjected to limitation of their allowance below the normal entitlement during nine of the past ten years of Mr Coxon's illness while he had been unable to find or hold down a job. The wage stop had been eased last year through the intervention of a nursing sister who had visited Mrs Coxon a year previously. Mrs Coxon said, 'We only had £11 odd a week for ourselves and the child, and then the nursing sister came to see us, and she got on to the welfare, and got us a rise to £14 odd a week, but since then they've took the wage stop off. They rose it when I was in hospital and a lady from the Child

Poverty Action Group, she got through to them and then they made our money up to £15.90, and when we got this rise, they had £1 a week rise on social security, and she asked us if we got it, and we hadn't so she wrote to them and we got it. Every time you have to fight for it.'

Other small incomes were also means tested. The previous year Mr Paton had earned enough to put in for a small earnings-related supplement, but on that occasion, 'When I got that £2 back the Assistance Board took it off us! So I was no better off. It was a waste of time putting in for it.' Several of the families we saw had had the same experience as Mrs Nottingly whose expectations of a rent rebate had been disappointed: 'The social security got our rebate. They put in for us. I mean we thought we would benefit by it, but they took it straight off us.' In Mrs McBain's case, the Supplementary Benefits Commission had left the family to claim on its own, but had deducted the amount of the rebate from their allowance without first ensuring that the family actually received it.

The proud poor

What sort of attempts were being made by officials to meet the needs which were manifested by the families we interviewed? Among the needy there were some who apparently found the system of applying for grants distasteful, so that they tried to live on the flat means-tested allowance. Mrs Weaver said determinedly, 'I don't have any debts, and I've managed on social security all these years. I never even bothered with the free meals, because, to be quite honest with you, I think if you train yourself to spend the money wisely, you can manage. They make it too easy for people. I'm sitting here, and I know it sounds very arrogant, but I don't owe the world a penny, and I haven't, all the time he's been sick.'

Mr Spain had also been reluctant to apply, although what he said about his original decision to look after his eight children himself revealed that he felt that supplementary benefit was marginally better than charity or total dependence on his relatives back in the West Indies. 'Going back to West Indies under the type o' conditions what I find meself in, it wouldn't make much sense, because to go and restart with eight kids behind me and the only way to start is people to sorry for you and to give you charity, and all these type o' things. I no up to that kind of fun, you know. In West Indies I got me mam, and I got people who'd really muck in and help out wi' me kids. But for meself, here we have financial, we have come through. I don't want no one to sorry for me, to help me. Because if it was that, when my wife died and it was in the paper I could get a lotta help. But I didn't up to the fun because people start to sorry for you and to give you charity. Well, they sent me a whole heap o' things here, and I clear them up, sling them, even cheques or something like that. You see, I don't mind taking help from people; you need help, in my circumstances you need help. But the type o' help that some people offer, that if you can't take it because it's like charity. Charity is a thing like this, that from the moment you start to take charity from people, you become dormant, you become bloody lazy. It set you up like you don't want to think for yourself again. You just want to live on underneath that system and they keep you to a certain level in life.'

But he found supplementary benefit only slightly preferable to a charity. 'Well, from that tragedy happened, the social security, it's about four times they visit me. Well, the first time, they don't say much really, because they know the conditions like, but the first time it was a bit embarrassing like. Well, I feel bloody horrible. I didn't even want to go to the post office. I feel funny, you know, to go in there and draw the money. They gonna treat you like you got pension! Like they say, "Yeah, he's a pensioner i'n't he?" Well, now it's a bit better, because to me, you've got to have a certain income to live off, to live. Well, as you know, and as I know that you paying for that, and people paying for that. It's not a charity. But on a certain level, and certain things that they gotta ask and explain to you, it's like a charity, you know. There are certain facts in life that you don't want to tell them. Although I'm not working I'm a bit independent. I don't go round and tell people and say, "Well, I'm in distress." I prefer just to keep that to myself, because, well, from a long time since I know myself I never do it, you know. It's very hard, just to break yourself in, because many times the social security come and they axe me many things, and I just skip them like. I don't tell them, because it look in a way really horrible, telling people a certain portion o' your life, you know.'

During the year he had been on supplementary benefit the officials had never asked him how he managed: 'Well, they don't axe me that really, they never go through that details with me. They only ask me what I'm doing, for the present moment, or what your circumstances are or something like that. Well, my circumstances don't change, innit!' When, with the help of a claimants' union who had become interested in his case, he tried to get help with the payment of the quarterly central-heating bill of £45 he was refused, and the bill was met by a private charity, through the agency of the Child Poverty Action Group.

Official reluctance to give grants

The less proudly independent, or bolder, families had met with various difficulties when they tried to claim grants. Several years back, Mr Lucas had sought help with the £7 removal expenses from the slum where his child had been taken ill, to a council estate. He remembered his visit to the office with anger. 'I've had a bit of friction. You wait and then you go in and see a young girl. I made her cry. She told me, "Oh no," she said to me, "why did you move!" As if to say, "Why didn't you save yourself £7 by living in dampness and rat-infested, black-clock ridden places." You know where she lived? Well, I tell you the type she was, she lived up behind the park somewhere. Probably went home to a steak dinner. She talked way above me, like, you know what I mean, the vocabulary was far better than mine. Mine just come out. I said, "You cheeky pig!" I said, "I've got one kid who's in hospital, he had a chest complaint with dampness. That's how I got this house." I said, "All I want is help to pay it." "No, we can't help you at all," she said. "You haven't been on our books six months." So I said, "I've got to be out of work for six months before you'll ...?" I said, "How am I going to move?" She said, "I'm sorry, we can't help you." Whew! I just lost me temper, and she started to weep. And anyway, I was shouting, like, and she said, "I'm not dealing with you." She threw me paper away and walked behind a wire screen, and I just sat there for about two hours, and this man come and he said, "What's the trouble?" He said, "Oh, they're a bit touchy, like," and he took it down, you know. Oh, they paid it.'

The poorest family said they had applied for a clothing grant but had received no reply. Mrs Coxon was worried that her son might miss school because of his lack of clothing: 'I wrote and asked the council when his uniform wore out, and the School Board man came with a note. He said, "Oh, we're in the red up to here," he said. "We can't give any more grants out," he said. So he said to take this paper to the social security, and we've not heard anything from it since. That's about two months ago, so what I've had to do, my clothing club that I had, I've had to get a cheque to get him a pair of trousers. I don't want him to lose too much school, you know. They lose ground so quick at school they can't keep up with the others, and then they have to go in the backward class. It makes them feel out of place with the others if they say, "Oh, you're backward." '

The other families who were on supplementary benefits agreed that officials showed great reluctance to give grants for exceptional needs. Mrs Miller said, 'Say you put in for a grant, they really do give you the first degree, when they come to see you, you know. We were pretty lucky to get a grant for shoes, because when they come and see you've got a nice house, you're less likely to get anything. He said, "You've got a pretty nice home. I can see you're trying to help yourself." We did get a pretty nice man, you know what I mean, we were lucky. Normally, to another certain person that we know, they went into the house and he sat and she told him all her troubles, and he said, "Well, I don't think you need anything meself. You've got a beautiful home. If you're that hard up, sell" – what was it he said? – "the sideboard, and when the money goes for that, sell that, and when the money goes for that, sell that." She said, "Here, while my husband was working, I paid for all this home," and you can't just go selling your home up, can you, and just getting bits and pieces?'

Mrs Ryan asserted that official reluctance to make grants had extended to an allowance for a diet for her stomach ulcer. 'They give me the allowance when I first come out of hospital, but they've dropped it now. The allowance was stopped this time we went on social security. They never said no more. And me doctor's note's been sent in. I told him, when he was here, the social security bloke, but he said, "You can't keep it up for life." But I'm on tablets for life.'

Confusion and jealousy among claimants

There was a great deal of confusion about what could be claimed. Mrs Nottingly said, 'They don't tell anybody, because I took the child to hospital, and I didn't know I could claim. I'd been throwing me tickets away, and somebody told us you could claim for it. I think you should get a big form with all what you can claim on. Well, half the time we don't even know what we're entitled to. I didn't know. We didn't even know about the grants until Jacky told us. He said you can get a grant after you've been on two months, a grant for shoes and clothes and baby clothes, blankets and things you need. You've got to get in with somebody that knows about it before you can find out. Then you find out you wasted a lot of money.' In another instance, it was not until three months after the recurrence of Mr McBain's tuberculosis that he had found out about the extra allowance to which he was entitled.

Would-be claimants guessed at what they were entitled to, and how assessments were made, by putting together scrappy bits of information and rumour. Mr Ryan insisted, 'Oh, you can't get a grant for clothes. You can get it for bedding, but you can't get it for clothes. That's what the lad told me.' His wife insisted, 'You can. Jeannie Robertson got £25.' Mr Ryan argued, 'But what did he say to me? "You can't get it for clothes." Bedding, yes, but not clothes. After about eight months you have to ask, you know. If you want clothes, you have to go to the W.V.S. We've never had it. I know the lad that comes from the social security, known him for a long time, and he said, "If you want a grant, never say for clothes, because you won't get it." Oh, I've known him for years, had a drink with him many a time. He's better than most of 'em. You'd think they were getting it out of their own pocket when you go down there.' In fact there is provision for clothing grants.

The feeling that they might be missing something that others were getting, or alternatively others' feeling that recipients of supplementary benefits were favoured with grants, seemed to generate jealousy and division. In an exchange between Mrs Lucas and Mrs Ryan, Mrs Lucas said, 'If you're no good and you're "on the game" or out on the town you get pounds.' Mrs Ryan said, 'You feel low, like. I do.' Mrs Lucas complained, 'Some people, when we first moved in here, we'd only got a bed and a table. Other people got canvas for the floor from the social security. We never got a thing.' Mrs Ryan said, 'All they give us was £3.50 for a bit of canvas. Everybody else's had fitted carpets I would say, bar us.' Ironically, families who had received no discretionary grant suffered from public rumours about the scheme. Mrs Coxon said, 'A lot of people think because you're on social security you get everything. As a matter of fact I was on the bus, and a lady was talking about having places done up, and she says, "Oh," she says, "it's all right for you on social security, you have it all done up for nothing." '

Financial commitments

Some of the families who were now living on supplementary benefits had formerly had fairly high standards of living, and in better times they had taken on payments for furniture, carpets, washing machines, television sets, and so on, which they had not fully discharged. Mr Spain said, 'Me and my wife used to have £40, £45 at least, you see, for the week. She used to earn more than me sometimes really, and we used to just balance it out. Well, I used to get overtime and I get bonus, like. Well, me normal wages, I used to come home with at least thirty. Well, we used to save a little bit to go on me holidays. If I knew conditions was going to be like this, maybe I wouldn't have these things, this furniture and central heating, but you can't forecast your life.' He now had an income of £30.35 for himself and eight children aged from one to fourteen years. Another family, the Nottinglys, when they first got married and set up home had both been working. Mrs Nottingly said, 'We didn't put anything down on the furniture at first when we got it all out, because he was on work for four months and we paid everything as much as we could like, everything was paid for then.' As we have seen, some of the other manual workers also recalled the good times in work when they had plenty of money, and Mr Ryan said, 'I like to be at work, so I can have me pocket money, you know what I mean. See, if I go to work, if I get £30 a week, I give her twenty of it, maybe twenty-two. Well, that's me pocket-money, see.' This family now had £21 a week.

Where wages had fluctuated a high level of living and financial commitments could sometimes still be maintained. Mr Miller said of a friend, 'He's the same as me, been unemployed for months and gets into debt up to his eyeballs. Before, we always found we pull out, in them couple of months when you get your money.' Mrs Miller agreed, 'All your life you're up one time and then you're right down the next, it's a feast and a famine.'

Slipping standards: debt

An immediate effect of dependence on supplementary benefit was that, as with the insured men, ambitions had to be postponed. Mr John said gloomily, 'We have plans that we wanted to buy a car and have enough money that we were able some time to purchase a place, but we just can't do that now because of my money.' And although Mrs Nottingly would have liked another child, Mr Nottingly said, 'We'll have have to wait till I get a job now. I can't afford to keep what I've got.'

Where the homes of men drawing insurance had been well furnished and well decorated, these homes tended to be barer, sometimes drab and dingy if the father had been unemployed for long. Mr Spain said, 'When my wife died, everything for the home stop. Since that time nothing. Well, to live off that type o' money, really, you must get poorer, because you don't have no other else income coming in. Under this type o' system there's only one bloody way o' living, you see, because only way you can live, you got to really economize and lead a kind of economized life, just to keep up for the week, or else you can't live at all. Because when most of my bills come I can't pay them.' He had a court order in, for repossession of a radiogram. Mrs Nottingly was also painfully aware that their home building had been frozen in comparison with what would have been normal for a couple at their stage of married life: 'We haven't got half as much furniture as we should do, and we've wrote to the company, I haven't paid for two months like, because we pay some of it monthly, and we're just, like, braving it out. Well, there's about £25 belonging to the carpet, about £45 behind on the three-piece, and about £20 behind on the television. That's just the months he's been out of work, like.'

After some years on supplementary benefit, the flat into which the Weavers had moved, in the hope of helping Mr Weaver's skin

trouble, was among the most bare, with faded, frayed carpets, dilapi-
dated furniture, tatty linoleum and dirtying wallpaper. Mrs Weaver
said, 'We haven't the money to put it right, you know, such as carpets. Well, everything will have to wait. I believe in good food and
we get plenty of that. I could do with furniture and carpets, but
you can't get everything, because there's only one thing important
to me, and that's food.'

Budgeting for some families had come to involve the calculation
of which debts could be missed this week, and court orders became
part of the way of life. Mr Lucas said, 'I've got a bill for that, like,
to take the washing machine. It's the wife is that. She's been missing
the bloody thing. I think meself, before that gets paid, in the corner,
the television or the washing machine, the fire has to be on for the
kids, like, that's our first worry! And this over our heads, pay that, and
food in. I say to her, "What you think you can manage on, and then
pay what you've got." We don't pay our debts every week, you know
what I mean. We have to miss the telly – there's a friendly man up
for the telly the other day for £2.75!' The Ryans lived in a state of
near siege. Mrs Ryan said, 'You sit here and you've no money, and
a knock comes at the door and you all have to fly in the airing cupboard, all of us, and the bairns. When we can't pay anybody we've
to fly in the gas cupboard and hide ourselves, electric men or gas men,
owt like that, you know. I've been out all day, I've been up to me
mate's (Mrs Lucas) in case the telly man comes for the telly.' Rather
than take the families to court the T.V. rental company apparently
found it simpler to enter the house and take away the sets. Mr Ryan
said, 'They come yesterday to take that out. I said, "You put your
foot over that door," as I was in. "You're not getting in here." ' Mrs
Ryan said, 'They'll come back tonight and take it out tonight.'

Because they were short of ready cash for lump sum payments,
several of the families adopted expensive budgeting methods. The
normal mode of payment for clothing and furniture was by club
cheques, where interest rates were high, but the most wasteful forms
of budgeting were illegal. Mr Lucas said, 'We generally have a club
and we sell it, a £20 club – which is against the law, by the way,
don't print that – you get people who want that, say, who're working,
they save £4. And I get £16 for me £20 club, but it's actual money.
Then I pay me electricity bill and me other bills. It's the only way I

can do it, like, where if you're working you'd just, say, pay it.' Mrs Ryan changed free milk tokens for food. 'Well, these don't like milk, so we go to this certain shop, and he gives us butter, eggs and all that like. He's not supposed to do it, like, he's liable. Fifteen bob for two coupons, like. He has a dairy, so he can say he's got 'em for milk, see.' The pay-off for the shopkeeper's risk in such cases is the custom, but sometimes also the value of the goods is only part of the value of the tokens.

Mrs McBain summed up the experience of these families from the north-east. 'You see, when you've been on the dole a long time little things build up, payments, things like that. Now he could start work, he could start work tomorrow, but it doesn't mean next week I'd be well off, because all these little things I've been backsliding, you'd have to pay them to catch up. And by the time you've caught up, they're finished work again, and you're back to square one. That's the thing about the dole. On these little jobs that only last a few weeks, you get yourself in a hole and you just start to get out of it, and you're back at the beginning again.'

Hardship

We have seen that these families had trouble in maintaining financial commitments for furnishings, but was there any evidence that they were having to cut back on spending on food or going short on essentials because of what they said was official parsimony? It was difficult to gain adequate and reliable information on spending patterns, but a number of the families showed signs of hardship.

Mrs Coxon said that a year ago, when they had been under the limitation of the wage stop, the nursing sister had called, and, 'This day we hadn't much here, and she said, "Haven't you got a better dinner than that?" And I didn't like to tell her at first, but she said, "What you going to have tonight?" I said, "That's all we've got for dinner."' But although the wage stop had since been lifted, at the time of the interview, so far as could be estimated, at the worst time of the year Mrs Coxon had only £4 a week to spend on food for two adults and a child, after spending on rent, lighting, bus fares for shopping, and a clothing club. And out of that small amount she spent up to £2 a week on milk: 'You see my husband practically

101

lives on that. In that pint mug he has that much, he has about eight mugs of tea a day. He has sugar and milk in that tea, and that really keeps him going, so if I cut down too much on that I'm really cutting down on the goodness. The Assistance Board did tell me to cut down on milk, but it's just that that's what he lives on, what's keeping him going.' Another reason why the Coxons seemed to be going short on food was because they spent as much as £5 a week on heating and lighting in winter. 'You see he's always cold, and he can't keep warm – even in the summer he's cold – and this room is always cold, no matter how warm it is outside, it's always freezing in here, damp, so we have to have the fire on all the time, summer and winter.' She also had to spend extra on fares to go shopping, 'You see, I have to go shopping every day because I can't carry a lot, and Dad can't carry a lot.'

Mrs Ryan was so deeply involved in club payments that she was sometimes in a worse position than the Coxons, with only £4 for food for two adults and three children – if she paid her clubs. On the Saturday before we called, Mrs Lucas and Mrs Ryan were already waiting for the family allowance to come before they could buy any more food, and they would have to try to borrow money. But here a contributory reason for the hardship seemed to be that Mr Ryan could not easily cut down his 'spending money' when he was out of work, although in this he seemed unusual among those we saw.

Like the Coxons, the other families we saw had budgets which differed markedly from those of the rest of the population, in that it seemed as though they could put the emphasis on one basic essential only at the expense of another. In spite of Mrs Weaver's insistence that they had good food, she herself was gaunt, and Jimmy Weaver was currently frustrated in his ambition to become a sailor partly because he was undersized for his age. The emphasis on food in the Weaver family seemed to be achieved at the expense of clothing and other items like furnishings. Mr Paton too claimed that his food was adequate, but boring: 'You see, today I'll go and get me dole, tonight'll be about the decentest meal we get. Our lass'll make a good meal, like, because it's dole day and she's got a few bob. Now tomorrow we'll probably get chips and something, chips and eggs. The next day we'll get chips and eggs. Then Saturday we'll get a

change, she'll say, "We'll have a change, we'll have egg and chips!" '
But his children were not properly dressed, and he had had to strip
the wires from the immersion heater because he could not afford
hot water. Mr Spain also put a great emphasis on food, cooking a
large meal each day for his children to eat at tea-time, because he
felt the school meals were inadequate. Even so, school meals were a
valuable contribution to his budget and he ran into severe difficulties
in the school holidays. And the great emphasis he placed on food
seemed to mean that he found difficulty in paying for clothing: 'Well,
they're getting a bit soggy now.' Also, as we have seen, he could not
meet his heating bill. Mr Spain found that the bills made him think
of his bereavement. 'The only time you dig your life up and you start
to think is when type o' financial thing occur, and then you say, "Oh
... if I was working." '

Other feelings of deprivation

Apart from debt and shortages of money for food, clothes and fuel,
the families felt deprivations in other ways. Even the Coxons, a
family which had never participated in the rising general living
standards of society, still felt the pull of general affluence. Mrs
Coxon said, 'We look at that, where he used to be working for that
measly money, now when he should be earning the money, we haven't
got the money coming in.' The Coxons' youngest son had only been
taken to the cinema once. And last year he had had to miss the school
holiday. 'He said, could he go, and I said how much would it cost.
He said £10. I said, oh, no, I couldn't manage that. They'd left it too
late. £10! If the school had told us at the beginning of the year ...'

Parents seemed sensitive to the problem that children might be
excluded from general patterns of spending, and usually mentioned
giving the children priority – they also tended to excuse any spending which they felt might be criticized by outsiders, such as T.V., by
saying it was 'for the children'. Mrs Miller's anxiety about her children focused on Christmas. 'When you think of Christmas and
you've got two bairns, then you do start worrying, you know. My
husband's been saying just lately, haven't you, and it's only, what,
July, isn't it, "Oh, Christmas is coming up." ' Mr Miller said, 'I want
£64 for a kick-off now, for two "Chopper" bikes.' His wife said,

'They're used to getting what they want. They'll have to, mind. He'll get a job. He'll do something. They never have been refused anything, we never have said no to them. We've always tried to get them what they want. They don't go short of anything.'

Mr McBain thought that most parents near where he lived tended to be indulgent with their children, 'Because it was so hard for them when they were kids. It's as simple as that. Same as I get fed up now with these kids, when I can't give them the things they should be getting. I mean really, now, to see a car outside everybody's house is nothing unusual. There's a bloke two doors down with two of them!' These two cars had been bought by a clerk – out of his redundancy money.

Mr Spain also worried about Christmas. 'It's a bit rough. Last Christmas gone, it's the first Christmas I spend that way really, and it was really rough. I couldn't buy nothing at all. It was people give them presents. Well, my welfare officer arranged, like, to get some toys for the kids, and I've got a lot of friends, like. I couldn't afford to buy it, because remember they don't allow you for these things, because a certain part of the things what you have, they claim it as a luxury, innit? You live on a means test. They only just want to know that you can get your food, and if you didn't wear clothes, well, I don't believe it would matter to them if you didn't wear clothes.'

Mr Spain had a solution, of sorts, to problems of being deprived of what others in the community enjoy. 'Well, they don't mind really, my kids really. I've brought them up that it's what I say goes, it's not what they said. That system wouldn't work with me at all, because I don't look because you have that I supposed to get it. Don't come to me with that. What I can afford, that's what I give them. It's like a woman, if you have a woman and she keep on asking and says, "Oh, I go over my friend house and she have television like that, and I want that," she make you bloody boring. And if you don't mind, she have you go up the bloody wall, because she want every bloody thing she see the next person have, and it's not a good system. And if you learn the kids like that, he's no good to hisself when he come up, going round and see people things and ask, "Oh, that one have, that one have . . ." It no good. No matter what you have, it don't matter to me. You could be rich, you could be poor, it don't trouble me. The only thing I want to live is a good life, that's all.'

To conclude, there were several people who appeared moderately satisfied with the level of living afforded by the means test. Mr Calvert, who lived with his wife in furnished rooms on an income of just over £6 a week after payment of rent, said, 'Well, we eat reasonably well. If there were any films that we fancied seeing I suppose we might miss them; we occasionally see a film or something. I mean things are financially very basic, but we get by.' Mrs Calvert agreed, 'I wouldn't like a whole lot of things to carry around. And we don't entertain. Our friends are so far distant, you know, really.'

Mr Dover said, 'We're broke today, but we'll be all right tomorrow. You see these days you don't need much for clothing. The fashion is to look scruffy.' He elaborated as he ate his lunch of boiled potatoes smeared with Bovril. 'Yes, I think there's enough money. I've got more than I need. I mean all you need is your rent and your food, isn't it? And when you're unemployed you've got a lot more time to shop for things. I mean us, we'll go out shopping, and it will take us three hours to get one thing. We go up here looking round the shops and commenting on things. Mostly we say how horrible it is. We go in the supermarket and we look at things and we shrink back in horror. Plastic food, we call it. If you had a lot of money you wouldn't buy that sort of food.'

6 Help and Disapproval from Relatives and Neighbours

In this chapter the workless describe how much help or disapproval they feel they have had from friends, neighbours and relatives (by whom we mean kin other than the wife and children, who will always be referred to as the family). Whether or not relatives and the surrounding society had given much support or expressed disapproval obviously depended to some extent on how relationships had stood before the men became unemployed. One point of difference is a general contrasting pattern between the mobile and the less mobile families. The more mobile families did not seem to differ greatly in the way they talked about their ties with their relatives, although these ties seemed to be more flexible and to be maintained at a greater distance than the same ties of the less mobile families. However, when we come to discuss links with neighbours and friends, we will follow up a suggestion from an earlier chapter that the less mobile families had stronger local roots.

Help from relatives

With families whose living standards were initially protected by insurance, the question of financial help did not at first arise. But where a family was needy the sympathy of relatives could be expressed in the most practical way through cash or gifts, and in some instances the hardships experienced by families living under the means test had been eased in this way.

For example, although they had perhaps a tendency to make too much of help received as a tangible proof of family affection, it was clear that the Coxons did get support from their married and independent children in various ways. They had two television sets because a son was in the trade. In earlier years the children had provided a small car, taxed and insured. At Christmas, Mrs Coxon said, 'Well, we was lucky this year. They all brought food, like, and tins of stuff. That helped us a lot. Otherwise we'd have had nothing. My sons and daughters are all good. Now you see, we've got the television, two shillings in the slot. Well, you see, if one of the boys comes up he'll say, "Here, a couple of bob for your telly," or perhaps say, "Here, a packet of cigarettes." Well, otherwise he wouldn't get ten a day as it stands. They come down at weekends, my daughter-in-law, and they bring a pot of jam or a packet of bacon, or something like that. Or she'll come down and say, "I've got too many loaves, would you like a couple of loaves?" I know very well they've bought it purposely so they can fetch it down. Or perhaps she'll send down a couple of pints of milk. They're all good to us.'

The affectation of surprise when these 'unexpected' gifts turned up so regularly presented some difficulty to Mr Coxon, as we saw when during one interview a son turned up bringing cigarettes. This provoked a histrionic response from Mr Coxon, 'Twenty! I asked you to get me ten! Still, thanks very much. They look after me, you know. Easter, the son-in-law came up and took me out to give me a few pints, because he knows that when he takes me out for a drink, once I get a few drinks inside me, he can see how I brighten up, you know. I get happy and cheerful. I invited 'em all up home, "Come home and have a cuppa tea!" you know, I'm very friendly.' But his wife said, 'Sometimes he won't go with 'em if he can't afford to stand a round, you see, because there's six or eight of 'em. Well, you've got to have two or three pounds to spend.' Mr Coxon said, 'They say, "It's all right, it's all right," but I hate to think ... I'm funny like that. You see all the others are paying.'

Help from kin had become built into the pattern of Mr Miller's work and unemployment. 'If it wasn't for her mother, we wouldn't have anything like. Her mother helps us a lot, with the kids' clothes, the bills, she pays for them, electric bill and things like that. She knows she'll get it back in time.' Mrs Miller said, 'You always seem to get ... I mean we write to me Mam. Well, we don't have to write. If she thinks we need she'll send, but it's just the thought. I mean we always get by.' If unemployment followed a regular cycle, the peaks and hollows of irregular earnings could be ironed out – as long as the hollows of unemployment did not last too long.

The main sources of help seemed to come from the grandparents (even where these were old and comparatively poor themselves) or from independent children. And relatives provided resources which could be mobilized in times of crisis to give support. Mr Ryan said, 'We got a letter through the door to say, if you don't pay they were going to come and turn the electric off, so I had to borrow the money to go and pay it straight away, for the children like. Me mother, she lent it like. She's helped us. She's on the old age pension. She lent me the money and I give her it straight back yesterday.' In fact, his mother turned up during the interview, refusing to budge until he gave her back the money.

Teenagers had been carried financially by parents who were working, and most teenagers seemed very dependent on the rest of their family. One mother said, 'He gets his pocket money, about £2 a week, and clothing, and if he wanted to go to anywhere with any of his mates, well, we wouldn't see him beat, you know. He's lucky. Both me and the Da work, so he's never been without anything what his mates has sort of got, you know, with them working.' A teenager said, 'I had money, like. Well me mam was giving us money, like. I used to get £3.60 on the dole, so I used to, like, gie it all to me mam one week, and she used to keep us in cigarettes through the week, and she used to give me it the following week. She says, "Aw, you can keep your dole money," and it used to go on like that all the time. It was canny, like. I used to go out practically every Saturday and Sunday night.'

Such support could carry the teenager through a bad patch, until he had time to find a job which was more to his liking. The father of a teenager whose pimples prevented his being accepted by the Army was quite prepared to keep his son until the pimples cleared up. Another mother had got her son into a government training scheme for a few months, and was now preparing to pay for driving lessons for him.

However, by the same informal rules of support, the workless man was sometimes called upon to support his own workless children, or to support children who were a drain in other ways, and one of the men we interviewed was 'lending' money which never got repaid to a daughter whose husband would not work but who was not registered for employment. At another time another daughter had been unemployed, and the father said, 'I was going to claim for her. I went up there to the exchange and I said, "I've got a big daughter to feed."

They said, "That's her bloody look-out. She should be at work, shouldn't she?" So that put the kybosh on that, which is fair enough really, although I had to keep her.'

So in various ways, because unemployed men and their families had a wider group of relatives they might benefit from financial help. More rarely however, they might be called upon to give it. Although cash help, or equally importantly the failure of such help, was probably most significant as symbolizing support or disapproval.

Disapproval from relatives

Once we leave tangible expressions of help such as cash and gifts we move into the area where the workless man's altered situation was brought home to him in more subtle ways, by jokes, or tone of voice and gesture. Mrs Vickers said that they had experienced no disapproval. 'With visitors we just sort of discuss the interviews for jobs. You know, they're like us, they're not really concerned about my husband being out of work, because he's not concerned.' Even so, Mr Vickers admitted that the family 'took the mickey' out of him, and, 'My brother-in-law envies me, he certainly does. He works at a place, he's worked there for thirty years, and he's hated every day of it.'

Expressions of disapproval from relatives might be brought to bear indirectly, on the wife or children, rather than being forthright and direct. Mrs Weston said, 'My family have said – when I've said my husband won't take a lower paid job – they've said to me, "I think he should take less pay rather than have nothing coming in at all." My sister, she knows everything what's going on anyway; once or twice she throws out a hint, you know, about him not working. "What does he do?" she says, "What does he do with hisself all day?" I says, "Well, he don't sit down, if that's what you mean." I don't have him run down. But at the same time, when I come home sometimes I think, "Well, I dunno . . ." '

As time went on, or where relationships were already strained and the husband was already unpopular with his relatives, disapproval might become more direct. Mrs Nottingly said, 'Me mother might say, "It's about time you got yourself to work." Well, me relations, like, me sisters and me Mam and that, they think it's him, that he won't find a job and that.' Miss Hebb said she was now isolated

w–10

from her relatives: 'They don't really know a lot about what I do, or what I'm like. My father won't speak to me because I'm unemployed. He says he won't speak to me until I settle down and have a regular job and marriage and kids.' But, 'I think my mother secretly admires me.'

Teenagers had sometimes felt similar pressures from their parents. One said, 'Me mother was on at us. She was always saying, "Get out, try and get a job."' Another, who was now working, said, 'Well, when I was on the dole this last two months she says, "It's about time you got a job," I say, "Oh, I'll get one Ma, nowt to worry about," and then I got this, she was over the moon like. Oh me Dad was saying, "Oh, if you can get on with that job, get on with it," and I says, "I'll get a job man, you've got nowt to worry about," and he's going on and going on, and he started to smile when I told him I was starting work. He says, "Aye son, it's best."'

When the workless were also needy an extra constraint could enter relationships with relatives. When the Weston family ran out of money, Mrs Weston noted bitterly, 'My relatives, all my sisters and that, every time they phone, "How are you?" But now they think we might need something, so they just all don't bother to phone. You see, my sisters, when we had money, we was the first to lend it to 'em, but you see I would never ask them. I would rather go without than ask them, because they know we need money, and I know they can afford to lend for weeks on end and not miss it, you know. But they just don't want to know. You see, I shall remember all this.'

At worst, either through repeated calls for help, or by reason of the exacerbation of other grounds for friction, families could become completely estranged from their relatives. Mrs Lucas said, 'My family look at me as if I was a lump of shit!' And Mr Ryan said of his wife, 'Her family, every time she goes down, they say, "What do you want now?" Every one of them has cash.' Mrs Ryan said, 'My mother and father won't have him in the house.' Mr Ryan: 'You go down there to ask for a sub. "What do you want?"' Mrs Ryan: 'Never think you're going visiting; always, "What do you want?"' Mr Ryan: 'Same as her – your father – he's been in here one day, that's when my bairn got buried. Never seen him since. Because I'm not working. You see you're a waster, because you don't work.' He added bitterly, 'Them docks, where they all work, you only have to go down, if you do no work, sign a form and you get £17 or £18 a week. But to get on it's who you know, see.' Mrs Ryan joined in, ' 'Cause they said they couldn't get a form, 'cause they didn't want to. They're getting *their* money, that's it.'

Other relationships: the mobile worker

Workers who had been more mobile seemed to lead lives which were less in contact with the surrounding estates where they lived. Mr Vickers speculated, 'When I'm taking the dog for a walk round the estate, I wonder sometimes, the people that are looking out the windows, I wonder what they do think, you know. The fact that I am unemployed, do they think ... *not* that it matters too much to me what they think, but one still wonders, you know.' When Mr Vickers saw friends, it tended to be visitors who came round to his home, and he was inclined to test them out: 'We had some friends round here the other night, and my wife made them a dinner, and I said, "We're not doing so badly for life on the dole!" They don't usually make remarks to me because I tend to take the initiative. I say to them, "It's tough on you, having to work." '

The Vickers family were not short of cash, and Mr Vickers could still keep up his regular evening out during the week. But for the more mobile any shortage of cash could have an isolating effect. Mr Spain liked a drink, 'But when I handle me budget, then it's nothing really left in me pocket. You get hold of yourself, say well, you see, well tonight I could, say, go in the pub and have a pint or something like that, or you're feeling like a little recreation – that's the whole point of your life, innit? – and you couldn't go at all, you couldn't afford it, could you? You're just stuck in the one way all the while. If a friend don't come along and says, "Well, all right, we'll take you out for the night and give you a couple of drinks," you know, I just stop inside, stuck inside.'

Mr Fellowes, who lived near Mr Vickers, had been upset by inquiries from acquaintances. 'People mean well, I suppose, but something sticks inside you. They'll say, "Hello, you're having a nice easy day!" and they don't mean anything, it's meant as a joke, and I take it as a joke, but there's just that ... some feeling behind it. They don't know how lucky they are. And if I go out shopping, we meet two or three people and they'll say, "Have you got a job yet?" I know they mean well, but if you've had a disappointment during the week, it gets on top of you. I know, I've felt that way myself when I've been in work, I've made a joke. It's harmless and you don't mean anything, but you don't know how it embarrasses people who are out of work.'

In these newer areas, however, it seemed to be the wives who were more in contact with the surrounding neighbourhood and who experienced direct informal pressures. Mrs John said, 'I got passed a remark when I went round my mate, "Oh, it's a year since your husband's been out of work, isn't he getting a job?"' Mr John, who sat at home most of the day, took violent exception to this: 'If they open their mouth and say anything to me outright, they know I can counteract that very hard and they know what I'm going to answer them! My answer will be so hard and bold and brief that they cannot, they, they, they cannot stand up to my, what you say, my argument, because I'm hitting them boldly!' However, nobody did make remarks directly to him.

More forcefully, neighbours' disapproval had come back to Mr Weston indirectly via his children, who met trouble at school. 'Obviously their parents must have talked, and the kids say, "Your Dad's all right, on the dole, raking it in."' Mrs Weston said, 'You see the kids have said it to Clive, because Clive came in the other morning, wasn't it, and he said he had a fight with a boy, didn't he? He said, "All your Dad does is sit around all day and lets other people keep him." This is what I mean, you see. It worries me.' Mr Weston countered, 'It doesn't worry me, because I know how blasted hard I work in here all day. I feel all right. If they look at me, that's their image. I mean the way I look at it, the circumstances I'm in are certainly not due to my fault, because I will insist I've always been a conscientious worker.'

The workless also encountered disapproval in more neutral settings away from home, with strangers, or comparative strangers. Mr Odell said, 'I went to a pub down the road, and we got into a political discussion and the landlady got furious with me. She said, "If you changed your ideas you might get a job." I said, I wouldn't change my ideas to get a job, because it would be hypocritical, and she insisted I was being hypocritical now!'

Mr Dover felt that the workless man had an inferior social identity in public places. 'When you're unemployed, it's as though you're not a person, as though you're not entitled to have any ideas. Often when I'm talking in a pub, sooner or later it gets round to, "What sort of job do you do?" and if you say you're unemployed, that's it: end of conversation! It's as though your opinions aren't worth knowing. You might be talking about Ulster, or something like that. As soon as they find out you're unemployed: end of conversation. It's as though you're not entitled to have any opinions.' Miss Hebb agreed, 'Yes, sometimes when you get friends of friends, who're conventional, they'll ask you what you do and you say you're unemployed, that's it: the conversation just stops. I've had people who've just walked away. I've said I was unemployed and the person just walked away, there was nothing more to say. It's embarrassing too when you're hitch-hiking. People ask what you do, and if you say you're unemployed, you can feel the tension and the antagonism.'

As a means of forestalling questions or warding off embarrassing situations Miss Hebb sometimes assumed a false identity. 'I sometimes say I'm a student, and then it's all right. I try not to lie about it. Like, I was having a lift with somebody and he said, "Where do you come from?" and I said Norwich, and he said, "Oh, University of East Anglia, where the students are," and I said, "Yes", but I didn't say I was a student.' Mr Dover's assumption of a false identity involved a costume: 'Sometimes when I'm walking round the town, I wear this old B.R.S. coat that I've picked up, and then it's surprising, I feel just like everybody else. If you're just walking about in normal gear, people look at you and wonder what you're doing, but if you've got a B.R.S. jacket on you might be delivering parcels or something like that. Sometimes I've lied about what I'm doing. People have asked what I do, and I say, "Oh, I'm working for British Road," and I'll invent journeys that I'm supposed to be going on.'

Yet even in the south-east, where workless men were more conspicuous in the day-time, and where those who condemned them were less likely to have experienced unemployment, Mr Haigh felt that rising unemployment was easing the pressures of public disapproval. 'One, two years back, if you were unemployed it was something awful, but now if you're unemployed there's nobody to point the

113

finger and say tut! tut! because it's all different people who're getting unemployed.'

Less-mobile workers in the north-east: a community of the unemployed

In the north-east there were families who had never moved to look for work, and whose social lives were a set of closely interlocking and overlapping networks of relatives who were workmates, and workmates who were neighbours. A man's life was lived more with his friends during his leisure hours, and less with his family. And the wives too spent more time together, out of the home.

In the north-east there were some indications that the workless retained a separate status, but local feelings were more sympathetic. Mrs Nottingly said, 'My friends just say, just, "I don't know how you manage it," and "I don't know how you can stand him all day ..." They feel sorry for him, like. They say, "Oh, is he still out of work? Is he still on the dole?" Some people feel sorry, but when he first came out on the dole, I was a bit ashamed, you know. I've got used to it now.'

The workless claimed to have much closer relationships with people in work. Mr Ryan said, 'Oh, they make jokes, but it's only in fun, "We're working to keep you fellers, and you're sat in the club," you know. We laugh about it, laugh about it. Now there's one lad there, Dave, when we were working, me and me brothers, like, we were dropping him, you know, on a Thursday night, and when he was working, he'd do the same for us, you know what I mean? You help each other out. I think that's what mates are for.' Mr Lucas said, 'You know, the lads who're working as much as think, "I'm fortunate," and the lads who're not don't get pushed under by them. You get beer bought by the lads that's working. They don't say, "Get a job," but "Here, get a jar," like, and just send yer a jar over, like regular, lads that you've worked with. They'll come in the club, maybe twice a month, and they'll say, "Are you having one?"'

So the social life of the workless men, and to a lesser extent their wives, still centred on the working men's club, which provided activities for the adults together, for the spouses separately, for the children and for the old people. Mr Lucas said, 'You get kids stuff. Every time we get chits for drinks, the kids get a treat upstairs, a film show or something like that. The other year the kids got ten bob apiece, apple, orange, and a ice cream and a film show upstairs. They take nearly £4,500 a week in that bar. The old people go of a Wednesday afternoon, they have a game of housey, cups of tea, sandwiches, and it's all paid for, the housey cards and everything; and they have a bus trip every other week, holidays, and it's all paid for by the club.' The chits referred to are a regular distribution of some of the bar profits to members in the form of free beer, which the unemployed, along with the employed, were entitled to.

On the other hand, there were hints that there might be recognizable distinctions in the club between the workless and those in work, as the Ryans' story of club life may show. They recalled how Mr Ryan's brother had come to be expelled from the club. Mrs Ryan said, 'Didn't he throw a pie at the Committee man?' Mr Ryan: 'A glass.' Mrs Ryan: 'A glass and a pie, at the Committee man. Well, they was having a party upstairs and they come down to the bar with the old stale pies for the lads on "skid row" like.' Mr Ryan: 'Like a box, see, with all the crumbs.' Mrs Ryan: 'His brother said, "You're not giving us old stale pies," so he shot a pie at them.' Mr Ryan: 'A glass.' Mrs Ryan: 'And a pie.' We asked about 'skid row', and Mr Ryan explained, 'That's as you go through the door of the club, and it's this side.' Mrs Ryan elaborated, 'That's all them that's not working, "skid row".' Mr Ryan: 'And they're all good lads an' all.' Mrs Ryan: 'If one of them has any money, they'll take the rest in, or if anybody's had a win on the hosses.' Mr Ryan: 'Say, I've got a couple of bob, you take each other in like that, and give 'em a tab apiece, or something like that. Always have done, that's what they call "skid row". You see one might sign on a Wednesday, and if I have no money I can go down and say to him, "Can you lend us owt till tomorrow?" Next one signs on a Thursday, and I can do the same on a Friday, don't I?'

However, any flow of cash from men in work to the workless on 'skid row' was probably small, and remained in the men's world, to subsidize the man's drinking. Thus when Mr Miller was extolling the value of mutual support among the men, his wife hastened to point out, 'That's not big, like, ten bob a time. We couldn't go, like, if he wanted to pay a 'lectric bill, we couldn't just go and ask.' Wives relied for help on other wives similarly placed to join them in economies of shared housekeeping. Mrs Ryan and Mrs Lucas had such an arrangement: 'One day she used to cry out, and I'd cook the dinner, and if she had the money one day, we'd go up to their house and get our teas, and if I had the money the next day, they'd come down here, and that's what we used to do.' These two wives who seemed to depend most upon one another for mutual support were married to the men who were most enthusiastic about the mutual helpfulness of the male drinking group.

Part Three:
THE SEARCH FOR IDENTITY

7 Pressures in the Home: Worker or Housewife?

      In this chapter the couples describe how the loss of work had influenced relationships in the home between the man and his wife and children. Whether the husband's presence in the home was regarded as an opportunity for a new relationship or as a constraint seemed to depend on the previous pattern of the marriage, so we will first briefly describe what we see as relevant features of these marriages, such as the sharing of leisure and household tasks. With the man at home there might be the chance for him to become more of a 'housewife', and for his wife to become more of a 'worker', perhaps to go out to work. If the wife went out to work, the couples might not spend any greater time together in the home. We also look, therefore, at the decisions and consequences of the wife working.

Patterns of marriage

Before unemployment Mr and Mrs Vickers had apparently enjoyed spending their leisure time in one another's company. They had watched T.V. together, entertained family visitors together regularly on several evenings a week, and had gone visiting and on holidays together. On the other hand, Mr Vickers had done rather little housework, but nor did his wife expect or want him to. 'He's never been one for cleaning. He's never been keen on that. Well, it is a woman's job really, isn't it? Sometimes he'll do a bit of shopping, fetch my odds and whatsits, and he'll come with me for the big shopping, to help me carry it. But if he does shop we only have disagreements because he's gone and got the wrong things, so I prefer to do it myself, so I can plan it.' Mr Vickers agreed, 'Occasionally I'll do a bit of shopping for my wife – very reluctantly.' His main activities in the home had been as a handyman, and he had a garden shed with a work-bench and tools where he had liked occasionally to work.

An example of a contrasting marriage relationship was that of the Ryans, who gave the impression that if they had spent time in the home together before unemployment this had been as much through inertia as through any very strong liking or desire for one another's company. Mrs Ryan looked back to those days with nostalgia. 'When he's working he's no bother. He's usually tired when he comes in on a night, he'd rather sit. I have all the bairns in bed when he comes in, and his tea ready, and he just gets a bottle of lemonade and sits and watches telly with me all night. That's us. We go out about eight o'clock to the fish and chip shop for our suppers and he never bothers about the club.' The question of joint holidays had never arisen; Mrs Ryan had taken the children off for days. Nor did they entertain visitors at home together: they saw relatives separately, Mr Ryan meeting his brothers at the local pub or club. When they went out for entertainment 'together' it had been to separate parts of the club, with separate friends, and an outing on the evening before our interview was apparently typical of what had happened on a number of previous visits to the club. Mr Ryan had remained downstairs on 'skid row' while his wife went dancing in the big room upstairs. He said, 'Well, they were all out dancing, and I had a few jars and I got half drunk, you know, and I went upstairs, like, and I told her, "Out!" I just said, "Out!" You see all the lads are in the bar, they're there to keep their eye on them – they're doing nowt wrong, like. But I got a bit drunk, like, it's just that you're in the bar and you're thinking about the dancing with men. I just thought, "The bastard! Away! Home!" Her mates were sat there, and that's what she's upset about.' In the home, by Mr Ryan's standards he had been quite helpful. 'I do a lot actually. When she was bad for six months, like, laid up in bed, I done the tea-cloths and everything, got the lads up and off to school and everything.' But from what we saw on several visits, rather little housework of any kind was done, and the house had more the feel of a base than a home.

The Odells seemed in some ways intermediate between the Vickers family and the Ryans. Mr Odell had moved with his family when they came over to work, and his parents and sister now lived near. He had married a local girl, with relatives near by, and now they tended to visit their relatives separately. Their marriage had settled down comfortably into a pattern where their social lives were separated, he involved in politics with his trade union friends, or going to the local pub; she going to bingo with her women friends or staying at home. They took separate holidays, he with his friends, she with her mother. Mr Odell remarked on how almost imperceptibly this pattern had emerged: 'I stopped in a pub the other night, and I never even thought, my wife might like to go out. I do try to get her to come out from time to time, but I think I've only got her out about five times for a drink since last July. Before she had the baby she'd go out, but you see even then the pattern was changing.' Mr Odell was in favour of women's lib and the broadening of family boundaries. 'I believe in the family, but I believe the family can be worked into a community system where there are adults and children living. You're one family, that's what you would call the brotherhood of man.' He did nothing towards the housework before he became unemployed.

Pressures in close marriages

Up to a point, in marriages which had previously been close, couples said they welcomed the extra time they could spend together because of unemployment. One couple appeared downstairs only after some delay to answer our call after lunch, and looking rather dishevelled and flustered they explained they had been resting upstairs. In another interview, Mr Vickers said, looking back on unemployment, 'Except for the last month or so, I can't remember how long it was – I should say in that time it wasn't too good really, was it; it wasn't too bad, but the shine was going off it, really, there – but for the vast majority of the unemployed period it was very good.' Mrs Vickers agreed, 'Really, I like having him around. I'm not like some women who want to be on their own. I prefer to have him at home. I'd like it if we had enough money so that he didn't have to work and he could stop at home all the time.' Other couples discovered that with the husband at home, the wife was freer to leave the children and go shopping.

However, a closer relationship for the adults was not without its problems for the children. One child, seeing his father at home all day with his mother, became reluctant to go to school, and his father said, 'He thinks it's unfair. Well, he's sometimes said – what does he say – "Why do I have to go to school if you don't have to go to work?"'

The burden of attempting to shield the wife from the full impact of unemployment seemed to put that much greater strain on husbands in close marriages. They were sometimes less cocky and confident about their prospects of finding work when their wives were out of the room. Mr Fellowes said, 'To tell you the truth, I think it's only just hit her, the feeling of what it's like. We don't talk about it much. I try not to bring it up, I try to play it down. She's very good, she's tried to understand. I don't think she did at first, though, but recently her attitude's changed, she's a bit down. She's pretty worried, but she doesn't say much. Sometimes she says, "Are you going round for the paper?" and I know the pressure's on her. But I don't want any of the pressures to be on her, or the kids. They've got to be on me.' And Mr Fellowes felt that he was also somehow devalued in his children's eyes: 'I think it has affected the kids. They're funny, you know, sometimes they'll make funny little remarks that show they're interested. Before when I was at work the kids were completely disinterested, couldn't care, but now I get the old ribald remark. If I say I'm going for a job the little girl will say, "You won't get it!"'

While the wife remained at home and in good health, there was little opportunity for the husband to become more of a 'housewife', partly because there was not enough housework to occupy two adults, but also because the wives still embraced their role. Mr Weston complained that if he did any housework, his wife merely manufactured more things to do. Mrs Weston said, 'I don't just let things pile up for him. I mean I like housework. In fact he says I work too hard.' Her husband agreed, 'You see, I maintain while I'm at home here, if I do a certain amount, it's something that she would have to do if I wasn't here. Therefore her days should be shorter. Does that make sense?'

Both Mr Vickers and Mr Fellowes said they noticed a change in the home atmosphere at weekends. Mr Vickers said, 'Of course the weekends are always vastly different anyway. I look forward to the weekend, because, you know, I'm seeing visitors at weekends.' Mr

Fellowes said, 'I find the weekends easier somehow. The pressure's gone, because I'm normally at home.'

The push out of the home

The pressures generated by the husband's unaccustomed presence in the home were greater in marriages where the couples had not voluntarily spent a great deal of time together before unemployment. The Nottinglys were a young couple in the north-east whose marriage was changing from the sharing of their courtship to the segregation of longer-established marriages. Mrs Nottingly was under pressure from her friends who seemed to feel that it was not natural for a man to be at home during the day, and she did not welcome her husband's attempts to get her to join in and dance to records as a break from housework. 'He gets on your nerves,' she said, 'I haven't the time.' Mr Nottingly explained gloomily, 'I muck the place up, and that's what she goes mad about, you know.' Mr and Mrs Nottingly said their marriage had deteriorated under the strain. Mr Nottingly said, 'Why, the first couple o' weeks, like, you don't bother, and then after a while you start to row.' His wife agreed, 'Yeah, you're like cat and mouse all the time, you know, "Why don't you get yourself a job?" You see, it's the money really that gets you down, and being on top of each other all day.'

Mr Miller tried to maintain that his behaviour was unchanged, but his wife insisted, 'You're bad tempered, irritable.' He replied, 'That's because I can't get out enough. Well, nobody likes to stop in on a nice night. There's a big night on at the club tonight. I've got a ticket in me pocket, but I can't go. I only had eight bob, and I went and bought the supper with it instead.' Mrs Miller said, 'Aw yes, you get sick of looking at each other, and you get to squabbling and fighting, whereas when you're working you don't see as much of each other.'

In the interview with the Ryans there was much evidence of bitterness and hostility between the couple, who quarrelled openly and violently over money as well as over the previous evening's humiliation at the dance. However, like his wife, Mr Ryan looked back sentimentally to the days when he had been working. 'We didn't quarrel then, like, because you're with each other all the time and

123

you're watching each other, you know, and you're fighting and niggling all the time, but when you're at work you only see them on a tea-time or something like that. When you're seeing each other, you're fighting all the time.'

In these marriages the couples developed routines where they avoided one another. Mr Nottingly went for walks down in the woods. Mrs Ryan felt that she detected a complete change in her husband's personality when he was unemployed, 'You see, he wants to go on the booze all the time when he's not working. There's nowt else to do. He wants to be in there with his mates.' Mr Ryan agreed, 'Like, I'm sat in the house now from nine o'clock in the morning looking at four walls. Now you go down there for a bit of walk, and that, and they'll say, "Are you going for a pint?" see, and that's how it starts.'

For their part, when their husbands were at home, Mrs Ryan and Mrs Lucas spent a great deal of time in one or the other of their houses where their husbands were not.

Apart from the fighting of the Ryans, there was other evidence of serious strain in these marriages, which showed that mutual avoidance had not contained the pressures generated by unemployment. Mr Nottingly confessed, 'She's left us once or twice, like.' For Mr Paton, separation through financial crisis had become a regular occurrence: 'Well, our lass is always departing. She was only away last month, for a fortnight, you know, fighting over things, money, clothes, things like that.' And Mr McBain was not joking when he said wryly, 'I've cracked the wife a few times, like!' Mrs McBain was embarrassed, 'Oh, you have not.' He went on, 'I've given her a belt. She goes on and on. She goes too far sometimes.' Mrs McBain admitted, 'Once you did. Oh, I just keep going on and on and on. I don't know whether it's through the circumstances that we've had over the years or what, but I mean I used to be dead peaceful, and dead quiet, but now I'm really irritable. The kids can't move. I'm on at them for the least little thing, aren't I? On edge.'

Wives as workers

Up to a point these tensions might be reduced if the wife went out to work: there would be more housework for the husband to do, more money coming into the home, and the couple would not need to see as much of one another if they did not want to. However, there were financial barriers against some women going out to work. For wives of insured men it was worthwhile going out to work, but the couples we interviewed who were drawing supplementary benefits described the means test in terms of a double poverty trap, which trapped the wife as well as the husband. The wives felt that the £2 which could be earned before deductions was not enough.

Mrs Miller complained, 'They don't encourage you to work.' Mrs Nottingly said, 'Well, I got a little part-time job cleaning, £3 a week, and they took it all off us, so I packed it in.' Originally, Mr Lucas had been drawing unemployment insurance for a short while, and, 'Me wife got a job in the chicken factory, it was £14 a week. The day she got her interview and passed her test, clean hands test, and all that patter, a letter come next day. My dole had expired, me stamps. So that caused murder.' Mrs Lucas said, 'If he was working, I'd be earning as much as him. If I hadn't to have a stamped card, I could have got a job here in the club. You know Sarah Green? She came the other day – I could have had a job £13 a week. I wouldn't even need a baby-sitter. That would be money in me hand, but I can't even get this money. Not while he's not working. And I love it! I'd go out to work all day, me, I would. If he was on the dole I could get £16 a week, but we're on full "nash", you see.'

We can gain a further impression of which wives were likely to go out to work if we look at their work in the past, and at the couple's feelings about the wives working. For the reasons against the wife going out to work were not entirely financial.

Mrs Vickers had worked before they had a family, but now she stayed at home because, 'My son doesn't like me to be out, he likes me to be at home. He comes home for his dinners.' Now, rather than work, she spent her spare time doing painting-by-numbers, but she intended to work later on when her son was older. This had been the pattern followed by the wife of another of the technicians, Mrs Fellowes.

In contrast, the wives in the less close marriages seemed to lay more stress on the money or the autonomy and separate life which work gave them. Like Mrs Ryan and Mrs Lucas, Mrs Odell said she enjoyed work; and indeed she had worked, 'Right up until I was seven months pregnant, and even though there was only two months to wait until the baby was born. I couldn't stand being in the house all by myself.' As the end of Mr Odell's insurance benefits approached, there was the prospect of her having to stop work, but, 'If I do stop work now, I know that I'll have to go out in the afternoons. I couldn't stop in all day. I'll get the housework done in the mornings and then I'll have to go out somewhere. Somebody'll have to go out, because I think we'd get on each other's nerves. We'd get each other down. He'd be depressed at not having a job, and I'd be depressed at being stuck in the house all day, and we wouldn't be good for each other.'

However, it was not entirely a matter of financial barriers or the wives' feelings about their work in relation to their marriages which determined whether or not they went out to work. Mr Nottingly said he would not let his wife go out to work while the baby was small, and tension arose in the marriage because he objected to her leaving the baby with relatives, or even going visiting. Mrs Nottingly complained, 'I've got two sisters living round about, and me mother, but I cannot go because I've got to be back to make his meals, and that's one thing, I cannot go out and leave. Like when he was working, I used to go out all day, and just come in and make his tea on a night, but I can't now. I have to be in the house.' Although it was summer, Mr Nottingly insisted on having a full cooked meal at midday. Later, when he found a job he was prepared to let his wife go out to work and have the baby minded by relatives.

Mr Vickers, looking back on his spell of unemployment after he had found work, admitted that he could never have allowed his wife to go out to work while he did the housework. 'You see, I've never lost my, sort of, *manly status*, if you like. That's what he's done, isn't it, the bloke who sends his wife out to work. Fine, O.K., if it's the only way of providing a reasonable standard of living, and the option is for both of them to both sit at home on national assistance and both be even more miserable. But at the same time you would certainly feel – well, I would – I would certainly feel as though I'd lost a bit of my manly status.'

Workers as housewives

There were several insured men who had agreed that their wives should go out to work. Mrs Odell had been very surprised at the way her husband had set about being a housewife. 'I said to him when I first went out to work that he'd have to do the housework, but I didn't expect him to do the washing. He's had to learn everything, how to change the nappies, how to put a nappy on. He'd never done it before. I always used to do it, even getting up in the night-time. I didn't want him to do it because I knew with him working, he was up at all hours and he'd be tired, but now he can do all that kind of thing. The other day he was supposed to go to the launderette and he'd only got 3s. for the dinner, so he washed them all by hand.'

However, although she admired it, it was clear that she did not altogether approve, and that Mr Odell was not very good at housework. 'Well, it's not right for a man, having to stop at home and look after children all day. I think that gets him down as well. Sometimes when I come in the door, usually it's tidied up, it may be a bit upside down with the toys that's been tipped out all over the place; but sometimes I'll come back and there's just nothing done at all, and I'll say to him, "What on earth have you been doing? What's the use of me going out all day to do a job, and then coming home to do another job at night-time?" And he'll say, "Oh, everything got on top of me, so I sat down and read a book."' Mr Odell drew on his political ideology and support for women's lib in insisting that there was nothing essentially feminine or degrading about housework. But he confessed nonetheless, 'I'm very bad at housework. It gets me depressed, so sometimes I'll leave it all and read a book until four o'clock. Then I'll start.' Of all those we met, Mr Odell was the one who most enjoyed the visits of the photographer, 'I had two really nice days actually. I'm sorry he's not coming back!'

Another male 'housewife' whom we saw was no happier in his isolation at home: Mr Fellowes said dejectedly, 'I'm here and the wife's out at work. It's a complete reversal. It's ridiculous.'

Worker as mother

We saw one other man who had taken over the role of housewife, Mr Spain, who had taken the decision to stop work when his wife died. Although he had some help from a Home Help and from a neighbour with the housework, he had also had to act as mother to his eight children from the time the youngest came home from hospital at the age of three weeks.

'Well, at the first I was panic, really, to see how I get on with that, but now ... I even panic and say, well, it look as if I would have to send for someone from back home to help me. We talk about it, so gradually I say, it's no use to do that for when that person come they don't fit in properly. I better start all over again, that's the best thing for me to do, and let everything gradually work itself out.

'Look, it's not a matter that I couldn't get a home to put them in, but I think for you to have a child, or anybody at all and to put them in a home, it's a bit of a handicap when they grow up and they look at it and they say, "Well, just because me mam died, and me father couldn't ..." you know, it's so embarrassing. You got to make the best of it, you know. I think, let the house go; if we live in poverty and not buy anything, at least the family is together. I do it all for the family, so they can have some family life together. Sometimes you get that feeling of running away, but if you respect your family, I don't think a man who respect his family and love his family will do it. They would prefer the family go down together, more than really leave them, and they would do it. Well, it don't make no sense, really, to have a family and then to care for them and to leave them with no one, innit? And that's what really happened to me. I help my wife really good, anyway, when she was alive. That's why I really take this on. She used to be a good girl to me, you know. That's why ... you got to get over what ...

'But it's a bit rough 'ere, boy, cor! Sometimes I don't know how I get along really. I just barely fight it off. You see, because look. If you have a woman, she have a big housework-doing, which way it's harder than to go out to work. Because going to work, you don't work so hard at all; it's just eight hours, and still between the eight hours you have breaks, you know. But not going to work, and inside here with eight kids – you want to come here and stop here and I'll leave you here all day with eight kids! – one day you have enough! You have enough with a day, you don't want no more than a day here. But it's an obligation I got to face up to really, so well, I gotta do it, not for my sake ...

'The only thing that I do that I really never did, really I never used to wash the clothes, you know. But you see the washing was a problem at the first time, and the thing that's a problem again is to get the kids them hair combed, you see. Yeah, it's a bit of a problem all right, but after a while I sort myself out and just adapt to that type o' work. Well, you gotta make your routine, really. Well, my routine is this. Wake up in the morning and give them their breakfast and go off to school. Sometimes I wake up about half six ... sometimes six o'clock, sometimes even half past five. When I get up, give them their breakfast, bathe Chris, feed him, bathe him. Like that, I do it meself. Yeah, he's special to me, he's the last one. Then after three of them have their bath, put on their clothes and move around a bit, and then sometimes they go back to sleep a bit. Then I start to do some washing, get the old brush out, there, and Hoover out. The small ones, comb them hairs, and get them going properly, and after I've finished that now, it's just time again for them to come home from school and they eat and all the washing up done. They always have a cooked dinner because they liked a cooked meal, you know – sometimes they can't eat the school meal, because most time they come here starving and say, "Daddy, I can't eat the dinner," you know, because a certain type o'food they like and a certain type they can't eat. Then after dinner they all do come in and sat watching television, and I put the big boy and the other one to wash the plates up, and then it be half an hour time I start again to tidy the rest up for bed, and that's it. I don't eat much myself, God bless what I eat!

'If I don't eat, I prefer to come inside here and see everything cleaned up and the place look all right, and you can walk round, it smell nice: I can't stand funny smell, you know. No, it's funny, if I come in here and I smell anything funny, I gotta keep on looking, you know, until I must find it. Because even the boys' bedroom, a certain time they take the dirty clothes off and they sling it one side, and go into that bedroom and me smell the bloody clothes! And I say,

"Come on, move the bed over. Take all what there is inside it," and I sort it out and I realize, you know, they mixing up the clean clothes with the dirty clothes. I have a woman, a Home Help, she come for an hour and a half, because the only thing I can't do is the hironing. I can do everything else, the cooking and the washing, and looking after the kids, but with the hironing, somehow, I dunno, the hiron is going clockwise and it should be going the other way, I don't know. So the Home Help does the hironing for me. But when she tidy up I have to go back over it, see, because I'm a bit fussy. I like to come in and see everything all right where it is, and if you going to do a thing for me and I see it's not properly done, I not going to insult you: I just keep you off, and try to do it myself. Well, my wife break me into that system, really, because the first time I couldn't have come in and lit a cigarette unless I have a ashtray there, like.

'I don't watch television, now and again. And I don't read books, that make you lazy, make you go out of the world, and you want to feel that you in the world. The only thing I would like to do is to sit down sometimes and relax and play some record, because that really make your mind relax, to sit down and listen to music, modern jazz or any kind of jazz. I like music that can make you look creative, like, that can make your brain think properly, because some time you just want to sit down and hear no noise at all, you don't want to hear no kids crying at all. Otherwise, the only boring thing to me is day to day inside here. Because we're talking, my kids they don't come from school, or somebody they don't come in, I can't get out for a coupla hours and says, well, even breathing fresh air. Well, I get all the kids together sometimes and get out and walk around and stretch me legs. But the point is this, I don't want another drama in my life. I just look after them the best I can, but I don't like to leave them with no one because I just have that feeling that no matter how that person might care for that child, there might be something go wrong and I'm not there, and I'd feel it.

'It's only a lazy person who like to stay indoors, and the more you stay indoors, the more sickly you become, because it's not good for you. You want to go out and work your limbs, burn off some energy, you know, get yourself fit. I only just use the allotment for an 'obby, like, you know. I only just try to keep fit, that I don't get ill or anything, because I feel if I ill, things will collapse inside me, see.

'It's a fifty-fifty chance, really, of finding another woman. Well, I met a lot of girls, really, and they say, they're interested, but on the other hand some woman only looking for security, like, what they can get for theirself. I'm not looking that type o' person. I'm looking somebody that really, they interested in theirself and they interested in what you ... you know. But some people not like that, and so you got to fight down the line and sort out a person properly before you can say, well, let one move in. I'm not looking.

'But I'd rather be working. What kind of life is this for a man, lookin' after the kids. And the little girl, when she shit herself, and I got to change her nappy. Shit, man! But I got to do it. There's nobody else. It's the best way for 'the family. Well, I tell you something now, the type o' work that I really miss is something that you enjoy to do. You just gradually put yourself into it, and you come in and it's a habit to you. It doesn't matter about the money, but you just look forward to that.'

8 Alternatives to Work: 'Fiddling'

In this chapter the workless describe in more detail what they did with their time when they first became unemployed, and as they began to realize that avenues into their preferred jobs were not easy to find. As we have seen, although they could not find suitable or acceptable work for the moment, they were still under various pressures from outside the home, or from their own families, to be workers or to keep up some aspects of the daily routines they had followed while they were at work. How did they reconcile these pressures with their own drives and views on what would be a worthwhile activity?

Individual activities about the home

Some workers, whose marriages we have already described as closer or who seemed in other ways to have a greater emotional investment in their homes, responded to unemployment by pursuing more energetically the handyman tasks they had formerly done around the home during their hours of leisure from work. Mr Fellowes said, 'You try to keep up a routine, doing little jobs here and there, decorating. I've done a bit of decorating. I make a few things, painting and whatnot, pottering about trying to fill your time up.'

Mr Coxon laid great stress on the way that – in earlier phases of unemployment when he had been fitter – he had never been idle. 'I didn't let it get a hold of me, because I used to be very handy then. I used to find somethink. I always had something to do with the kids and that. I had a little piece of wood and I used to make this and make that. Do you realize that them candle-lights with a bulb and a wooden holder, that was my invention! I had a load of timber, and like a load of, like, handles, and I was sitting down and I thought, "I dunno, I'll make it into little boxes." I used to sit down thinking what I could do, and I made them about four inches long, put them into the bottom of these little boxes, put the wiring in and up through the pole . . . And I made about three or four hundred of them.'

The most striking example of someone who intensified a normal pattern of handyman activity about the home – combining with it some of the skills he used at work – was Mr Vickers, who set about making an amplifier in his garden shed. When we first met Mrs Vickers, she complained a little that now her husband was out of work, although she had expected to see more of him, 'It's not much different. I never see him. He's always out in the shed! To tell you the truth I get a bit cross about it sometimes. He'll get up at eight o'clock, quarter to, sometimes. Then he gives David his breakfast. Then when he comes back, straight into the shed until lunchtime. Well, David comes home at twelve. Then he has about an hour for lunch, and back into the shed until five o'clock. It varies, sometimes I can persuade him to come out for a bit, say if I want to go up the town for an outing, or some shopping, he might come with me, but I've to persuade him. I wouldn't like to tell you how I persuade him – I'd rather not go into that!' Mr Vickers claimed that what he was doing was almost an ideal existence: 'I think I wouldn't work if I didn't have to. I think I'd like to set up my own little workshop, with a bandsaw in it, and a lathe, and turn out bits of furniture, even if it was only to give my wife, and then I could sort of pick that up and drop it when I liked, really a sort of extension of what I'm doing now. The shed, well, it's a place where I know pretty well where everything is, and when I go out there to do a job, I know pretty well what I'm expecting to achieve, the day's target, and that's where I come away frustrated if I fall badly short.' However, although Mr Vickers insisted that he was not exactly lonely at home, he said, 'I miss the people at work. Even the people I didn't like, I miss them.'

Another man who combined skills from work with skills from handicraft around the home was Mr Weston. After the failure of his attempt to become self-employed through his usual work, he had begun to make pictures for sale. 'I've had ideas ever since I was made redundant, actually, but it's finding out something to do that's novel. It's only through being actually out of work that I've thought about this. The girl next door gave me an idea. She was doing what I would call galimaufrey, putting a load of rubbish on a board and spraying it. And I thought to myself, if you use nails and stuff . . .

The first one I tried was that church, that's an actual picture. Trouble with the girl's, all the stuff falls off; she puts it on with Polyfilla. I found that when I first started, I was talking to the bloke down the shop, he said, "That's unusual, isn't it. How much do you want it to sell for?" I said a fiver, but anyway he brought it back, it had all fell to pieces. But he'd put £7.50 on that, so he must have thought it was worth something. I do designs, ships, buildings, bridges, houses. The only thing I can't do is animation, you know, drawing animals. I'm hopeless, you know, a mouse looks like an elephant. That's the sort of thing I could do, though, flowers.

'If you'd seen me, how hard I worked the other fortnight on these pictures and other stuff, a damn sight harder than when I was *at* work, but I enjoyed it. Now these pictures, these pictures are really things that I want to do, but unfortunately the only setbacks I've had from making these pictures has been work! I've got to keep my family at the same time, you know what I mean, but every time, without fail, I've got a collection and somebody's seen 'em, they've said, "Right, I want one of them." So I do maintain that if I could get off me backside to go and sell 'em ... Well, I could mass-produce 'em, but once you make a mould you're finished, I think, because it's been done so often before. Mine are all originals. That's what I want to do is to keep originality. You see, there's a lot of aspects to it. Someone might discover that these things are a work of art, you never know. It happened, well, the "Political Prisoner's" a work of art, which is a load of old rubbish. Well, someone might pick one of these up and say, "Cor!" – you know, some crank, I don't know if they're all cranks or what – say, "That's a work of art." Then I'll become purely an artist. Another thing is, I might become big commercially, and I'll get such an order that I can't cope with it by myself. I'd have other workers to join me, and get different premises. I've got four pictures away at the moment, which should net me £12 today. You see, what I don't want is to spoil myself. If I sell 'em privately, selling 'em for £5 making a load, go to the dealer and he'll say, "Well, I've got to make my profit," and V.A.T.'s coming in. Actually I ought to make them as a bargain, because the way I'm doing 'em now, I'm going to start doing 'em quicker. I take about five or six hours, that, about fifty pence an hour, but after all it's something worth doing, isn't it? I enjoy doing them, so if I work ten

134

hours a day, I'll make about £6 a day, six days a week, it works out about £35.

'As I say, since I've started on it, these other little jobs keep turning up that's never allowed me to get a collection. Oh, consciously I don't worry. I mean this situation now, it's either whatsit or bust, isn't it? Well, now, I'll be perfectly frank with you. Work has gone right to the back of my mind there, because I feel so free doing these pictures, that if I can make a living wage without the dole, I just won't be interested in going back to work. I get more satisfaction out of doing pictures. When it comes out good, I feel real chuffed. My mind is getting more keener because I've got to keep on me toes to live. I must go out to sell these pictures. Ever since I've been made redundant I feel far happier and far freer. This is why I would like to make a go of pictures.'

There were two further examples of activities which combined some individual creativity with attempts to make a bit of cash on the side (illegally, since the individuals were on supplementary benefits). Miss Hebb had made some grotesque Heath masks for sale, and some pottery; she also made clothes. And she had on display in her room two very interesting *art nouveau* tea sets: 'You see that one there cost £2 10s. and that other only cost 50p, so I'm going to sell the two for £28 and that will be next month's rent. I got a bit of a shop downstairs, actually. There's, er, old clothes, I done a bit of business like that. I get quite good things from jumble sales, old clothes, you know, and sell 'em to students, coats and things. Well at one time I actually had ideas of getting a shop, but it was so difficult to get premises. I, er, spent about six months looking, but just couldn't get one, but now we've got the basement.' Mr Dover was making kites to sell on the beaches next summer. And in this context of small-scale business activity we might also note that Mr Haigh, who had wanted to start his own mail-order business, was filling in his time by helping to organize a bulk-buying scheme on the estate where he lived.

Finally among the workless who spent their time at home in individually creative activity there was Mr Calvert. He said that when he and his wife, who had studied photography, became unemployed together from their routine clerical work, 'We both decided at the time that we would use the time, if it was a month or, you know, three months or what, that we would use the time to get our own work together as much as possible, so that when the period ended we'd have something, you know, saleable. Well, I tend to feel bad, daily, if I don't do some work at this, even if I'm totally, you know, um, even if I've got huge reasons why not really. Well, I tend to do things more or less to suit my work, because, you know, it's difficult to drive yourself regularly. If I'm into a good reading mood, I just read until I feel, like, really collapsed. This is one of the advantages about having a job, because if you do have a job you're more businesslike automatically, and, say it's two o'clock and you don't have another lecture until four, you do two hours. But the compensating advantage of not having a job is that you can go on productive bursts.

'I feel busy with this, and I think it's pretty destructive to think, to conceive of myself with relation to regular unemployment. Personally, I can only say this. My being unemployed, just not being involved in anything, would be very difficult to conceive if I hadn't been working away at this. I mean, if I wasn't doing anything, I mean, at the moment I feel O.K., but if I wasn't doing anything, I'd feel in a very fragile situation. I know that that's not consistent, but one feels that if one is doing something, that one is not in such an untenable position. I mean, I think that this is just something to do with mental health.

'I think in about three months or something I'll be in a position to start hustling, sort of, publishers and then, I don't see this as a big, sort of, golden horizon, because probably it just begins there . . .'

A trade unionist out of work

During the time when he was a 'housewife' Mr Odell increased his activities with the local claimants' union. Mrs Odell said, 'I suppose that's why he goes out so much in the evenings, because he's cooped up inside all day. He feels as though he needs a bit of fresh air.' But for Mr Odell, going out to the claimants' was more than this.

'I became much more active in the claimants' after I got the sack. I was first in a trade union when I was nineteen, but there was a sort of big jump when I got the sack. The contact with all the others who'd been messed about by social security, and to meet people

136

who'd been messed about by local departments sending them from one to another, I was very annoyed. Now I think they've accepted us, the social security. A lot of people have been for clothing grants and they'll say, "We don't do clothing grants," but they don't do it when we're there.

'It's completely different in the claimants'. You see, I'd rather see the union, you know, the trade union, built on similar lines to the claimants' union. You see, in a trade union, so much of the work could be, I think, to change that union, to make it become a workers' movement again, which it's not, it's become a carrier for so many people. Whereas the claimants' unions, there's no leadership or anything like that. There's no election of permanent officers. More of the people take part in the discussion of what has to be done. One person can't decide a certain direction and say we're doing this. It has to be thrashed out. It's the same with every claimants' union.

'A concern with social security's a stage, to my way of thinking, that we've got to get over, because all we are at the moment is something to change the mistakes of social security. You see, more than that, we've got to unite with the employed worker, and get rid of this feeling that the man in work has about the man on the dole that he's a lazy so-and-so, getting about seventeen or eighteen quid a week, just that feeling, so that it will eventually develop into a complete workers' movement. That's my idea, I don't know what the general attitude is. I believe we should picket factories that are doing overtime and things like that, or where there are redundancies, cut the working week without the money, that's a step to workers' control, I think, can be. By work-sharing you can get *people* together, you wouldn't have the social competition and the jealousies between them. It's a big step, if you worked at it right, if you organized the factory right.

'I get depressed occasionally at the moment because we can get the, kind of, leafleting, the basic work at the S.S., we get eight or ten to do it. Meetings, our average attendance at meetings was twenty to twenty-five people, and it's dropped. It's about fifteen people now, mostly students, and I think I'm one of the oldest. Before, I blamed the lack of unemployed people on the intellectuals, like there was one of the students, and International Marxist Group people who were trying to take over the claimants' unions, but they've gone, and there's none of their organization blokes there now. Something's gone wrong somewhere. We're not getting them. We're *getting* them, a few, but it's still this thing between the student and the working man that left school between fourteen and fifteen. You see, he wants to leave everything to the student because he's embarrassed, you see.'

Group activities out of the house: 'fiddling'

Some of the less-skilled workers of the north-east worked together doing jobs around their local neighbourhood, earning money illegally – 'fiddling'. (For this short section on fiddling we will not use the false names by which our informants are identified elsewhere in the book.)

These men said they had come to fiddling only after the search for regular work was exhausted. One wife said, 'When he first came out of work, he used to go out every day. He was out looking from morning till night.' Her husband agreed, 'I *was* worried. I went looking for jobs for four months.' She continued, 'And it was all bus fares, during winter, going round these factories, he was all over, down the pits, you went all over, didn't you, just wasting money, because he was getting nowhere.' Another man described how, 'It takes a certain type to fiddle. You get blokes who, out of work – mind you, good workers – but just cannot fiddle. They don't like knocking on doors for, like, coppers, you know what I mean, like, "Do your windows?" Or they don't like going on the beach for coal and selling it. Maybe call them proud.'

In response to the question of who fiddles, one man said, 'Them at the top most!' Another justified himself in simple economic terms: 'Well, I think meself, like, I'm a man with children. The Assistance won't give me no grants for shoes. A man should be able to work and earn money for to buy shoes for his children without getting done, as long as he puts down on a paper how much he made, like. Also, we'll say I made £3 today: well, say I went down and said, "Right, I'll buy you a pair of shoes for £3 with me bonus." Now I'd get the bill and I'd show them that. Now I believe in that, like, but I don't believe in a man who neglects his children and goes out fiddling and drinks it all the time. I don't believe in that, like.' In fact this man saw fiddling as a comparatively innocuous alternative to the only other way open to him to get money – theft. 'I mean, I've been in prison, like, but I'm not ashamed of it, like, you know, because I went out stealing because I had to, just through worry. So what's the best? Going and doing a little bit of fiddling for yourself instead of breaking and entering, isn't it, and being a thief?' However, this man also stressed that there were other rewards from fiddling. 'Other blokes, like, just go out and fiddle just for to get out at work. Well, like a mate I had, when he was on strike from the pit there, couldn't stop. Used to walk from here right down to the beach, get himself a bag of coal, and he used to carry that bag of coal right from the beach back here every day. And he didn't have to do. He had coal in his coalhouse. Just to do summat, see. He's never been off work in his life. He couldn't sit in the house.'

Other men supported these views that fiddling had started only after the failure of the search for work and with the build-up of financial and other pressures from unemployment. One said, 'Well, when I first was unemployed I just went round looking for jobs; that's how I killed me time, but when the places ran out to go to, you either sit in the house, and I'm no gardener, as you well can see, like, I haven't got a clue as a gardener, and I just wondered what I was going to do. I had a breakdown, a nervous breakdown, just sitting in that chair, looking at that box and that, got me down, like. In the end I didn't dare go to the door. I didn't dare get on a bus, and I couldn't breathe. It was an anxiety state, it was the state I was in. I just tried to fight it off. I went to the club one night, and I just sat there and I panicked. I thought everybody was looking at me. I couldn't experience that, like. I just stood up. I said, "Here, you'd better get the doctor. I tell you what, I'll go meself," so I was that worried and frightened I walked to the Royal, and I went in. I see the coloured doctor, I said, "You'll have to help us, like," I said, "I'm going funny, like, here." Took me in, five weeks, and the missus broke down one night, couldn't manage, so I signed meself out.

'Well, I come out and I've never looked back since. Yeah, well, I've got a little bit of a fiddle, window cleaning. Champion! Champion. You just get up on a morning – don't get me wrong – I can't make me wife a fiver again, you know what I mean – but now I make me own baccy money and me own couple o' pints, and I guarantee I won't see the Royal Infirmary again. My bother was looking at the kids. You know what it's like, having to miss the rent to pay the coal, and the little bit, the few bob I make now, we don't have to, you know what I mean. On a fine week I would say I make about five or six quid, like. You won't have to mention that, like, or else me dole's stopped. You see what I do, I give me wife all me dole. She has no baccy to buy for me, and no beer. I take no pocket money at all. We're just ticking along nice. Now if I hadn't had a few windows, she'd give me a pound pocket-money, I know she would, just for baccy alone. And sitting in the house Monday, Tuesday, Wednesday, Thursday, Friday, don't tell me she wouldn't say, "Here, go and get a couple of pints. Here, go and get a few pints," like. It's nothing, like, a pound. You can only have a packet of tabs out, and a cup of grog, out of a pound, you know what I mean, like, so that's, like, £2 she'd be worse off. Whereas with the windows, which is not much, it gets me a few jars and a tin of baccy, and if I come in and she's a bit short I generally give her half a quid, and she gets a big loaf, or a packet of margarine, a packet of sugar. We get over.

'Yes, I am frightened. If you get found out, it's stopped, but what do you do? Do you sit here, like? Where do you go for a job? What do you do? You might fill forms in, but they just put 'em in a drawer and close the drawer.' His wife agreed: 'You don't mean to say that there's people going to live and let their bairns starve at weekends, when they can go out and fiddle for a day.'

In another interview, a look of fear and apprehension crossed the wife's face as her husband described the temptations which unemployment offered for a man to turn to theft or become a 'layabout'. He said, 'I'm the type, if I've got nothing to do, I've got to have something to do. I've got to go out or somewhere. The last time I was out of work I got into trouble. You see, when you're out of work you start drifting, like. I pinched some cigarettes. You see, you can't afford anything, and I used to smoke about sixty a day when I was at work. Well, it's to pass the time away, and for adventure as well. I've been tempted to do things like that, but you have to watch it. If you see things lying about, if there's anybody's door open and there's nobody in, like, I'm tempted to go in, like.' The marriage had run into difficulties, and the husband admitted privately that their sexual relationship had deteriorated during this first period of unemployment. But now, the wife said, they had ceased to argue as much and the marriage had taken a turn for the better, although she was guarded at first about why this had happened: 'It's just one of them things, now, just recently we've stopped arguing about money because it's no point.' The husband agreed, 'Before we used to be arguing all the time.' She said, 'You'd never go out. Well, now he goes out.' At this point her husband must have decided he could trust us: 'I go out and do a bit of fiddling on the side now, you know.' Later he made a point of telling us how his sexual relationship with his wife had improved since he had begun to go out and earn money again.

The invitation to fiddle

The man who had had the nervous breakdown said, 'I had the chance to get a kick off a lad whose mate started work, travelled, had to go away to work. He said, "Do you fancy making twenty-four bob this afternoon?" I said, yes. I went down, I made twenty-four bob. Well, I know people who's on the dole who's got colour televisions as well – mind the same person's got a good mate, he's on to a good "feed" man, you see.'

The 'feed' or man who had the task of finding the jobs had to 'know how to go on' and to have 'the talk', 'the patter'. The theme of the invitation to fiddle coming from another man recurred several times. And as with other information about work, the working men's club was an important centre. As one man explained, 'You get all the patter that's going round, like, you know. They'll say, "I know where there's a fiddle, where you can get yourself ten quid," you know what I mean, get a bit of copper, or something like that.'

Invitations and opportunities to fiddle also come partly from the local community, which must provide the work. One wife explained, 'I think once you get one job like that and you can get in people's houses and sit and talk to them, they'll say, "Well I want this doing, and that doing," and gardens and decorating the house.' Other men spoke of being accosted when they were out fiddling with queries like, 'Do you do gardens?' Another said, 'We're all in the same boat, I would say. Nearly all the lads who clean windows on this site, they'd rather help you than hinder you, like. They give yer houses; they say, "There's a couple of houses up there wants doing." They tell yer a woman asked, a woman passes yer, "Do you do so-

and-so?" You say, "No, but I'll tell so-and-so, who does it, like," you know what I mean.'

Apart from neighbours, invitations or opportunities to fiddle also came from employers. Mr McBain recalled one such invitation from a self-employed plumber who was trying to set up in business, but who could not yet quite afford to pay the going rate for a plumber's mate to help him. 'He wanted me to go fiddling with him, on the dole, but to work for him, do you get me?' Some of the wives felt compelled to fiddle, and they were sure that employers acquiesced in their fiddling to get cheap labour. The wives pretended that their insurance cards were 'at the labour exchange' – and according to the wives the employers pretended to believe them: 'They must know. If my husband was working I wouldn't go out cleaning every night for £4 a week, which is obvious, no woman would. And if we handed our stamp cards in, they'd have to pay more for all the stamps.'

There were several instances where workless individuals had done jobs mainly to fill in time, but had found themselves earning money as a result, because others paid them for their produce or services. In a previous spell of unemployment, Mr McBain had gone in for gardening on a big scale. 'I used to work hard, like. I had about 8–900 bloody chrysanthemum cuttings, and about 400 dahlias. I used to make a bob or two. If I had it now I could make more than I used to then. Then I used to, maybe, somebody'd come for a couple of pounds of tomatoes, I'd maybe give them a bunch of flowers as well, like. Well, a bunch of flowers would be worth six bob, the tomatoes were half a crown, so I was out of pocket really, a bad businessman, you know, like. I really wasn't interested in making money.'

Jimmy Weaver, who was too small to get a job as a sailor, had nevertheless become one. 'I cannot really say that my life's boring all the time, because that would be a lie, like. I go out sailing on the yachts. Oh, it's most fun in the winter, like, when you get a bit of bad weather, that's when you get the real sailing. There's one old bloke, like, an old age pensioner, and he's got a gaff-rigged ketch down there. I get up about eight o'clock, if it's really rough we still gang out. That's when all the fun is, when you're really travelling, but I prefer these old boats to the new ones there are. It's harder working, you get more fun out of them, like. It's hard work, like, but because it's something I want to do I enjoy it.' He, too, would sometimes earn money, from fish he caught. And he was not the only teenager who had earned money from a job started principally to fill time, at the invitation of others.

The official detection and informal control of fiddling

To catch men who were working, the Department of Employment and the Supplementary Benefits Commission have special investigators out making inquiries. There were also regular home visits from officials checking on the family's circumstances, so the prospect of being caught was something of a deterrent. One wife recalled, 'Now one day, all his mates were window cleaning on the flats. We had a letter saying the "nash" man was coming. When the "nash" man come, I had to fly behind the flats and tell all the lads to tittle off, and when the "nash" man went away, I went and told the lads, so they started on the windows.'

On the other hand, the fear of getting caught by officials seemed to be lessened in several ways. There were the safeguards in the procedures the investigators had to follow to substantiate a prosecution. A man described how one of his friends had been caught: 'Oh, they followed him with a van, three of them, lads like yourselves, educated like, government jobs, good jobs like. They were agents of some kind, that was their job, like, finding the likes of lads like me on the fiddle. You could be shopped, I could be shopped now for all I know, but the patter is they've got to follow you for a fortnight. They've got to see you collecting an' all.' Not all the men caught in this way were punished. Another man said, 'It happened over there, the other week, you know, a lad got trapped. About three of them drew up in a car, the agents, and they warned him, so he went to the dole and declared it, and the dole man said. "Looka son," he said, "go away," he said. "They won't bother you again," he said. "I don't mind you making a bit of baccy money as far as I'm concerned" – that was the feller behind the counter, like.' Another man, too, was sure that the authorities were not making an all-out drive. 'They've only got to stand on top of the labour exchange with a pair of binoculars and they'd see hundreds of them. You can do anything and get away with it round here. I don't think they bother, meself. I mean if I was an investigator from the social security, why I'd find loads of people on the fiddle, like.' This man's wife complained, 'I *am* worried. At the social security they don't seem to try to find anybody that's fiddling. He'd be better off if they found him a job. If they found him a job it would be a lot better, because other people's going to pack their jobs up just to do that. They'll think, "Aw well, he can do that, I might as well pack my job in, just to do what he's doing. He's making more than me!"'

Some couples seemed more afraid of the informal sanction of an anonymous letter sent to officials by hostile neighbours or workers. One couple described an incident (with the Electricity Board, but it could have been with social security officials): 'There's one over here, an enemy. We had our lights turned off by the Electricity Board. My husband put them on when the child was ill. Her over the back went down and spragged us.' Her husband said, 'You don't know it was her.' He went on, 'It was on about three nights. The next night they brought the detectives and the electric man copped us.' His wife insisted, 'They said they'd had a phone call, somebody'd been up and said the lights was cut off. She was the only one up here that knew our lights was off.'

The limitation of the will to work

Fiddling did not carry for these men the same demands for all-out effort as a full-time job. One window cleaner said, 'That's not a bad game, but it kills you, that going up and down kills you. When I first came here, I could have made £40 a week, easy, on the windows, you know, but you get sick of it. It's all running up and down the ladders, you know, it kills you, man. I used to pull me shoulders out every week, you know, both me arms used to just hang. I couldn't lift them up, with stretching, you know.'

Others, including Miss Hebb, felt that state support took the edge off their needs for cash, which otherwise might have spurred them to get their businesses off the ground. The man whom we described earlier as being tempted towards theft said, 'All the men what's down here at the exchange, they've been on the dole for years, they don't want jobs, like. When you talk to some of them, they say, like, "If I can get money on the side, you know, doing other jobs, I'm not going to get a job," like, you know, "You're better off on the dole."

I'm getting like them now, like. I do something on the side now, like, I'm not bothered. I never bother going for a job now. Aw, if you can keep your dole and make £10 a week on top o' that, who's going out to work?'

Within four months this man had found a job and was back in full-time work.

9 Changes in the Morale of the Workless

In this, the last chapter concerned directly with unemployment, we attempt to trace how the morale and identity of the workless changed over the time when they were unemployed. We were able to follow a number of the men during the period when the changes were taking place, and the remainder who had been unemployed for various lengths of time described changes they felt they had undergone.

First reactions

To men who had never previously been out of work, unemployment was an unfamiliar, even an unreal, experience. Mr Haigh said, 'At first it feels marvellous. It's as though you've left the rat race, you're not in it any more and you can look at it and wonder why people bother. You look at them setting off in the morning at 7.30 and coming back at night at half past five, and you think, "Why bother?" The first few days you sit at home and relax, and it's like a holiday.' His wife said, 'You know it's happening, you know he's unemployed, but it's like a dream. It's as though it's happening in a dream. The bit when you're asleep is your real life, and when you're awake, that bit's like a dream.'

Initially the more skilled had been confident that a new job would not be hard to find. Mr Vickers said, when we first met him, 'At first I thought it was great! I'm looking for a job – not hard enough my wife thinks!' He and his wife exchanged a smile, but he was quick to defend himself against the charge of exploiting the system: 'If anybody accused me of not caring, I've got this' (his careful file of applications). 'I'd show them this; I'd give them a right mouthful.' Mr Odell, too, was inclined to a bit of bravado on our first visit, and said he was not worrying much about a job: 'Well, I'm too happy at home. To tell you the truth I was looking forward to getting the sack. I thought I'd get a lot more of my books read, although I think I've read less.'

However, the sense of ease and holiday did not take long to wear off. Mr Haigh continued, 'After a bit you get bored, and by the end of the first week you're bored stiff, and you realize you haven't a place in life. You're not contributing anything; you're not doing anything to help the community along. You're a drag on everybody else really. You're a drop-out.'

Mr Miller, who was more accustomed to being out of work, had taken the onset of unemployment more philosophically. 'When they first come out of work, you'd think somebody had cut their throat, wouldn't you? You'd think somebody had chopped their hands off. For a person who's never been out of work, I find them more worried. They like it on the outside, but really inside ... I mean there's him over there, been at the steelworks twenty-odd years since he left school and he's just been laid off redundant: "Oh, it was champion." But you should have heard his wife, like. "We'll have to get a job. We don't know what we're going to do," like. He has a lot of redundancy pay, but she said it wasn't the coin. She said it was all right now for maybe a couple of weeks, but after that ... For myself, well, since I've left school I've been on and off. I've never really had a steady job, d'you know what I mean. I'm not a man, like, I've been somewhere all me life and when the crunch comes worries, "Ooh, what am I going to do now?" I always know summat'll turn up. Something always does in our game.'

For the young school leaver unemployment did in fact slowly grow out of a holiday. One mother said, 'Mind, I don't think it was so bad last year, because a lot of their mates had just left school, and the six weeks' holidays, he just went on his holidays with us, and they were just used to being bored with school, and they were free for a few weeks.'

Growing anxiety

Mr Vickers's morale while he was out of work clearly went through a number of phases. His relaxation when we first saw him turned out to be partly a result of disappointments in his search for work, which had led to him putting more emphasis on his 'work' in the garden shed. He said, 'I take all the local papers. I don't read them straight away. I used to, but I don't any more, I leave them until the evening.' A little later, however, Mr Vickers spoke of the way his routine of work in the shed was beginning to be disrupted by the increasing anxiety of finding a job, although he still insisted that the routine would be resumed. 'I dunno, I've just sort of slackened off some-how. My work's gone to pot a bit. I've had several weeks when I've looked back and said, "What have I done this week?" you know, since, sort of starting doing nothing. Well, if you looked in the shed this morning, well, just take an example, my kid's bike has had a puncture for about a week now! Well, normally I would have stop-ped what I was doing, mended the puncture and got on with it. Now, looking for a job has got a bit out of hand. When I first started out in the shed, I wouldn't have let my day be interfered with at that stage. You see, then the first priority was my work, the second was finding a job. In other words, I'd spend the evenings and that time that was available after I'd finished my day's work, whereas now that's sort of taking second place, and first place was looking round for jobs.' He was also under growing pressure from his wife, who said, 'I suppose this last week or two I have begun to nag him a bit and to get on to him to come out of that shed and put in a bit more time finding a job. There must be more papers he could get, with more jobs in that he could apply for. You see, I don't quite see things the same way as he does, and I don't think his work in the shed's that important.'

Mr Weston's attempt to become self-employed through making pictures began to meet similar challenges from his wife, who said, 'It's all right being free as long as you've got the money coming in. These pictures, I don't disagree with him doing them, but I can't see us making a living out of it, that's what worries me.'

Mr Fellowes, with a despairing helplessness, described his increas-ing anxiety and the failure of alternative activities. 'You don't realize, not until you've been out for a couple of weeks. It costs money, decorating, and you can't keep it up. Mostly it's just pottering. I get bored stiff. Well, Monday arrives, maybe I'll go fishing. I always used to do a bit of fishing, but this weather it's a bit cold. Tuesday and the local paper comes out, so the first job is to go out and get that. I read that for an hour. Then the rest of the day I just potter about. Sometimes when you're working you wish you had a bit more time to do things, but I'd rather be working now and have no time. Sometimes I get to walking up and down with my hands in my pockets, walking up and down on the carpet. Wednesday I go down to the firm to collect the pittance they pay, and I meet a few people there. Thursday there's some more papers to scan – that'll take about two hours. Then perhaps I'll make a phone call about a job. And there's the labour exchange. Friday there are four more local papers that come out. I get them and then I work like a bomb until I've covered them all. A man *needs* work. If a man hasn't got work he's half way to being defeated.'

Problems with sleeping and eating

Anxiety sometimes appeared in physical symptoms, in problems with sleeping and eating. In any case men accustomed to doing heavy manual work and regular drinking found difficulty with sleeping. Mr Nottingly said, 'I keep waking up. I usually watch the telly till about one o'clock or something and then I go to bed. When I was at work I was always in bed about eleven o'clock, then, wasn't I? You can't do it when you're working. Well, when you're unemployed, you're not tired at one o'clock. You can sit up all night and then just go to bed when you feel like it.'

Initially the men who had done hard physical work had tended to wake early, but as the workless spell stretched out routines began to slip. Mr Miller said, 'It's what you're used to. If you're working for a few months and you have to wake up about seven o'clock, then I'm like an alarm clock. I wake up automatically at the time for work. But then you gradually get off it.'

Eventually wakefulness at night was followed by sleepiness in the day. Mrs Nottingly said to her husband, 'You do get tired. Now when you're on the dole you could go to bed in the afternoon, couldn't you? He says he feels, he's walking about, "Aw I feel tired." Well, he was never like that when he was working. He seems to be more tired now than what you did when you were working.' Mrs Miller said of her husband's tiredness, 'I think he's glad to get to bed to sleep and forget about it. But I mean they must feel guilty, well, not guilty, but, I don't know, I think it makes you feel a bit awful when you're not working.' A teenager said, 'It's crap being on the dole. You had nowt to dae all the time. It was all right at first, like. Then after a couple of months you started getting lazy, like you cannot be bothered to dae nowt, just feel like stopping in bed all day.'

Some of the men also began to experience loss of appetite or indigestion. Mrs Odell said, 'Oh, he'd love to get a job. Some days you can see he's really down. I think when you're unemployed, the people outside they look down on you, and that's bound to get you down after a bit. Some days you can tell. You look at him and he looks really tired and ill, and he hasn't eaten a thing for four days. I'll make a meal and put it on his plate and he'll take a couple of spoonfuls and say he doesn't feel hungry.' Mrs Miller said of her husband, 'He's complaining with his stomach all the time, and he's edgy, like, he's on edge all the time.' And Mrs Vickers said that her husband had also had problems: 'It's only been in the last few weeks I noticed it. I could see him looking depressed. He's even got up in the night with indigestion, which he's never done before.'

Trouble with eating seemed to be also partly a consequence of the lack of money. Mrs Coxon said of her husband, 'Very often he'll go without his dinner sometimes, to make sure we have it.' And Mr McBain blamed the recurrence of his tuberculosis on, 'Being out of work and not getting enough grub. I was getting so I wouldn't eat. I mean when you're out of work you worry, and you don't feel like eating.' His wife said, 'He'd come in at tea-time and I'd give him his tea, and he'd say, "I don't want it," and he got really run down.' Mr McBain went on, 'I worry a lot, I mean it may sound daft for somebody out of work, but I worry a lot about the kids, like. I'm that type, but when you've been bad like me you worry a lot, and I think I got right down, then, not getting the proper grub and that – well, we couldn't afford. I was thinking, "Well, if I'm eating it, the kids aren't," and it puts yer off eating, and you get to the point where you don't really feel like eating any more. I think your stomach shrinks. I didn't want it. I just used to pick and poke, like.' Mrs Ryan blamed her stomach ulcer on the stress of living on a low income: 'That was through not eating four meals a day. I was not eating all day, and then on a night I was just gulping meself on

150

packets of crisps. I was nearly dead, the last sacrament and everything.'

Apart from these instances, there was Mr Lucas, who seemed to be
cutting down on food in order to go out and about with his friends.
'I don't have no dinner. I just find I can live on one meal, like. These
have a good meal, school dinners, but I can live on one meal and a
couple of pints.'

Slipping standards

As time went on and access to suitable or acceptable jobs still seemed
blocked, the men's requirements for work began to slip in all respects,
type of job, starting wage, locality, prospects, and a change appeared
in men's increasing preparedness to be 'flexible' and to sell themselves in interviews.

Looking back later, Mr Vickers felt that the period about three
months before the end of his insurance benefit had been a crisis
point. By that time other men who were redundant with him had
begun to get jobs, 'And at that time my morale definitely did take a
knocking. Another three months and you would have noticed one
hell of a change. It makes me shudder really, to think about it now.
Everything started happening then, you see. This friend of mine
phoned up, just to inquire how we were getting on, and to tell us
that he was coming this way to have a look. And you know, he told
me an example of how his boss would react. He wanted to interview
somebody that they had down, an African, and his boss said, "Oh,
don't bother with him, you know, he's been out of work three months
now, he can't be any good." So my friend said to me, you know, if
that sort of attitude prevails in industry, you know ... It shook me, it
did. If that sort of attitude is fairly common. Then again, although I
preferred *not* to work out the exact date when my money would run
out, I could see, having subtracted about £120 from my bank balance
to tide me over the first month at work until I received a salary, you
know, it didn't look as though there was much left. You know, time
was running out, in other words, and having had *nothing* in the
months that I'd been looking round, what were the chances? The
chances were that I wouldn't get a job in the time that that money

would run out. And then I'd be starting looking round for some sort of income like bank loans or something horrible like that.'

When we had interviewed him as he approached the end of his savings, and before he had found a job, both he and his wife were apprehensive about what the lack of money would do to their relationship. Mr Vickers said, 'Yes, I think it'll be pretty grim. I think it'll have some effect on you as a person. You'd lose ...' Mrs Vickers joined in, 'Well, it certainly would to me. I'm quite a content person as long as you know there's enough money there to just jog along, you know, just to have the necessaries of life, but once that money has gone and I can't have the necessaries, then I think I should be miserable. For one thing, I think we'll start arguing then.' Mr Vickers agreed, 'Yes, for one thing we'll have to compromise on what we spend. I shall start questioning everything my wife spends.'

Mr Vickers became more anxious in the interviews – although at the time he still insisted that he was confident. 'Now I'm more cautious, more careful about what I say ... I'm more nervous, wondering how the boss will react. It's becoming more important that I get the job. Whereas before, even on the way to the interview, the last thing that was on my mind was what I was going to say in the interview. I'd be thinking more of what a pleasant journey it was. But this last time I suppose I was much more serious, if you like, you know. Well, the fact that I'd taken the trouble beforehand to gen up. I was *prepared*, I was well prepared, so to speak, for being asked technical questions. Whereas before, you know, I was quite, I'd convinced myself, you know, that I'm ... you know, as I stand I'm good enough to walk into that other job, that I didn't need to put in any extra effort to prepare the interview, if you like.' He also changed the sorts of work he was prepared to consider. 'My attitudes are changing all the time. When I started out, I thought I wouldn't accept it unless it paid what I used to get. But at this stage if I see any prospects of advancement, I'd be prepared to go in at a lower level.' He also began to think of temporary jobs. 'Now this other job at Bedford, they phoned me up and they said, would I be interested in a supervisor's job on the afternoon shift, two till ten. Well, my first reaction was, "What money?" I don't mind what it is as long as it's reasonably well paid, and it would enable me to use the mornings for interview.' In desperation he thought once again of emigration: 'I think that's one of the things that I will do, if I run out of money and I still haven't got a job. You can't get back in a family emergency, you can't do it, but ...' He was disappointed, yet relieved, that another of his last-resort jobs, the R.A.F., was closed to him, because he was too old, and he also had a rejection from a firm he used to work for years ago, but which he had left to improve his prospects – he now regretted not staying with them.

Finally, just before he got a job, he became prepared to consider work on building sites (although as yet he did nothing about it): 'Well, I always like to think that because I'm sort of skilful with my hands, I like to think that I could make out on a building site. I've always loved building, even building the patio for instance. And I fancy that because I like hard work – I don't stop once I start, I keep on going – I think I could, I'd be able to make out at sort of carpentry, or something like that. Mind you, it's the initial stage of getting started that's the, sort of, problem. Nowadays, you've got the unions and the apprenticeships. I'm not sure I'd be allowed to do it.' He was then still not thinking of labouring, but looking back after he got work, he thought he had been getting to the point where he would consider fiddling. 'It's surprising how easy it is when you're in employment, to sit back and condemn people, you know, that are, you know, dole fiddling and this sort of thing, you know, drawing the dole and got themselves spare-time jobs. But there's no two ways about it. I would have done that, that's *exactly* what I would have done. Certainly, and I'm honest, I'm *very* honest, but when it comes to that.... Probably what I would have done would have been to get a part-time job on a building site, or something like that, which would have meant an even greater worry then. It would have incurred a greater worry on whether you get caught. There must be a lot that are forced into this kind of thing, and once it starts, it's difficult to get back into things again.'

Mr Fellowes described how his minimum requirements for a job had slipped back over the months while he had been out of work. 'It goes in stages. The first couple of weeks it was like being on holiday. You get through the papers and you go through the motions to see if there's a job. But then when it's gone on week after week, it begins to sink in, "This is it," and jobs that in the past you've skipped over and you've said, "I can't do that," you begin to consider them. Take this man next door. He lost his job and he went to work, shift work, and all he does is fill up holes, and I thought, "I couldn't do that!" I couldn't bear the idea of going into a job where I wouldn't use my mind again. But I met him recently and he was saying to me, "You ought to come up here. The money's good. I'll look around, and see if I can get you a job like mine." It's only filling up holes, but it's got to the stage now where I more or less agreed that he could look round for me. If you go for some jobs, you have to be careful about how you tell them about what you've been doing, because sometimes if you seem to be overqualified they don't want to know. Sometimes I play it down, and sometimes I play it up. I think I'm at a peak now. I sit here dead worried and I think, "I've got to get a job," but in a month or two I'll be saying, "I can't get a job." ' Mr Haigh said of Mr Fellowes at this point just before he found work, 'Poor old John. He's applied for so many jobs and he's been turned down and he says he's unemployable now. He's unemployable.'

Mrs Weston increased the pressure on her husband still further, drawing his attention to adverts in the paper. She said, 'I look, mostly every night I look, and find him some.' Mr Weston protested, 'I mean, she says, "Here's one, £18 a week." Now how could you live on £18 a week?' She went on, 'Sanitary man, cellar-hand.' He scoffed, 'Yes, there was one, laying paving stones, self-employed.' His wife persisted, 'Round the corner they want a barman, evening work.' Mr Weston resisted, 'But I wouldn't work in a pub as a barman.' But his wife was desperate, 'If you want money you've got to do anything. That's what I'm trying to tell you.'

As the end of his insurance approached, Mr Odell also began to think of himself on building site work. 'There's not much more that I can do, because I've tried every place that I want to work in this town, and two of them have got my name down and I can't see anything coming from them. I won't try any factories or anything like that. I might sort of go out on the old digging for a while ... I think I'd be all right. It's just hard work, and I've done harder work before. I did harder work in the factory. I believe the most important thing about a job is whether you like the job, it's not the money.'

Mrs Nottingly said of her husband, 'I think he'd take anything. When he first came out he wanted a painter's job, but now I think he'll take anything to get a job.' The suspicion that self-employment might be an opportunity that he had not the 'go' to take up was a cause for argument between them. Mrs Nottingly said, 'That's what I say about him, he hasn't the go. He says he has, but he hasn't. He was thinking about it.' Mr Nottingly agreed, 'Oh, yes, I was thinking about it.' But his wife insisted, 'I don't think he has the go. You haven't really.' He protested, 'You have to have the money, mind. You have to have some money to back you up.' She objected, 'I mean you said yourself you didn't have the responsibility, and you haven't.' He tried again, 'If I had the money I would.' But Mrs Nottingly had the last word, 'I don't think you would,' and he ceased to defend himself.

Blocked opportunities and loss of identity

So far individuals have been describing the relatively early stages of unemployment up to about six months, during which they retained some confidence that they would work again, however much that confidence was shaken. But among those we saw were people who had suffered longer spells of unemployment, and whose experiences of searching for work had been more discouraging, so that they now seemed to regard as blocked the avenues into any sort of work they would like. Their urgency in looking for work seemed to have passed the peak which some of the workless have just been describing, and they had begun to feel that their whole identity was changing.

MR JOHN

'Well, of course, because this thing that happen to me it brought about a hell of a lot of pressure on me, physically, psychologically, and financial hardship and everything. I go for a walk, and try to do some reading if I can, but it's very hard for me to get the brain functioning properly, because, as I say, things is not the same as before the accident. It's caused a lot o' upset.'

Mrs John said, 'I can't get on with him at home. He's always moody mainly, and he gets on my nerves that way. When you see a man with a long face where he never was like that type, and lately you've only got to do a little thing, or if anything'll be out of place, and he snaps at you for no reason. That's the moods he gets in, through the accident, because he never was out of work before, in ten years he's never been out of work. Because he hasn't got a job, because what man likes to stay at home and sit indoors while their wife goes out to work. No man likes that, to know he's supported by his wife.'

Mr John agreed, 'I'm so *moody*, you know. Not only housework, a lot more things, simple things, the fact that the whole damn accident itself had bring about a despair on me and distressful and it's affecting me. The fact that I'm not able to carry on further studies what I wanted to do. I'd rather be self-supporting, and to find out over a year which one don't in a position to do so, it's very frustrating.'

MR MCBAIN

Mr McBain's working life had been broken several times by spells of unemployment lasting up to two years, apart from many other shorter spells. He takes up the story where he was sacked because he took time off work to get married, when he was living with his in-laws.

'My mother-in-law was a very intelligent sort of woman, and she was a bit too quick for me at times. You know, she'd say something to me, and I'd say, "Are you trying to be funny there?" and about five minutes later, I'd realize what she'd said ... whew! Talk about bloody Andy Capp wasn't in it. I was opposite to Andy Capp, me and her mother. She'd start singing, she didn't used to say anything, she'd find an apt song and sing it, and if the cap fitted, wear it. She'd start singing, and I'd say, "Look, it's got nothing to do with you. Mind your own bloody business." "Lah, dah ..." and sing some bloody horrible song about ninety year old in a mournful voice. I used to go, "Aw, out!" She'd say, "Will you do the wallpapering for us?" So I'd start, and I'd get it all ready, put a piece on and smooth it off, like, and her father'd walk in and say, "By, that's a good job that. Marvellous that," going like this, you know, peering, pretending he couldn't see the join, straining his eyes. "But, if I was you ..." Aw, and I used to say, "Off, out!"'

'I was about a year, and I was trying all over the place, and the new factories that had started on the trading estate, I tried all them. No chance. Actually going in the factory, in the back room, in the offices – they were factories, machine minding. No chance. Well, I was getting knocked back that often. I was on a bike sort of thing, and riding from here to the other end of town, you know, it's a bloody long way, you know, the next town, and get a bloody puncture, you know. I'd have to walk about five mile that way to come a mile this way. You get knocked back each time you do it. You get fed up.

'I bought a garden anyway, and I was in the garden for two bloody years, lost in the garden, wasn't I? There was another eight lads, like meself, they were all out of work and they liked gardening, but there was nowhere else to go. We never used to go out socially like that; a bottle of stout maybe, we used to send up to the off licence, like, when we were sitting round in the cabin. It was another little house. I had a ceiling in it, the lot. I done it out like a house. Eleven o'clock most nights I used to come home – her mother used to say I had another woman. Stopped even looking for a job, really, in the finish. I did, really, in them two year, I lost all interest. I think at that time, I become a little bit of an hermit. I think if I hadn't been married, and no responsibilities at all, I think I'd have just walked out, probably just went on the roads or something at the time. I really believe I would have done it. I believe it.'

A relative found him work, but then later he was unemployed again for two years. 'I was in the garden again, because I didn't drink, and all I did was go in the garden. I lost meself like a bloody hermit, you know, to a large extent. I had the lads during the daytime. There was about five or six of us in the same position as meself, and we used to sit and talk, and tea-time we'd just sit there, either taking cuttings or just pottering about like a bloody old man, lost, bloody utterly. I stopped even looking for a job. In them two years I lost all bloody interest. I thought, "What's the bloody point of it all, anyway? What's the reason for it all?" Then you start to become, well, deranged ... I can't pronounce the word when you're thinking about things, I can't get it out ... psychologically. You start thinking about it, "What the bloody hell's the point? Why are yer here?" I lost me interest in me religion, you know. There was a time when I thought, fair enough, there's a God and all this, that and the other, you know, but I never went to church. Now, well, I don't believe there is a God now, me. Well, anybody who thinks there's a God, he must be a funny bloody God, not my God anyway. He works the wrong way for me if there is one. I think he should look after everybody if there is one, like. I don't think there is.

'Well, I got to thinking to myself, "Well, why am I here? What's the bloody point of it all anyway? Some people have got everything and I can't even get a bloody job." I mean I didn't want the work. All I wanted was a job, so that I could hold my bloody head up. Because I still think that if you're on the dole, you know what I mean, you've no rights, you know. I dunno, I can't find the right words for it. When you're on the dole, I don't think you're the same as when you're working. You haven't got that certain . . . I think you start to lose your identity in yourself, and you feel inside what yer are, you've got to think you're something, and, like I said, there's times when, well, "What's . . . what am I?"

'I have a lot of trouble getting work on me own game now because of me brother being militant. He can't get a job anywhere hardly. He's very militant, doesn't mess about. You see, if I changed me name I'd get a job, I daresay! And this area, it's been used and used and used until there's nothing left now, you know what I mean, and you'll find that when new industry does come into this area now, you find that there's not a lot of local men get started on them. I think the reason is that the people who belong in the area, this particular area, have been used that much in the past, by the process, their grandfathers, their fathers, that's been handed down, till they've got to the point where they say, you know, bugger it, and if there's any trouble on a job they all suddenly say, "We're not having it," like. They've become a bit on the militant side, but the employers won't allow them in, have you got me?

'I don't know, I think I've changed completely to what I used to be when I was a kid, like. I mean, now, I'm starting to notice things, things that I do, and I know for a fact it's things I would never have done years ago. Well, I think, like, with the kids, that gets on your nerves all the time. Me father was a bloody bad'un, you see. He used to knock the hell out of us, like, really old-type Victorian sort of a feller. He's took the bloody belt buckle to me many a time, just on somebody's say so. He wouldn't try to ask me whether it was right or not – sometimes it was right and sometimes it was wrong, and I think most of the times it was right, it was, because he did it when I was wrong, sort of thing. But now I'm starting to realize, I'm starting to take his little ways now. I don't know whether it's something to do with being out of work, or not, I think it has, like. Well, about six months ago I done something I would never have dreamed. We had a new telly, didn't we? There was £13 to pay on it – it was £80 odd and I paid £40 down, didn't I, because I'd had a bit of self-employment, and I had a few bob, and I thought I'd have a decent telly for a change. Well, I walked in the house. She goes round the bend through me being out of work, you know, she starts niggling at me. And I'd just got the telly mended, hadn't I? It was brand new, and anyway I must have been strung up or something, me nerves must have been strung up – hers was, I know that, and she started on at me – and I walked over to the telly, picked it up – I didn't bother pulling the plugs out or owt, I just walked into the garden – the telly was on – and slung it in the back garden and smashed it to smithereens.' ('And jumped on it – he said he didn't want me to watch it again, and that's the type of thing that stretches you too,' added Mrs McBain.) 'That's what I'm looking at, when I said I think you start to change. That's when I realized.

'I mean there was a time I wouldn't tell a lie for anybody. I'd sooner get a smack in the face first, or I'd sooner smack somebody in the face. I wouldn't tell a lie. But now I would. I'd tell as many lies as I could, to be honest about it, as long as I could further me own ends without actually hurting somebody, like. At one time I wouldn't do that, because there was one thing about me father: he was hard, and he was rough, but he would never tell a lie to anybody – he would to me mother, he'd tell lies to me mother, but he wouldn't to anybody else. He was as straight as a die. Well, I never swore. I lived with me mother-in-law – the outlaws! – all them years. I never swore, because I used to cop that much language from me father, I used to say to meself, "When I grow up, like, I'm not going to be like him," and I didn't swear until I'd been on the dole for a long stretch, and then I started to.

'You start to lose your standards, I think. You do, don't you? And put up with things that you wouldn't normally, and your standards start to die down all the time, you know. You'll argue with somebody that you're entitled to something and they say you can manage on a dollar or ten bob less than that, that's the way of making you psychologically lower your sights, and it's, well, not only moneywise, I mean, anything. It's not something you describe. It's just, well, your life, the way you go on.'

'Oh, it's boring. I used to play football or something like that, sit about the house and play me guitar, and I just got fed up.'

'Oh crap! Like you're in the house on a Monday, on a Tuesday. Wednesday you gang down the dole. On a Thursday to the dole to sign. That leaves you with Friday, Saturday, Sunday and all the way like that again, the same week. Only one day you get out and that's a Thursday. Well, I got up, went down to the shops for summat, like. Went down to the dole, just signed, went back home, and that was it. I was in till the following Thursday.'

'Got up round about ten o'clock, half past ten. Play records till round about half past eleven when the bairn used to come in for his dinner. Put his dinner on, take him back to school again, and I was in the house all afternoon, and I just used to watch the telly, like, pass me time away.'

'Bored all day. Naebody to talk to apart from me Ma like.'

'You were just stuck in the house all day and all night, because you've got nae money to go naewhere. Bored stiff.'

'Oh, it was boring, murder, nowt to dae, bone idle. Oh I was up early every morning. I didn't lie in. I used to go for walks. Boring. I was doing nothing, like, except the gardens, painting away at the front doors, like. Now and then putting records on. I used to play football in the square, like, cricket, with a couple of lads next door, like, when they had their days off on a Wednesday afternoon.'

JIMMY WEAVER

Jimmy Weaver's father said of Jimmy's year-long spell of unemployment, 'It's getting far enough. I'd like to see him getting a job now. I'm frightened of him getting used to it, that's what I'm frightened of, that's the danger, because I've witnessed it meself. I've worked at Wearmouth colliery for forty-three years now, continuous employment there, and I've never lost a day's work hardly, just maybe the odd day here and there, through a cold maybe, in all that time, previous to these last few years when this come on, and I've been off a series of thirteen month and five month and fourteen month in the last three or four year. Well, I've got to a stage where I didn't want to ga to work, and yet I've never lost a minute's work before this come on. I got really lazy. The situation's desperate. They're definitely on the scrapheap, you know. I think the bairns is disillusioned. He was keen, he thought he was going to get on a boat, you know, that's what he was after, but as he said, he'll take anything, because they're beginning to feel at a loose end, you know. He's been finished a year this week.'

Jimmy himself said, 'Oh, I get bored sometimes, but it's not that bad. I don't really get bored to tears, like. But the point is, like, when it comes to the crunch, like, you know, I've got to get a job. That's what I'm feeling lately, like. You know, when you get a job, you're going to find out how hard it is, definitely, when you've been out of work a year. Obviously, when I'll be getting work it'll be strange to us, you know, but I'll just have to get used to it, that's all there is to it. On first leaving school, like, I could have getten well into the job in two or three weeks like, where going on the dole, like, it's even different to being at school. If I was starting work from school it would be different, but leaving school, going on the dole, and starting work, it's three different things, you know. I wish I had a job, well for the money, like, I want some money, but it's just the job I want an' all, like.'

MR COXON

For the chronically sick Mr Coxon, the full impact of unemployment had crept up only slowly over the years. 'At first I didn't realize. I thought I would be all right and go back to work, but when you can't do a full-time job, you can't do this and you can't do that, then you can't go to work really. I mean I thought I could go to work, because I've been after jobs. I've been after a job a couple of years ago, I've been after a driver's job, driving a big fifteen tonner, up in Finchley, and that bloke took me out on test. I had a nice drive around the houses, I took it back, and he said, "Do you know another driver to go up to Liverpool?" I said, "Yes, my son-in-law." He said. "All right, I'll give him a job an' all," he said "£20 a week," and I came home and told my son-in-law, but he said no. I think he didn't want to take it on because he knew I couldn't go to work. I could have got a job like that, got a job anywhere. Now I can't because they've brought in the H.G.V. licence. You see, and the tying over and the sheeting over, I can't do that. I could drive all right, do driving all right. It's all heavy lifting on them jobs, such as like delivering televisions. Just imagine me getting a job like that where you cart televisions up to the top of buildings. It'd kill me. It'd kill me with empty hands going upstairs, let alone televisions. You see I can't do the driving and unloading. I'm going to mess meself up unloading.'

Mrs Coxon said, 'In between he's been after jobs, but he's been out so long, when he tells 'em his age ... He's even been for a tea boy's job, haven't you, on a building site, but they said he was too old.' Mr Coxon said, 'Sometimes I get so chokker, with these jobs, where they say I'm too old. It disheartens me, so I'm just waiting now to see what comes round, if anybody likes to give me a couple, three hours work, you know, I'd do that.' Mrs Coxon recalled, 'He tried part-time work, but two days of part-time work and he was ill in bed again.' Mr Coxon agreed, 'I can't do a full-time job. I know I can't. I thought I could, but now I know I can't.' Mrs Coxon said, 'He knows in his own mind he can't. Oh, you did do a little job, didn't you, up the pub.' Mr Coxon became enthusiastic, 'Oh, a pubman's job. I liked that, I did, yes, collecting the glasses, and at weekends, but the people what had it moved out and the new people didn't want no pubman, so they finished me.' Mrs Coxon went on, 'But they're very few and far between, those kind of jobs. You see, he could take his time, see. If he took a job where if he feels bad he could stop. There's not many jobs around like that.' Mr Coxon grew enthusiastic, 'Even them people used to like me. Everybody in the pub used to like me, the regulars, you know.' Mrs Coxon laughed, 'They used to hold their hand over their drink and say, "Go away!" He used to be so fast the drink had gone before they noticed, because if they had gin or something in the glass he couldn't see it. He used to pick up the glass and take it.' Mr Coxon nodded, 'Well liked, you know, well liked.

'No, I'm not troubling now. Another four years and I'll be pensioned right off, you see. That's what I think they're doing now, not troubling, just keep in touch with me, like, and that's about all.' The nearest he now came to driving was to go with his three sons, who were all drivers, on a long trip. 'I went up in the new "Artic." eight gear change. Beautiful. I couldn't have a go though. The night driving, perhaps that's what I should be doing, the European service, if I was still on.

'What I do now, I do the bits and pieces in the place. I do my own washing, I do the washing up, I do the sweeping up. I might go upstairs. I might go out in the garden to do something not heavy, I don't do any heavy work. If I do a job and it takes the peace of mind to do, I get tired out, and I tire myself right out before I stop. I don't sleep. Sometimes I get bored, well, everybody gets bored in a house, I don't care who. I want to go out; I make myself a promise that I'm going to do what I want to do, go out tomorrow for a nice walk and stop out for a while, and perhaps when that day comes it's pouring with rain, and then I'll get all worked up. Sometimes I haven't been out for a whole week, I stopped in for a whole week sometimes. Well, I've got the telly in here, and I sit and watch that telly, and if there's a gripping play on I'll go, "Aw!" and turn it off, and I'll go upstairs, for the sake o' going up there. Or I might moan about something. Perhaps the boy's left a load of stuff all over the place. Sometimes when I walk in this place here I'm off, "What the bloody hell ...!" and I shift the sugar and I shift the cups. That's how I get, like, and I go in the bedroom, and I chuck me coat off on the bed and I just sit down and maybe have a smoke. If I get anything on me mind, I'm off, see. It's only because I worry about something. I might be worrying about a bit of money or something like that. With lots of things I worry more now, but mostly I worry about how will I do a bit more better than I do now. I'd like to have a few pounds in me pocket, when I go out and see something. When I go all round these shops or go up to London, but I can't. I can't do that. That's why I only walk round here, because you've got nowhere else to go.

'I do still think about work, because I *must* think about work. I want to try to get a job driving. You see, what I'd really like for a job, I'd like a van, a small van; a good one, not an old crock what I got a lot of trouble with, no worry. Load up with small parcels, like, and trundle out in the morning, Luton, Bedford, somewhere like that, and drop the load off there, and pick a load up and fetch it back. A job like that only lasts about six hours. Take your time and that's it. But you've got to go a long way to find a job like that, see, even a part-time job.

'It's lorries barmy I am. I like lorries. You ask your friend who took the photographs. I took him up one of them footpaths where the motorway is, and I stand up there, I do, and I see the lorries coming up and overtaking and flashing their headlights, and I think to meself, "I dunno." I watch 'em go by, I stand up there for hours sometimes, if it's nice, if it's not raining, it's nice and warm. I'll stand up there for hours, watching 'em, the old lorries, overtaking and flashing lights.'

MISS HEBB

'When I try for a job they're all very, sort of, governmental jobs and things like that, and when you fill in the forms you've got to have references and then you state what your previous jobs were, and I haven't got a chance when I start sticking things down if I stick down the truth, and I'm not much good at lying, you know, to get a job. I feel, you know, if I lie for a job I probably won't like it anyway.

'I would love a job if I felt happy in it, and it was really something worthwhile doing. I liked working on the adventure playground. I liked that a lot, but I mean the hours and conditions were so bad, and the pay was nothing. I can't see very much future. I don't go much on the future. I don't think about the future. I need some kind of stimulus. "I've got a great future behind me," and I just can't get started again somehow. While I'm here on S.S. I've got my rent and I've got my food. I can't see anything coming out of this situation. It'll have to be something that comes out of myself.

'It drives me to screaming point sometimes. I was all right when I was on the adventure playground arguing with people and fighting the kids' battles, that kept me going. But once you stop doing things and you've got your food and rent provided, then it's your mind takes over and I can't stand it.'

MR DOVER

'I think you can apply yourself a bit better when you're older, so I *thought* I could get on to something at the local tech, they were advertising a place there, you know, a course there, and I went to see the lady and she said, "Well, you need some A levels, really, you know," so I went down to the place here to see about some A levels, and he said, "Well, you need some O levels first," you know, and I've been on an O level course before, just for one, and it's so bloody boring, it's incredibly boring . . .

'So, I'd been on social security before that, but they hadn't paid me my full whack every week, and then I got my arrears through the claimants' in one go, so, the winter was coming and I had £25 in my pocket, so I split abroad, you know. But I got mixed up in the Bangladesh war, and I got a bill, £120 to pay off. I was flown back by the R.A.F., you know, and I can't have my passport until I've paid it, so, er, I'm really sort of beyond, below zero again now. I'm just sort of existing on social security hoping to make some money in the summer time, beaches, selling things on beaches, you know.

'I find I change slowly over the years. I can see two ways stretching ahead of me in life and I don't know which one to jump on yet. Basically what I'd like to do is travel around a bit. I'd like to get up to Burma, I think it's a good country to be in, or Mongolia. I had a plan to go to a little Mexican village. I'd like to go and see Mexico before they completely fuck the place up.

'But I don't know, I seem to be changing as I get older. My attitudes are changing. You get to like the home comforts, a roof over your head and a bed to sleep in. I don't feel as much like sleeping rough any more. I'm feeling bored, you know, for the first time in my life, I think, but I'm finding it difficult to do anything about it, you know. I've got to get some money to get my passport back. Once I get the money together, I'll have the chance to decide whether to go back to Asia, or I've a chance to go to Mexico for a year, or whether to invest in a few more G.C.E.s.

'I don't believe in an alternative society any more. And I don't take drugs, not in this country. The cannabis has got no kick in it. Anyway, I think drugs are artificial, people who use drugs, they're looking for something. Me, I suppose I'm a bit different, with being a bit older. Somehow I seem to act like a father figure to a lot of these guys. I did believe in an alternative society at one time, but now I believe you've got to have a big group of steady guys who'll keep the thing going, and society produces a number of guys like me and they'll have to tolerate a certain percentage of us. I think we keep things going, and we do lots of little jobs that wouldn't get done otherwise if there weren't guys like us. Well, er, washing cars, window cleaning, doing a bit of removing, working on adventure playgrounds.

'We're free by conventional standards, but I suppose after a while you make your own conventions really. Once you start to build up routines, and then you start trying to break away from it, really, you know. I think I have more routines now in a way. We have a routine on everything except timing. We've got no clock, but we have fixed routines. Our routine is basically to get up *some* time, you know. We never stop in bed all day. I was going to stop in bed today, but the sun started to shine and I got up. But whatever time we do get up, this is the sort of routine. We go down to Spratt's, or whatever his name is at the bottom of the road, and buy a newspaper, and then get some bread and next door to get some milk. It depends; we bought the *Sun* today, because we felt like a giggle. Because if you buy a quality newspaper you feel obliged to read it, and I didn't feel like it. I used to be interested in politics at one time, but I don't bother much now. Up to about 1969 I would say. It was about the time I was leaving my wife. I don't know. It all seemed to be the same old scene, you know. Sometimes when we get up we've got no idea what time it is. We ask the man at the shop what time it is. It might be seven o'clock, it was seven o'clock this morning; I was surprised. Or it might be three o'clock in the afternoon. Sometimes I say, "D'you know what time it is? D'you know what *day* it is?" and the guy looks really surprised. We haven't much sense of time. Sometimes we'll be sitting here and we'll say, "Let's go down for a game of darts in the pub," and we'll go down to the pub and the pub will be closed, and we'll think, "Christ, fancy the pub being closed." Apart from shopping to pass the time, we've taken up gardening. We've built a little greenhouse. Well, that's a commercial proposition with tomatoes the price they are, but it's only a small garden. Another way of filling the time is to write letters. I write fantastic long letters to people all over the world. And I have developed the capacity to do nothing, absolutely nothing, but it worries me a bit. I really don't know what I do with my time. I was writing a letter, and I began this letter and I got broken off, and when I went to finish this letter I looked at the date and it was four days between starting and finishing. Christ, man, four days! Where's it gone? It wasn't until recently that I suddenly realized for the first time, hell, it was as if time suddenly caught up with me, you know.

'I get bored now. I mean once you've got your rent and your food, that's it. You start thinking, and I don't know how to pass the time. I felt a bit down yesterday, and the only way I can get rid of depression is to go out and have some beers and get really stoned.

'You know when you're in a field sometimes and you look at the insects and you see them all scurrying backwards and forwards, and you're up in the air and you're like God, you feel as though you could reach down and squash one, and they're all busy going backwards and forwards, all going somewhere. Well, just recently, just this past year, I've had this feeling about people. I'll stand at the top of a hill sometimes, and you look and there are all these people rushing backwards and forwards, driving cars, riding on buses, going into shops, and they're all going somewhere. They've all got work to do, or they've got journeys to make, and I feel, "What's it all about? What's it all for?" I feel outside of it. It doesn't make me want to join in, it just makes me feel different. I really admire these guys who can get up and shave, and have breakfast, and make a journey to work, and come home again, and have meals – guys who can do all that in one day! I don't know how they can manage it. When I've got to sign on, or anything like that, just do the one thing, it bugs me all day. I'm rushing backwards and forwards. I can't seem to settle down. Or if I've anything to do, if we've got to latch on to the time thing for a bit, say to catch a bus to go somewhere, it's a real drag. We can't seem to get with it.'

10 A Postscript: Work Regained

Some of the men whom we interviewed did eventually find work during the course of our study, although not before their confidence had been shaken. We also interviewed two groups for whom subsidized work was provided specifically to rescue them from unemployment: some teenagers doing paid community work of various kinds, and disabled men working in a sheltered workshop.

Although we have already introduced the teenagers, none of the disabled men from the workshop have yet spoken.

The workless return to work

Mr Vickers told us triumphantly over the phone, 'I've got myself a job, mate!' In a subsequent interview he described his feelings on being offered work after six months' unemployment. 'That was the first time I've experienced an offer then and there. Oh great! I came home feeling pleased that I'd got the job. I called in at my in-laws on the way home and let them know, because they'd be wondering how I got on.'

However, asked if he would have taken the job when he first became unemployed, he said, 'No! I wouldn't have done. I should say just solely because of the salary.' But now he was glad of the work in spite of longer hours, shorter holidays, occasional travel away from home, a longer work journey, and a reduction of status from staff to hourly-paid. 'It was a lot less money than I'd hoped for, but at least it was more than one of the directors was outlining to me at the first interview. And I can manage on this, and in fact with overtime by next January – and as the manager said, they all do manage, you make sure you get your overtime ... It has its advantages in that I shall be paid weekly and I won't have to go one month without income. I suppose it's because it's a complete change of jobs, and I like that idea, so I didn't feel too bad about clocking on. There's no aspect I don't like, really. There's a little bit of a problem with home life. My wife's been used to me home at pretty regular times, and certainly never having to stay away from home, whereas I shall certainly sometimes have to stay away at nights on occasions.

'But I think my wife's just the same as I am. She's so relieved that I've got a job that she's quite prepared to make the sacrifice of not having the car.' Mrs Vickers agreed: 'I was very excited, very thrilled, yes! Well, I was more pleased for him, not even from the money point of view. It was just a relief to think that he's got a job, you know, just for him, for his morale. He was getting worried.' He said, 'I tell you, I'm mighty grateful for a job because since they've offered me this, since that – I tell you, I was a bit apprehensive about accepting this, really. When I got it, it renewed me with confidence. I thought, well, I don't know, I can probably do better than this. I'd got loads of jobs, I *felt*, still in the running. I told him I'd ring him next day, having phoned Stevenage, where I thought I was in with a better chance than this. I just told him, "Look, I've got other jobs in the offing, you know, I want to see how they're going. I don't want to have to turn round and say I'm not taking it after all." But I did phone them up, let's face it, and told them I'd accept it, but I still had it at the back of my mind that should another one come along, you know, I would have no hesitation about taking a better offer. Well, Stevenage, they phoned me back eventually and said they advised me to take this offer. But since then there's these three, four refusals come in since then.

'I suppose I did feel good, you know, going into work, to make a start, but, in effect, the thing is that the first week went so badly that I never really got an opportunity to enjoy it. By the second day, Tuesday, I thought, "This is a bit off" – as at that time I'd been introduced to one bloke, Bill, and he was teaching me how to test these boards, a very routine and basic sort of operation, and in fact when I told him something of my past, you know, he tended to talk down to me, if anything. I was just a bloody lad looking over his shoulder, you see – and I'd been introduced literally to one bloke at this time, and I thought, "This is not on," so I had a word with the boss, and said, "How about somebody showing me round the firm and introducing me to people?" And so he turns to Bill and he says, "Good idea. Can you do that, Bill?" So of course, Bill's no confidence or status or anything else to do the job and we stand outside somebody's office, like, and he hasn't the courage to go in, you see, if the bloke's on the telephone or something, and he says, "Do you want to see this bloke?" I said, "Nah, forget the whole idea."

'And then, anyway, about Thursday, we had to go out in the field, and I spent a day watching this bloke servicing some equipment. Most of the time, the whole morning, we spent waiting. He pressed all these buttons, and I didn't know what was happening to it. So Friday I was supposed to go up there again, and I thought, "I've had just about enough of this," so I went and saw the boss again, and I said, "Look, this is a complete waste of time, as far as I'm concerned," I said. "This whole week, I just don't know anything, I don't know what the hell's going on." And I told him, I said, "The way I'd like to do it is, I'd like somebody to tell me what the thing does, so that I know how to make the thing perform and then find out how it works." And he admitted that this is how he'd like to do it. Anyway, he went off and had a long chat with this bloke, Jack, who I'd been assigned to, and it all came out that I didn't think much of the way I'd sort of been treated in that I wasn't being shown round the firm, and Jack came out after this talk and apologized for dumping me in the lab, and he was bending over backwards at the time to make amends.

'I said to my wife at the time, "It's a good thing I spoke," I said, "this could have gone on for weeks and weeks and nobody would have bothered." So anyway, and after that, and also the fact that I did some overtime and I worked out how much it was worth, that was four and half quid, you see, plus my expenses. It's surprising, you see what fantastic change of heart after ... Well, I was getting so depressed, and my wife was. I was coming home and complaining. I didn't actually take it out on her, but it was just the fact that I was a bit miserable, and you see it makes her terribly miserable, you know, it's a sort of downward spiral, it gets worse and worse.

'I should say the weeks go past quite quickly now, but I won't say I'm never bored because that's not true, because I get frustrated at times. I tend to be frustrated and a little bit bored at times, because I don't know what to do with my time next. It's not so bad at the moment when I keep getting the odd hour or two's instruction, and then I find something to do. Mind you, it's still not as it should be, because I keep saying to them, you know, I expect to make rapid progress, and generally, sort of, er, bulling them up, you know. That's my attitude after all, because as far as I'm concerned, this is my money, and until I'm really on top of the job I can't really expect much money, can I? At the moment I'm not worth anything to them.

'Another thing, I could always go in the canteen at the old place at any time of the day and there'd be somebody there I could talk to. And I would find a very good atmosphere, I would think, if there was a load of service engineers, so there would be a certain amount of tie there, even though, on average, the service engineers are not as, none of them, you know, as well-qualified as I am or anywhere near it. Well, at the moment I'm in a machine shop sort of atmosphere. Well that's not, er, it's not me.

'But I mean, even if I'm still thinking of moving on, I've got to at least give this a twelve months shot – I'm convincing my wife as I'm talking to you! I think I shall give that a rest for a year. I'm *sick* of looking round. The thing is, knowing what the prospects are that I will probably have to go for so many interviews before landing a job, not only will I not be getting paid for it, but if they get a sniff that I'm still itching to shift off, that I'm just using it for a jumping platform, well ... Mind you, I still think they're getting a bargain. I still think they're getting me for a lot less than I'm worth.'

Mrs Vickers sometimes looked back nostalgically to the days of unemployment: 'I like him here all the time now – where before when he was at work I used to allow him to go out in the shed one or two nights a week, now I don't want him to go out at all.' Mr Vickers's work in the shed had ceased.

Of Mr Vickers's fellow workers, Mr Haigh got a job with a satisfactory contract, but he had to move house and maintain two mortgages for two years. Mr Fellowes took a job with inferior pay and conditions.

Among the other skilled workers, Mr Weston had the offer of some work which he accepted because the family had run out of money, but reluctantly: 'I mean, even though this chap's phoned me up and I'm morally obliged to accept his offer, it's a form of defeat, you follow what I mean.' His wife told us privately, 'He doesn't want to go back to that job. He'll be ever so miserable if he goes back.' However, Mr Weston was hoping to be able to keep on making his pictures in his spare time.

Mr Odell found himself a job as a bus-driver in a neighbouring town, where he had to hitch-hike to work in the dark hours of early morning. He also suffered a loss of wages, more insecurity, and poorer working conditions. Although he had wanted a large firm, the new establishment was small and shaky. He was virtually the only full-time employee, and could only make up his former wage by overtime working. 'I've had a couple of reports for going too fast, but I was travelling just within the speed limit. It's incredible because the boss won't tell me off or get annoyed with me because I think the position is that he needs me more than I need him. I don't like to take advantage of that. I've got an old van now, and he ran into trouble and he's got one driver there with no proper licence and there are a couple of cars going round with no tax on them, and there's a couple there of the part-timers who refuse to drive these things, so I sometimes lend him my van. The last few weeks I suddenly realized I'm not getting any journeys on Saturdays, except when he gets stuck or when he wants to go out for the evening, and he annoys me because he's not sticking to what he said about overtime. One of the reasons he made me think there was other drivers there was he said, "Of course, full-time drivers get first choice of work," so I'm not getting first choice.' Mrs Odell said, 'The boss never pays him, you know. He never gets his wages regularly on a Friday like he should do. Sometimes he don't get 'em till the middle of next week. Then he started paying him by cheque. They stopped one of the cheques in the bank, the money mustn't have been there, anyway. I don't think he gets very good overtime, and he was only saying the other night his boss had underpaid him by 6d. an hour.'

Mr Odell complained, 'I mean, even though I do less work here, I've got to spend the hours, and you don't see anybody. Most of the time I'm in the yard on my own, like. Except sometimes I'm borrowing a car, and burn up around the country! I sometimes wish I was unemployed again. Oh, I miss the claimants' union, and not having to go to work. I was thinking about a milk round, because really I like driving coaches better than I do buses, and on a milk round you finish early in the morning. I'd be able to get more involved again with the claimants' union, and I'd be able to do a bit of coach-driving as well.' Shortly afterwards he did become a milk roundsman and stepped up his claimants' union activities, although the union remained in the doldrums.

When he got back to work he ceased to do any housework, even though his wife was now working full-time. Mrs Odell said, 'The thing that gets me down, I have to do everything in the evenings when I come home, wash and iron. And whenever I get a day off, I'm always working. I sometimes wish he was still off work.'

Finally, among the more skilled, Mr John got a job where he had to live away from home. 'I will be travelling off to a firm and this firm have passed the test and they will be paying me what I think is a good fair starting wage to start off, which there will be no employer round this place here will pay.' He had become a travelling man.

Teenagers in community service

The teenagers we interviewed had been unemployed for periods from eight months up to a year, and they now worked in jobs like decorating old people's houses and digging their gardens, or other jobs which had an element of service.

'When this job came along, I was really pleased. I like the job we're doing. It helps the old folks and I like it.'

'You're helping the old folks and it learns you for when you're married, like, you can always do the house, where other people don't bother.'

'I like digging it over, and I like cutting the grass. It's just the particular parts I like. Some like digging holes and burying things . . .'

'This job, it's better than being on the dole, really, like. It gets a bit boring at times, like, but better than being on the dole.'

'It's a job, like, and it's money . . .'

Jimmy Weaver said, 'It's painting and decorating, it's £10 a week, like, and . . . I'd like it, but it's not particularly the reason I'd . . .

Well, you're doing some good for somebody, but, you know, painting and decorating, it's not my idea of a perfect job, like.'

The disabled in sheltered work

CHARGEHAND

'Well, I was actually in and out of hospital until I was eighteen, and then I was at home. Up to that time I'd never given work, keeping meself, any sort of thought. You know, at home, mum and dad, always had a pound in me pocket, never had to buy anything. Me and work had never been introduced. I'd never had to worry about this. Then when I was sixteen, I went down to a training centre. I done about eighteen months there, they trained me as a welder. I came home and got a job in a small one-man band near home, but quite honestly, the job he was doing, there wasn't enough of it, sort of fortnight's work and then nothing. After that I more or less gave up looking for a job as such. Nobody wanted to take the responsibility of somebody, I used to walk a bit then on crutches, badly, but a bit. I just sort of gave up.

'A hopeless marriage prospect I was, no job, no prospects, no nothing, no income, no nothing. I had this homework that I was doing through the sheltered workshop – this was the first time I got to know about the workshop, I was going down to the labour. I couldn't claim money in those days, though, I'd no stamps, I hadn't done any work. I don't think national assistance was on then, from what I can remember. I used to cut the excess rubber off mouldings, boring as hell it was. You used to get 7/6 a sack. The trouble was you could never get enough of it. I could have earned money at that job, but you could never get enough. They had a hell of a problem to get work and they used to share it out, you know. That was about a year or something.

'And then I got married, so I had to make up me mind to do some work by then, you know. It was that thing called love. My wife was working at the time. I don't think I'd have given much thought about it really, you know, stupid days, living with mother. I think I sort of made up my mind I'd have to get a job, and they introduced me to the workshop, you know, and from there, I reckon they've been bloody handsome to me.

'I did think of outside work, and I have had a look round over the years, but to be honest, I think I'm frightened, the fear, would I fit in? And the other thing: there's a lot of people, you've been in the job so long you're frightened to change. Although I say to you that I quite honestly think it's wrong for all disabled people to be in a club as disabled, I know that I can come here and I'm recognized as Dick, you know, and who the others are. But I don't know if I'd like the idea of wheeling down the factory floor full of girls, and that, you know, all running around.

'Unfortunately, I'm afraid that you're never allowed to forget for long that you're amongst the disabled, you know, I do resent this. Well, they're forever reminding the fit that we're disabled. Unfortunately, this is one or two characters that do this quite a lot, and I've never been sure that disability on its own in its own little world is the right thing. I think it breeds the wrong thinking inside. "We're disabled. We must have this, we need this, this is our right." Which for my way of thinking is a load of old . . . First of all a bloke's got to have something inside of him, because otherwise they just keep take, take, take . . .

'They're not allowed to compete with outside workers. Take the hearing-aid we make. I'm confident that those boys could hold their own in the outside world. Unfortunately this is the same with most sheltered workshop work, that it could be classed as women's work outside, but these'll hold their own against women as well.

'I think the government subsidies are there as long as there's a job, and at the time they like doing the job they've been asked to do, you know. But once again, you get a flow of work, it may be packing postcards, or packing cigarettes, first of all it's a bit of a game, but after a week you're bored to tears. And then you'll get the same about the assembly job; that's caused quite a few rumpuses. You get to hear that some feel that the men on the assembly job have been on it too long. But here you couldn't blame just management; you've got to blame men, because these men are so jealous that if the work gets shared out and there's not enough for them to earn top bonus – and this goes for all of 'em, not just the assembly job, because it's been said just recently about sharing work out, we're a bit short in other directions. The system that's being run at the moment, I can't understand it to save me life. They take blokes on, they tell us they're forced to take blokes on, it's not their fault, it's government policy. And yet there's not a cat in hell's chance of finding work for 'em at the moment. I can't understand why they do it. I don't think anyone else can, except the powers that be. This is where the men on the assembly job start to look after their little corner. There's too many to share it out with.

'I think there's quite a few blokes here, who, financially they're comfortable, but they do come for the work. Take him over there. He's an ex-serviceman, and financially he's laughing. His wife's working and his daughter's working. If he stayed at home he could claim extra, but if he stays at home he'd go potty, so he does this. Let's put it this way. I think his income, even if he was at home, would be in the region of about twenty-five quid a week, and it is a bit of a struggle to come to work but he comes. I mean if he wanted to swing the lead he could con the national assistance into quite a few bob a week, but I think they do need the work. I don't think the people here would honestly say to you in words they're grateful. I think most of them, unfortunately, even those who you look on as thinkers, will knock. But if they told the bloody truth they *are* grateful, because they can either come here and be bored occasionally, or stay at home and be bored to tears *all* the time, you know. I expect now and again you get dissatisfied with your lot, but on the whole the workshop's done bloody marvellous.'

SKILLED ASSEMBLY WORKER
'Had I been like I am without the workshop, I would have had to stay at home. My wife would have had to wash me, dress me, help me to the toilet. Without the workshop, *finish*! You see I have, with my wife, localized myself to meet my retirement. Now it could be at sixty-three, -four, -five, -six or -seven. I'm ready for it, but ... I would like to stay here until I'm sixty-seven. I don't want to be around my wife's feet all day long. I enjoy myself here with the repartee that we have, and as long as I'm able to do my job, providing I have a job to do and I can do it. On my job it's a steady flow, and has been for the last six years. Now over there you have a different situation, where there isn't enough work. Now if you was to ask me if I was on his job whether I wanted to stay here, taking his money, I'd still come to work, rather than stay at home doing

nothing, because I get something out of the workshop. I do, as an individual. Some people say the workshop should be burnt down, and the people are making money on disabled people's backs and all this business. I don't mind how many people make money on my back, providing I am taking home something I can use.

'This particular job, for the last six years, I *used* to dream about it. I've got many books on it, but I find there's no need now. It's far better to get on with your job, enjoy your job and go home of a night-time, have a wash and put your feet up.

'Oh, I think there's still plenty of time for a better workshop, but it's a slow process, you see. It will come, it will come. The only thing where it may not come is if we have a terrible recession. Then you might have the sheep separated from the goats. By that I mean you might have your better people stay here and the other people will have to go to the wall. I hope not.

'When you come in the factory and you see quite a number of disabled people it makes you feel fit yourself. It doesn't solve your problems, but it makes you feel a lot better in yourself. By and large the people who are able to use their brains and their hands are the mainstay of the workshop. Those people who are disabled ... Now look at little Alice over there, she's one of the most marvellous creatures you have ever met. Now she does all the work at home, she does all the housework, all the laundry, all the cooking, the making the beds, she does cake-making, she can do anything, she can do work as good as what I can on that bench. And yet if she went outside to a firm to be given a job, they wouldn't look at her. There's Cyril over there and Alf over there, they both belong to the local basket-ball team. But because you're disabled, this is what annoys me, because you're disabled, it doesn't mean to say you're block-heads. There's a chappy over there, n O levels, but because he studied and studied, he had a mental breakdown, and although he's quite a nice chap in his way, but you've got to keep pushing him. The chargehand'll call out, "Get your bloody arm down," or some-thing. He doesn't take umbrage. If a fit person says that to him, he'd take umbrage, but because he tells him and he's in a wheelchair. When he hasn't got any work for a while he likes to have a little sleep. There's a little chappie over there, he's got a wife and three children. He could stay at home and get more money than he does now, but he doesn't, he comes to work. He can't work, he's multiple sclerosis, he shakes all over the place. All he does is just sticks these on. I daresay he comes to get out of the way of his kids most likely! See that chap there. His arthritis has caught up with him badly in this last two years. He doesn't have much to do, which is lucky in his case, you know, the job he's doing. Quite honestly, even if we got a full batch, I don't think it would give him a full eight hours a day graft. He's one of those, well, it's just the job he's been asked to do, you know, all he's doing, he takes the finished assembly and just inspects that there's no faults on it, the final inspection, gives them a rub with a duster, puts them in a box. He doesn't pack the box or anything, and you know, ten assemblies like that he can do in two minutes. I mean I think he's wise enough to realize this is fair enough, this is, and anybody would be mad to expect him to do much more.

'When the unions say, "What can you expect for wages, you're doing women's work," we tell them, "What are you talking about? I don't care whether we're doing women's work at all. We are the same as you in effect. My clothes cost me the same, my electricity, my rent, my food, my petrol, I have to do the same on £15 a week as you do on £30 a week," and this is a fact. What I'm saying is this: we have to pay the same for our shirts, our ties, haircuts, anything you like, the same as them.

'By and large, it can always be made better, but I wouldn't have anything taken away from the workshop.'

SKILLED ASSEMBLY TESTER

'I went to a rehabilitation centre when I left school, but that was no good. Then I used to make wigs at home, about sixty or seventy wigs a week, but I was exploited. I used to get about £7 a week. Then that went bankrupt, the Japanese ruined the trade, they brought out machine-made. It was quite a good job really. It was indoors, no expense. In my little way I was quite happy really. My mother used to go to work, she used to go to work about eight. I used to start work at nine, and pack up at four. Lonely? No. I'm the sort of person, I don't need company. I used to have a wireless, and we used to have a dog in those days, and strangely enough that was company. I had a chair, but I didn't really have the strength to push the chair outside. I used to work in the garden when the glorious weather was here, and that was a big help that was. Then the wigs went bankrupt, as I said, and I was out of work for about six months. Strangely enough, it came on very gradually. The work didn't stop dead, it stopped slowly. One week I was on social security, next week I was working, next couple of days I'd be working. So it came on very slowly. I don't remember really. The weather was gorgeous that summer. I used to go in the garden, I should say, to pass the time.

'The money was fantastic to me then in them days. The first week I was here, I had £12, it was gorgeous. I didn't find the company no advantage. Everybody here said, "Oh, ain't you better working with people? Isn't it better coming out to work?" But ... they used to think I was mad, because I used to like working indoors on my own. Funny really. I'd not really worked with people before, only at the rehabilitation centre. I was there six weeks, you can't really call it working. I've got a personal thing, that you can't have friends, more acquaintances at work. I don't know, it's possibly me again.

'If it hadn't been this particular assembly job, but one of those others where they haven't enough work I would feel like I was being supported. I think they must be. Let's put it this way. If you were working outside in industry, because you'd be working with "normal" people – I don't say "normal" people, I don't honestly know – but I always get the feeling that because you were working with others you was not getting full money. If you was working outside, I don't think you'd be getting full money, but you'd be classed more as a *person* working. I mean you say, "Where are you working?" Somebody asks you, and you say, "Sheltered workshop." "Oh," sort of thing. You know immediately what passes through their mind, you know, charity, or something like that, which it *is* in fact. I'd like to have a try at working outside. Let's say, I don't think this is my limitation. I did try for a job at a firm, but they told me, they was pretty ... They took one look at me and said, "You can't work." They're not prepared to give you a chance, sort of thing. I've had that once or twice.

'I wouldn't mind packing up work and have my own little business, but you need capital. We would like a shop, selling commodities.

'I met my wife on holiday, really. I went to Italy with the Welfare, and my wife was a Welfare Officer, you know, and it just grew from there. I couldn't have gone on holiday with the Welfare if I wasn't working here, because of the money, it was about £32 to go to Italy for two weeks. I think work's been a help, but it's been a help that I could have missed, so to speak. I think so, apart from the money. I don't think I would have got married, but apart from that.

'If this job was to go out of the workshop and we get back on the flat money, the flat money is reasonable to live, but about exist on, but as for social security ... Although I do feel tempted sometimes to pack up work and live off the country. Well, I had a week off over trouble with my car, and I got £15 from the social security. Here I get twenty-two. We couldn't really live on £15 a week, no new clothes or anything, and we've got a car, that costs fifty quid a year, and then there's maintenance, insurance. Though I think if I packed up work we'd get a telephone paid for by the Welfare. We'd get a television paid for by the Welfare. But that's not the point really. I don't know how I'd feel if I packed up. I've never tried it. Well, if I stopped at home, the wife's at home with a baby, so I don't think I'd *miss* working with people. One of the things I find in coming to work, you get up at seven o'clock in the morning, ten to seven, you're up. Saturdays and Sundays we've both got a bad habit, we get up at eleven o'clock so the rest of the day is wasted. So I feel that if I didn't come to work, and I didn't *have* to get up, I wouldn't get up and most of my life would be spent in bed, wasted. Saturdays and Sundays are just, sort of vague – feelings. You get up at about eleven o'clock, and you have a row because you're both dog-tired with staying in bed, you know what it's like. I think if I was out of work and home all day with my wife it would be one massive row all the time.

'If they offered me a pound or two less I would accept this pound or two less and stay at home, but I think this is just me, you know, just laziness. I think I would probably get bored, but I'd be able to overcome it. Trouble is, when you're out of work, you don't have enough money to do things. I think you need a drive. Some work is the most boring thing on earth, but because of the drive, you just do it, sort of thing. But then again, if my wife did work, I think I would be dead jealous, if she was earning more money than I was. One half, I think, would feel useless, stopping off work, but the other half would enjoy it.'

UNSKILLED ROUTINE WORKER

'I mean the job in this workshop isn't in my stage, let's face it. I'm a heavy-lorry driver and humping sides of beef. I mean I've never had a light job, but I just get on the best way I can. I mean I've always drove heavy vehicles, and humping hind-quarters of beef. Get up at half past three in the morning, start at five, get home at two o'clock in the afternoon. That has been my life. I've never done a factory job before. Much as I'd like to get in the outside world and get on with a bit o' graft, not to be boastful or anything like that but I am one that's liked a bit o' graft, and I've got this disease of the spine in respect of this, an ageing spine. I'm not trying to pull any strokes or anything, but if I've worked with men twenty years my senior I've always liked to do twice as much as them, and maybe this is the results of this.

'The D.E.P. done what they could, but as I say, my age seemed to be my obstacle. I'm getting on for fifty-seven. My outlook was trying to get a messenger's job. I used to read the paper and write after jobs, letters, but the majority of them, the adverts, said, "Messenger required, forty-five years old, physically fit," and I had it both ways, fifty-seven and not physically fit. I registered at the labour, I registered at the Alfred Marks Bureau. Very distressing, 99 per cent of them, they say, "Name and address, when was you born and why, and what nationality, last employment for three years." Well, I hadn't had any. Whether they thought I'd been in gaol or something, I don't know. "Well, you fill in the form and we'll let you know." When they say that, you've had it. I mean I haven't been to work, on and off, for six years. I got to the stage 1968, '69, that I finished up having shock treatment at St Bartholomew's Hospital, which I've been in and out for the last nine years, which is our depressive state, out of work.

'People don't pass remarks to me about being disabled, because I'm one for being a bit wary of people, because my wife had had it before me, and that put me more on the ball than what I was. I mean she said, "I met Mrs Kent down the street and she said there's nothing wrong with you, the way you walk round," sort of thing. But as I say, there's nothing to show for it. Well, my wife had one or two various rows. I thought I had friends till this last six or seven years. That's why I just want to keep myself to myself.

'Since I've been penalized by this disability, if that's the word to use, I've not looked for that money. I've been quite happy to take a reasonably local job for about eighteen or nineteen, where before I could get twenty-five to thirty. I'm glad to go to work. I wouldn't be frightened of saying I was working in a sheltered workshop, far from it. I'm glad of a job! Much as I'd like to be out there with a six-ton lorry under me. I'll be quite honest about this, nothing would give me greater pleasure than walking out of here to get under a Rover or underneath a quarter of beef. Fiddly work is out for me, I'll be quite honest with you. I find it much harder to do than another person sitting beside me. His hands might be more nimble than mine, but probably him getting under a quarter of beef would be much harder than for me. That's it, some people are more adaptable. I work as hard as I can, as fast as I can. Assembly work I do here; nobody chases you, you get on as best you can. It's not a question of I'm not keen. I find it, what shall I say, more of an obstacle, fiddly work, it's the smallness of it. But as I say, one has to accept it, and that's it.

'We've only just started work now. We had ten weeks sitting around playing draughts and cards. Oh, that was deadly. The first couple of weeks might have been all right, but after that you lose a little bit of heart. You think, "Where's it going to end?" like. Anyway, fortunately enough, a bit of work come in and that was all right. I was here the first ten weeks and then doing nothing for ten or eleven. Then I thought to myself, "Well, at least I'm going backwards and forwards to work, and meeting people," sort of thing, there's that to it, you know what I mean. But nothing else really to occupy your mind except cards and draughts, the day seemed sixteen hours instead of eight hours, so to speak. You ran out of talk, you ran out of games, there you are. There's one person who started here the same day as me, Mr Jameson, we teamed up quite well as regards working here. That's as far as it goes. I don't say, "Well, come over and see me some night." But as a work friend I find him quite a nice chap. I've felt much more contented in me mind, much more contented.'

UNSKILLED PACKER

'I was eight years out of work. I worked in the leather factory before. I was a sprayer, and I got this, rheumatic fever actually, but it spread to arthritis. I went sick of course, and I stayed there, oh, about eight years. It felt a bit, sort of, degrading, if you know what I mean. You go for a job. "Oh, no, we haven't got room for you," sort of thing, because you were either in a wheel-chair, or you was on crutches.

'I didn't think much about moving from Devon up to London. I was just glad to get a job actually. I wouldn't like to stop at home very much. There's nothing much to do at home. By the time you've pottered around and tidied the place up, you've had it ... You can't go out all the time, you know. I don't have to do much here. I do get bored with it, but then, there's other things going on around which break it up a bit. You do get bored. I suppose every job does get a bit boring after a time. Well, there's usually a bit of something to do, they've just hit a bad spell, that's all. I've had a couple of days when I've had nothing to do. Well, you can just sit down, read newspapers or something, as long as you're not making a nuisance of yourself, charging around interfering with other people that have got work to do, you can do virtually what you want, sort of thing. You see, if there's no work here you can't get the sack. They take a certain number of people to lie idle, put it that way, in case they've got work here and they need it pretty quick.

'There's really no satisfaction in the work, only that you're doing something. You're not a sort of cabbage, sort of thing. You are trying to earn your living. You're not living off somebody else's back. That's the only satisfaction you get.'

Part Four:
WHAT THE WORKLESS TELL US ABOUT
THE SOCIAL CONTRACT

11 Who Breaks the Social Contract between Society and the Worker?

As we saw in the introduction, in the public debate about
unemployment it was assumed that in various ways the workless
were failing in their duty to work. We have now heard a small,
selected group of the workless describing their experiences of
work, social security and unemployment, and our interviews
confirm that such accusations were faced by the workless in their
own self-doubts and in everyday relationships. In this part of
the book we ask, what sorts of answers can our small study
provide to the large questions which were raised in the public
debate: how did the workless themselves see the honouring of
the social contract between society and the worker?

Our interviews were selected on the basis that those who had
done different kinds of work and who had received different
levels of reward and support from employers and the State might
experience unemployment differently as a result. And we found
that the workless do indeed experience their situations differently:
what they say about work and social security is shaped by visions
of work as it might be or ought to be, and by personal judgements
of who was breaking the work contract.

THE SOCIAL CONTRACT OFFERED BY EMPLOYMENT TO THE
MORE-SKILLED WORKER

We infer that for the more-skilled living in the south-east, work
had been interesting, adequately paid and in good supply, so
that it could be largely taken for granted. Work was arranged in
a pattern of ascending career lines, with increasing seniority,
pay, autonomy and control over the work situation, and security
provided for those who had increasing skill and specialization.
Appointments and promotion were on individual merit. Jobs were
widely advertised and applicants for jobs must furnish credentials
and attend a personal interview. The more-skilled men's search
for work was individual, to be mastered through their own efforts
and diligence in searching through advertisements and sending
off applications. Expenses were paid for interviews, and removal
expenses and sometimes houses were offered to successful
applicants.

The ideology underpinning such a view of skilled work is that
the individual can make choices, work presents a structure of
opportunity to be scaled by his own efforts to maximize his skills
and talents, and individual worth will be rewarded. (Such an
ideology has strong affinities in the Protestant work ethic, which

was associated with the nineteenth-century capitalism from which we inherit, in an attenuated form, some of our notions of the value of individual effort.) The important elements are that the individual seeks his own salvation under the protection of employers in an industrial and social order which is unchangeable, well ordered and just. He is invited to be ambitious, trusting, optimistic, loyal and honest.

THE SOCIAL CONTRACT OFFERED BY EMPLOYMENT TO THE LESS-SKILLED WORKER

In contrast we infer that the work experiences of the less-skilled men living in the north-east had been that the work activity itself offered few intrinsic rewards, that only very hard or dangerous work was well-paid, and that the supply of work was irregular and contracts only short-term. Work could not be taken for granted.

Once the initial step of entering an apprenticeship had been missed, there was (at least in the area where they lived) little opportunity for promotion or pay increases with seniority, since there were no career lines to follow. The less skilled who had tried to move into more-skilled work felt that they had bumped up against barriers, of skill and educational credentials (some of which were imposed by the unions), of colour, age and physical disability. Some workers in less-skilled work had lost their jobs when they tried to innovate in an attempt to improve their jobs or working relationships.

Jobs were not widely advertised, especially in times of high unemployment. The less-skilled men's search for work was often collective, and getting work depended on personal visits to employers and on finding information from friends in work who would use personal influence with employers. No credentials other than strength were required. No interview expenses were paid, nor were there offers of removal expenses or housing in other areas. The only invitation extended to the less-skilled worker had been for him to leave his family and work away from home, living sometimes in a camp or isolated group of migrant workers, with no security or responsibility undertaken by the employer. In other words, the best offers they received were cash in exchange for strength with no commitment on either side.

So in their descriptions of their work experiences less-skilled individuals gave little indication that there had been any attempt to convey to them that there were opportunities of reward for their worth. There had been no invitation to them to consider work as a sphere where ambition, trust, loyalty and honesty had any place. The implication which they seemed to be invited to draw was that industry and society were not ordered in a just manner.

THE STATE'S HONOURING OF THE SOCIAL CONTRACT:
THE ROLE OF THE EMPLOYMENT EXCHANGES

When men are out of work one of the ways in which society may be seen as attempting to honour its side of the social contract is in providing job-finding services. Here again individuals with different skill levels had different experiences.

Out of work, the skilled workers who wanted to regain a job with comparable financial rewards or the same skill as their previous job had found that the State employment exchanges were of little help. The men had been offered occupational guidance on how to train for other skills, but were not pressed to retrain. Some had found that the possession of skills and the backing of credentials was a defence against occupational 'guidance' into other work or pressure to take work inferior to what they wanted. However, the more skilled had other sources of help in finding jobs. They were satisfied with the exchanges to the extent that they were left alone and could sign on without too great a chance of being identified in the queue, and thereby classed with others who they felt might not be looking hard enough for work (or who made them engage in self doubt). There was a suggestion that the atmosphere of the exchanges and the sense of stigma might differ from locality to locality, depending partly on the clientele who lived in that area.*

The drop-outs who had skills or credentials which they did not wish to use, and who were registered in occupational categories for which the exchanges had no jobs to offer, had discovered they were in a kind of administrative limbo. They would not be found jobs but for the moment there was no threat of withdrawal of support.

For the less-skilled workers the employment exchanges had been of little help in finding jobs which they wanted or were prepared to accept. The workless felt that in applying through the exchanges they had less chance because they lacked the personal influence they needed in times of job shortages. Moreover, these less-skilled individuals (and the more skilled who remained out of work longer) had felt that they were under pressure to take jobs they did not want. They complained that the jobs they had been sent for were inferior in pay or working conditions, or that too many men had been sent and the job had been taken.**

---

* The Department of Employment now has separate job-finding services which are intended to promote the mingling of the unemployed with the employed, and thus to reduce the stigma of job-finding. But the workless are still required to sign on at the exchanges, even though payment is increasingly made through Giro orders. (See Chapter 12.)

** From the official's point of view there might be good reasons for sending more than one man, since a number of the workless

In some instances a less-skilled man's current relationships with the state services could only be understood in terms of his long struggle to improve his job, thrusting up against the barrier of what he felt was the failure of officials to sympathize and their insensitivity to his demands for recognition of his hard won, if minor skills. As with the skilled, again the possession of skills was seen by the workless as a defence against official pressure to take inferior work, although union backing was necessary for the defence to be effective. However, other individuals less abrasive in character had found that such pressure could be circumvented by negotiating with the employer to get him to pronounce them 'unsuitable', or by behaving unsuitably in the job interview. The drop-outs did not need to behave unsuitably: it was clear to employers that they did not fit.

Teenagers' experiences of work and the Youth Employment Service were similar to those of the less skilled, but if anything the Service had shown them less evidence that they were valued as individuals.

THE STATE'S HONOURING OF THE SOCIAL CONTRACT
THROUGH INCOME MAINTENANCE

Even the more skilled had found that job protection and compensation offered privately was not large, and they were mainly dependent on income from State schemes. A combination of State *and* private redundancy arrangements and insurance benefits, *and* tax rebates, was adequate in the short run to meet the needs of skilled workers. The money had to cover a substantial domestic and financial stake in society, through a commitment to home building and an adherence to the life styles and consumption patterns of the estates where they lived.

However, the skilled came to realize that after a period of time State support would be reduced and even withdrawn. More pressure would be brought to take inferior jobs, regardless of whether or not the workless individual had been looking for work or whether suitable work was available. In the long run, partly through fears of the failure of State support, the skilled had all taken jobs which were inferior in some way to those they had had before. Their redundancy pay, which was based on their past work record rather than the real disturbance they suffered, was inadequate compensation for the loss of their previous jobs.

Out of work, the less skilled had found barriers to obtaining

---

might have claims on the job - the long-term unemployed man who needs a boost of morale, the new man who is still eager, the newly released prisoner who needs a job to keep him from turning to crime. But what is at issue here is how things look to the workless themselves.

State support. They had gained the impression that officials cut through the complexities surrounding their loss of work and presentation of their needs by refusing benefit unless and until their demands proved sufficiently persistent. In striking the balance between the deterrence of abuse and meeting need, it appeared to the workless that social security officials loaded the balance too far towards deterrence.

Further, while the less skilled were looking for work and drawing supplementary benefits, in various ways they were made aware that there was a ceiling against which they banged their heads when they tried to get more income. The restriction of wives' earnings was felt to make working not worthwhile, and trapped the wife as well as the husband in a 'double poverty trap'. Several of the workless were too proud to apply for extra grants, and among those who were prepared to apply there was much confusion about what could be provided, a confusion not helped by what appeared to be different judgements by different officials. There was no evidence of officials taking steps to seek out need, and indeed there was a suggestion that they were operating informal rules to cut down on grants for which the regulations made specific provision. Applicants could not decide whether it was best in applying for grants to let standards slip and appear needy or to keep up standards and risk being ignored or refused. They pieced together the workings of official discretion from a mixture of hearsay, gossip and rumour, and among those we saw there were feelings of discontent and jealousy; myth and half-truth were being encouraged.

The living standards and financial commitments of the less skilled could not be adequately maintained on supplementary benefits. Families slipped into debt, with a routine of court orders and growing dilapidation of their furnishings. For a proportion of the families there was real hardship, with a shortage of food, clothing and electricity. In one family this was probably due to the inflexibility of the father's demands for money for personal spending, but more common were instances where men did not eat properly because they were worried that their children might not be getting enough to eat. And in other ways it was feared that their children might not be benefiting from the current rises in general standards of living in the surrounding society. (In spite of their apparent budgeting difficulties some of these families had incomes which they did not declare of £5 to £10 above supplementary benefit rates in some weeks.)

Only drop-outs - who had little financial or domestic stake in society and who disapproved of conventional expenditures on supermarket food, neat clothing and consumer goods - expressed any satisfaction with the levels of supplementary benefits payments.

The conclusion we draw from what the workless said about the State's honouring of the social contract is that their experiences with social security to some extent mirrored those they had had with employers and work. The skilled had received more favourable treatment, while the less skilled had had more adverse encounters.

191

But for neither group was the state service adequate, and for both the experience could be devaluing and even degrading in its sense of powerlessness.

THE BEHAVIOUR OF THE WORKLESS IN HONOURING THE SOCIAL CONTRACT: WAGE REQUIREMENTS

We now turn to the behaviour of the workless in honouring their part in the social contract. We look first at the accusations that in their demands for work they were unrealistic and inflexible, particularly in respect of wage requirements.

When they looked for new work the workless, skilled and unskilled alike, were indeed inflexible; they tended to treat their previous best wage level as the basic requirement within which they looked for a job. They did not question the justice of the wages they had been receiving in the past, and the best wage was felt to be nearest their just reward. Initially at least, some of the workless seemed too proud to stage-manage their encounters with employers. They gave the impression that they felt they had compromised in work far enough, as if they were saying, 'I must be taken as I am.' The more skilled felt they needed the higher wages they had had in the past to the extent that they had financial commitments in home building which they had taken on while they were in work. They felt they 'deserved' their money, and even looked for an increase: several refused 'on principle' to take cuts in pay in their old or in new jobs. (We should, however, note at this point that other larger studies of redundancy seem to indicate a less intransigent stance by the average worker, in that workers do tend to say they will accept a cut in pay – although the exact form of what they say would depend on how the question is put and what are the alternatives offered.)

An even more powerful sense of the importance of cash from work comes from listening to the work histories of the less skilled for whom work could not easily be taken for granted. Some men were quite explicit about the way that 'grabbing' or 'grafting' in otherwise little rewarding work had brought the cash they needed for that particular stage of home building or for travel and sex. Through their need for cash to pursue other interests even overt nonconformists had to some extent become keyed into work and society. Less-skilled workers also tended to say they needed their higher pay to cover their commitments (to pull them out of debts they had incurred partly through living on supplementary benefits), and that they deserved their money for the hard and sometimes dangerous work they did: the rigours of such work could only be compensated by substantial 'pocket money' for their personal spending.

One very important consequence of the less-skilled man's desire to earn a high wage could be that the only option open to him was to take a job in contract work where there was no employer responsibility and indeed where there were no union rules to

prevent a worker from exploiting his own strength. There was
some sort of option to get higher pay, but only at the expense
of security and decent working conditions and responsible employer
relationships.

We conclude that clearly money had taken on for the workless a
deep personal and even 'political' significance. They seem to have
learned that men are valued in our society by the money they
receive in wages. The workless wanted not just money-to-pursue-
another-interest, but money-from-work as a measure of their
worth and a reward for their commitment.

Only the drop-outs - who had no fixed conventional 'needs' -
were not very explicit about their starting wage requirements.

SKILL REQUIREMENTS

The inflexibility of the wage requirements of the workless imposed
an inflexibility on the kinds of skills they could look for in their
new jobs, because of the way jobs are organized into hierarchies
of skill levels. The more skilled gave the appearance of wanting
to be flexible, and they did not wax very enthusiastic about the
occupational skills they had practised in their last jobs. Yet the
more specialized they had become, the less chance they saw of
doing a different job for the same money. Indeed a skilled worker
who had been willing to move and switch his job could find that
he was less well established in work and was the first to go when
the recession arrived.

There were also several skilled men who, by reasons of disability
or official disqualification, found the return to work in their old
skill difficult and who seemed to cling to their occupational skill
the more on that account. (We wondered whether the other skilled
workers would have been quite so casual about the value of their
skills, had there been any real chance that they must change.)
We suggest later, however, that the attachment of these workers
to their skills was not entirely to be explained by the insecurity
of their position.

Some of the less-skilled workers also were inflexible in their
skill requirements. They were inclined to stress relatively minor
skills: for even jobs classed as unskilled labouring might call for
the exercise of a surprising number of skills which made for
variety, and men officially classified as unskilled might possess
a whole range of small skills. These men hoped that such skills
might provide a ladder - albeit a short and crowded one - enabling
them to climb out of the ruck of labourers who were now scrambling
for jobs. Further, we have already noted how the skilled and
unskilled learned at the employment exchange that skills might be
a defence against pressures to take work with lower pay.

In short, in various ways the workless had learned that flexibility
in occupational skills could mean a loss of income and diminished
security.

REALISM OF JOB CHOICES AND FURTHER CONSTRAINTS ON CHOICE

Were the workless being unrealistic in the jobs they wanted? In fact they looked at first for the sorts of work they had already done in the past. And the less skilled could continue to hope for such better jobs partly because of the lack of any sort of information from employers or employment exchanges about what sorts of jobs were or were not available.

Indeed, the workless individuals' first choices of work were conservative compared with the work they would really have liked to do, as was revealed after a time by the emergence of their ideal job choices. Significantly, a fairly common ideal at the back of their minds was self-employment, for the freedom to earn and autonomy it could bring; and another ideal was improvement through increased qualifications or skills. But those among the workless who did try to make and attain more adventurous choices of occupation found that in various ways they were again defeated by barriers of credentials, skills, colour, physique or age.

We suggest that there were probably also barriers to the possibility of a change of job through self-employment which stemmed from the limit set by the regular economy upon the type and amount of work available. The regular economy already occupied most of the areas where activities might be profitable, and any workless individual who wished to become self-employed must carve out for himself a fresh crack - this at a time when there was a slump in business. Mr Weston was an interesting object lesson in such difficulties. He had been bankrupted once before, by a wholesaler who resented fresh competition. He was then unlucky in losing his office to another employer, and his attempts to make money from his pictures brought him below the level of income where he could live independently. Before this last attempt foundered he was already beginning to meet competition from imitators of his line of picture making.

WILLINGNESS TO MOVE

Willingness to move appears to be sometimes taken as an indication that a workless person is more interested in fulfilling his obligations to work, even at some inconvenience to himself. However, our interviews suggest that factors other than a sense of duty are involved.

None of the workless wanted to move at first; the wives were more reluctant than the husbands and laid more stress on the importance of ties with relatives. But the more-skilled men felt that they could move after work again because they received offers which would enable them to move (although they had some difficulties because of an unusual arrangement of tied house purchase).

Further than this, the fact that they had been willing and able to move in the past seemd to mean that the more skilled, more mobile workers had fewer ties and loyalties in the surrounding neighbourhood. Links with relatives were either more attenuated or more flexible so that they could be maintained at a distance, and the families had cars and phones.* Also, partly as a result of the moves but perhaps as a cause too, their marriages were closer and more cohesive so that the couples and their children were more easily able to move again as one compact unit.

In contrast the less skilled, who said they had never been given the chance of moving except as travelling men, had developed and retained stronger local ties: roots. In their friendships were embedded both the information about possible jobs and the influence for obtaining new work. Partly in response to the hardships and uncertainties of work and the help which friends could offer in the face of such hardships, the men had tended to band together. The wives, too, led lives more in company with others - but apart from their husbands. The marriages of the less skilled probably became, and remained, less close.

So these families were less cohesive when it came to a question of moving. Moreover the further strains imposed by unemployment sometimes threatened to break up the marriages altogether. Couples complained they quarrelled more because they were short of money. Their marriages were perhaps less geared to avoiding and containing conflict because the couples had never been used to spending much leisure time together. Although they developed routines for avoiding one another there were still outbreaks of violence and signs of incipient marriage breakdown. The longer this conflict continued, the less possibility there would be of the family moving as a unit, although the man might become more willing to leave his family and work away.

We conclude that willingness to move is not simply an indication of an individual's sense of duty, but may be heavily dependent upon the economy's valuation of his worth and upon the way this valuation has become built into the whole fabric of his relationships, even into his marriage.

---

* Although we believe our emphasis is correct, perhaps we should be careful not to exaggerate the difference found in our study between the skilled and the less skilled. The skilled sometimes had relatives nearby, and in one instance a number of members of the same family had moved to the same new area, helping one another with information about work and housing. Conversely, in the north-east there had been some disruption through rehousing, although moves had been short or families had moved together to the new area.

THE EFFECT OF INSURANCE BENEFITS UPON WILLINGNESS TO WORK

As we have seen, the combination of private and State social security was adequate in the short run to meet the needs of the skilled, insured men. And although these men had found work not unrewarding in itself, when they came to look for new jobs they were unenthusiastic about the skills they had practised. While the cash lasted out, they tended to stick to their demands for high pay, and several engaged in activities which they said were more satisfying than the work they had been doing. Their relationships at home had been close and companionable. Does all this confirm the suspicion that the level of insurance benefits was keeping unemployment high by reducing incentives to work?

We believe not, for out of work the skilled men showed in various ways that they were still subjected to pressures and internal drives to find work. Marriage relationships proved in the situation of unemployment not to be very flexible or capable of sustaining very much more companionship. In the past, closer companionship had not meant that tasks in the household were more shared; instead, the husbands had been used to expressing an emotional investment in the home through the handyman activities which they carried out there. And with the onset of unemployment husbands and wives retained and even intensified their conceptions of what was man's work and what was woman's work. The housewives still tended to do the housework, even embracing their household chores and manufacturing extra ones to replace those done by the husband. As a result there was little for the man to do at home.

The husbands in closer marriages tended to protect their wives from worry, and said they felt a sense of pressure in the home which was only relieved at weekends when they would normally have been at home.

Some of the tensions in the home might be temporarily relieved because the wives of men receiving insurance benefit could go out to work. But the husbands of working wives showed a sense of being devalued. Even where men had a sustaining ideology or sense of purpose, housework and life at home with the children could prove tedious and dispiriting. Men were likely to feel isolated, and to become more aware of how they had valued the companionship at work of people whom they scarcely knew or even did not like. They now realized the value of sheer routine in work.

These men appeared to be pushed into doing masculine or otherwise self-justificatory activities about the home. And it was our impression that although several people claimed to be satisfied with these alternative activities there was quite a lot of hubris and insecurity in their claims. The activities tended to have begun or intensified only when the search for a regular job had failed. They were justified as 'working hard'. Sometimes they involved the skill, and in one instance even recreated the whole routine, of work although they could not recapture the relationships of work. And as time went on they came under stronger challenge and were to varying extents abandoned in favour of looking harder for regular work. In the most striking instance a very absorbing and time-consuming activity was more or less abandoned, and was not restarted after work had been regained.

The skilled men showed evidence of the pressure to work in their changes of morale. They had begun unemployment with a feeling of holiday and unreality, although they nevertheless still looked for work. But they did not worry immediately if none was forthcoming, and the initial failure of the search led to more energy being put into the alternative 'work' activity. But after a while anxiety began to build up, the more so as the insurance and redundancy money threatened to run out. The men experienced physiological symptoms of stress, such as difficulties with sleeping, feeling 'lazy' and tired, and loss of appetite or indigestion. They became more worried and depressed, and efforts to find work, which had fallen off a little after the first rebuffs, were increased again and became more desperate.

Continued failure to find work led to a slipping of the skilled men's requirements for a job in every respect. They came to consider work in other localities at the same money, self-employment, less-skilled work, temporary jobs with a view to continuing the search for work, and eventually building work and 'fiddling'. All these changes were accompanied by a severe loss of morale. It was as though when they became 'flexible' their best hopes had been defeated.

We conclude that although insurance benefits were partly successful in their aim of giving men more time to look round and find work which suited them, there was no evidence that benefit levels were so high that they reduced the incentive to find work, or indeed that they were very important in relation to other drives. Insured men continued to look for work while they were unemployed, and had they been able to find jobs they would have gone back to work much sooner than they did.

THE ABUSE OF SOCIAL SECURITY: FIDDLING

We did find that some of the workless were working at small part-time jobs for earnings which were above the permitted limit but which they did not declare to the authorities. Fiddling creates some dilemmas for critics of the social security system, who tend to stress the small scale of detected abuse. A study such as ours can give no firm indication of the extent of earning by those drawing social security benefits, for, like the recent official studies, we dealt with only a selected group. However, what the workless told us leads us to question whether their working should always be regarded as an abuse of the system. (What we say now does not refer to men who work full-time, of whom we found none in our study.)

197

The less-skilled men who fiddled by earning money in part-time irregular jobs said they did so in response to a number of changes in their lives. The official allowance kept them short of money, so that their families suffered financial hardship. There were strains in their marriages and pressures from their wives to work and earn. Skilled, insured men said that as they approached the end of their insurance benefits they had become prepared to fiddle. The workless who actually were fiddling were drawing supplementary benefits: for several, crime was a real and threatening alternative way of meeting their needs.

The less skilled said they had only become prepared to fiddle in response to·rebuffs from employers. And they tended to start fiddling when they received invitations from friends who were fiddling; also from neighbours for whom it was convenient to have a supply of cheap labour, and from small employers struggling to start businesses.

From what men said, fiddling filled a number of needs. It brought them once again the sense of control over their lives which some of them had clearly valued in work. It brought money that was their own and not the State's or their wives'. It brought freedom to spend once again, because the extra money from fiddling insulated the men's drinking and social needs from the family budget.

Both in the work and the freedom to spend, fiddling brought male companionship. Workless men's drinking is seen as a form of abuse - paradoxically drinking is regarded by the public as indicating at one and the same time that benefits are too high and that men are leaving their families short of money. But on the evidence of our study, less-skilled workless men went out drinking partly because of pressures in the home. Out of work they were strongly drawn to the masculine world of the street corner, the club and the pub. And also they needed to maintain social relations with the work group to keep in the running for jobs.

LIMITS ON THE SCALE OF FIDDLING

Although we can say nothing about the prevalence of fiddling, our study did tell us something about the sorts of controls both formal and informal which exist to limit the scale of fiddling. The perceptions of the fiddlers that official surveillance was low may reflect the situation of over 10 per cent unemployment in the area, where it hardly made sense to mount a massive campaign of detection with a view to reducing any supposed disincentive effect of fiddling on men's will to seek work. In fact from what the workless said, fiddling was closely policed informally by local public opinion and by anonymous letters from neighbours if a fiddler was thought to be getting more than his fair share of additional income.

As with attempts to become self-employed, there were probably limits to fiddling imposed by the availability of work. Because the fiddlers were working in the cracks of the regular economy there was only a limited amount of extra work to be done. The more of the workless who fiddled, the smaller their individual rewards would become. This was especially the case with high unemployment, when there were more men to fiddle but comradeship demanded that the work should be shared out and that no one should be too greedy. (On some estates where there are full-time window cleaners depending on their earnings for a living, they have to be prepared to physically fight to keep their rounds free from encroachments which would dismember and diffuse their jobs in a larger number of small unviable bits.) So it might be suggested that, paradoxically, in times of high unemployment the less vigilant the authorities, the more tightly will market forces operate to keep down fiddlers' gains from irregular work. (This of course does not apply to employers who are prepared to offer men full-time work without checking on their cards, and the Department of Employment attempts to close loopholes by dissuading small employers from employing men without cards, although the advantage to the employer of hiring such workers is large.)

FIDDLING AND THE INCENTIVE TO WORK

Although supplementary benefits were insufficient to meet the needs of these families, there were public fears that with additional earnings from fiddling the workless might find the incentive to work much reduced. Indeed, as we saw, some of the workless themselves were inclined to overlook (or were unaware of) the barriers to self-employment and to forget the lack of work, when they said they felt that fiddling reduced their will to work and made them lazy. And what happens if the work they could expect to do was not very rewarding in itself?

The evidence of the persistence of a will to work in spite of earning from fiddling runs somewhat along the lines of our previous discussion of the skilled workers. Although in talking about work the less skilled had laid such an emphasis on cash, there were various indications that even quite arduous work had offered them other satisfactions or fulfilled other needs. A stress on physical effort was among the hints in the work histories of how much these men had valued the masculinity of the work they had done; another was their desire for outside work and their objections to going into one of the indoor factory jobs in the area (in what were locally disparagingly referred to as 'knicker elastic' industries). Now, viewed from the unstructured life of unemployment, men found that there were attractions in work: they missed the division of activity from leisure, the achievement of autonomy within a structured framework and the control of the pace and timing of work and its rewards by the exercise of sheer physical strength.

Initially the less skilled had taken the loss of work more

philosophically than the skilled. Their efforts to find work also went through cycles of activity and inactivity, but with less confidence and enthusiasm, though some desperation. They, too, lowered their sights. They became prepared to take work which was even less skilled and more arduous, to travel away, to accept lower-paid but steadier work. Eventually they said they had become prepared after long spells of unemployment to accept 'anything', although evidently they still needed enough money to live.

It seemed that fiddling did not reduce, and indeed through fears of detection might increase, all the informal and internal pressures upon a man to find work. Worries about 'laziness' proved to be evidence of a continuing desire to find work. Paradoxically, even complaints about the authorities' lack of vigilance could be evidence of worries about becoming too dependent on part-time work: the man who most feared that he was becoming a layabout through fiddling subsequently went back to full-time work. In these areas a 'layabout' seemed to be a man who was thought to be too lazy even to fiddle and get money for his home and family. Fiddling kept alive an individual's self-respect in the face of evidence that employers did not want him. Fiddling was a protection against the charge that he was 'doing nothing'. We conclude that for some of the workless in a very real sense fiddling was work.

CHANGES IN ATTITUDES TOWARDS WORK AND THE SOCIAL CONTRACT: SOME INDIVIDUAL SUMMARIES

Finally in this chapter we ask did the willingness of the workless to work reflect the social contract they had been offered; and how far were their attitudes towards working an expression of a degree of integration with and commitment to the wider society? We have already been exploring these questions as they relate to questions in the public debate. We now want to focus more sharply on what might be termed in the widest sense the 'political' orientations of workless individuals.

We recall that earlier in this chapter we had to say that we 'inferred' what learning experiences the workless had been 'offered'. This was because when individuals themselves described their experiences they did so from a number of different perspectives, which showed that they had approached and learned from those experiences in very different ways. Certainly individuals had not always taken up the perspectives of society and the ideologies which we suggested that (in our opinion from the comparison of a number of separate instances) their experiences had 'invited' them to adopt. We can best illustrate what we mean by giving here some summaries of how differently individuals and groups had learned. Each of these summaries may represent aspects of the experiences of very much larger numbers of the workless.

The technicians had begun by trusting their employers and

moving after work, and by making a financial and emotional investment in society in home building and in their adherence to the life style of the estates where they lived. These skilled workers had seen the breaking of their work contracts as a breach of trust by their employers *and* the government. The protective and paternal relationship they used to enjoy with the firm crumbled after a take-over by an American head and in the face of increased foreign competition. In work the technicians moved away from their faith in the company and towards collective combative action. They formed a union and the atmosphere turned to one of conflict and recrimination. Out of work they became less optimistic and they postponed cherished plans. They became more chary of moving, and when they found that their specialization meant that they might have to move they spoke of their skills as if these had been a sort of duck decoy, lulling them into a sense of security which was false, and narrowing their freedom of choice. They thought of self-employment and emigration to escape from what they now felt were the restrictions of working in industry in England. And although at first the activities they carried out at home still expressed some kind of individual trust in work, as time went on they became demoralized and were eventually prepared to behave in a way they had previously thought dishonest, by fiddling. The return to work was a renewal of personal confidence and faith that the system would reward their merits. But Mr Vickers, for example, felt he had been forced to sell himself too cheaply. In his relationships with his new employers and work-mates he showed some insecurity, prickliness and resentment, along with a new impatience, ambition and status-consciousness.

As we look closely at other skilled workers the pattern grows more complicated. In work Mr Weston had been a trusting employee who had slowly learned to be ambitious. But he had also been something of an innovator, apt to criticize employers and to clash with them on that account. He gave qualified support to union activity as a goad to employers, but he was also a 'rate buster' who was criticized by his workmates for working harder than they felt the employers deserved. For him, too, redundancy had come as a disillusioning breach of contract between a conscientious worker and what he had previously taken to be responsible management (again the take-over followed the introduction of American economic values into a paternal British firm). However, Mr Weston also held the unions partly responsible for the loss of his work. Redundancy, in fact, crystallized the frustrations of his working life, and he came to feel that in work there was 'nowhere for him to go': he must try to become self-employed. There was still another twist to his story. Out of work, as in, he remained independent and an innovator, so he fell foul of the employment exchange through his refusal to compromise. In his attempts to become self-employed he came up against barriers, and his return to employment was, he said, a kind of 'defeat' for his ambitions. Yet there was little sign of any really deep disturbance of his will to work hard, or of any growth of cynicism.

Mr Weston seemed to live somehow within himself, independent of other's opinions and esteem.

Another fairly skilled worker, Mr Odell, had come from a monastic tradition of meekness, self-effacement, and work for the service and salvation of others. The impact of factory piecework with what he saw as its selfish and materialistic individualism had been distasteful. He had slowly derived political lessons from his work experiences, latterly helped by trade unions and claimants' union friends. His initially religious philosophy became transformed into a full political ideology: the one fitted the other like a glove. His energies became directed towards improving work for everyone and thus improving society. Getting the sack had been an almost depersonalized incident in what Mr Odell saw as the general conflict between workers and an industrial system which spoiled life. He became categorized by the employment exchange as 'unsuitable' for the very job on which he had set his heart, but this did not make him bitter or stop him looking for such a job. He transferred his energies to a claimants' union but found their activities peripheral to the political struggle to improve work for everyone. He found himself a new job, but it offered no outlet for his political energies nor any kind of trusting relationship, and he left it to work again with the claimants. He seemed to be slowly growing more marginal in work and more committed to collective action outside work. Incidentally, when Mr Odell described the sense of power and achievement which he gained from driving large vehicles fast and expressed his antagonism towards the passengers, work seemed to hold an extra and quite unusual charge. We could not help wondering about the way those biographies of power politicians on his bookshelf hinted at qualities in his nature which were expressed in his driving but which were taboo in his personal relationships and political ideology.

Another fairly skilled worker, Mr John, the West Indian, also came from a strongly religious background, but a different Christian tradition. In him we thought we saw the clearest example of the trustful, individually ambitious worker whom we have described earlier. Coming from a primitive-Christian background in a society in an early stage of industrialization, Mr John had seen British industry as an opportunity structure to be scaled by individual ability and effort. His urge to work had been as if towards a personal individual salvation, ambitious, stern, Calvinistic. Work seemed to hold for him the key to a wider degree of acceptance. This was obvious from his descriptions of the delights of arc-welding, his eagerness to be accepted as a skilled man and paid at the proper (white) rates, and from his ingenuous delight in his successful performance in the trade test. Prior to his accident his lack of formal credentials, his colour, his eagerness to rise, and his sensitivity to perceived slights from his superiors, had led to frequent changes of job. His accident and subsequent unemployment and possibly permanent disability came as a very unwelcome interruption to his long, lone strategy for self-improvement and personal advance. Yet, perhaps significantly, although he himself laid little stress on the fact, Mr John remained a member of the local Conservative club. The lessons he had drawn from the way the work contract had failed to offer him individual opportunity seemed primarily religious. Although he had lost his faith in the divine order he still clung to his original goal of acceptance as a skilled, white worker. He had become gloomy, less optimistic, less certain of achieving his ambitions, more mistrustful of employers and his destiny. Yet as we left him he was preparing to renew his faith in a fresh employer who would pay him what he considered a good rate. There seemed no possibility that Mr John could see collective action as a solution towards his problems in work.

The other West Indian whom we saw, Mr Spain, had also suffered adverse experiences and received little recognition in work. He came from a less strongly religious background and was less ambitious, so that he seemed more accepting of his setbacks. Nonetheless he too preserved a strong desire to work, even in a mundane job.

In sharp contrast in the political lessons he drew from work was Mr McBain who came from the north-east. It is perhaps tempting to speculate on the possible links between Mr McBain's childhood (which sounds to have been harsh and authoritarian, dominated by a father who himself worked in a harsh and authoritarian setting) and Mr McBain's abrasive confrontations with his employers and officials. Yet to concentrate on personality factors would be to discount the rigours of his working life, which exemplifies the way the social costs of unemployment fall heavily on a minority of individuals. The very early part of Mr McBain's working life clearly shows the impulse to work hard at unrewarding jobs, and the sense of personal failure and guilt which his first experiences of unemployment had brought. Like other men in the north-east Mr McBain still talked about the idea of the 'good worker' who, like his father, worked until he dropped. But Mr McBain was convinced by the time we saw him that his earlier attitudes had been blinkered and that the industrial order had given him 'no chance'. The social security system he saw as just an extension of that order. He had gained a political education through his own experiences of work, but also from the example of his oldest brother. From being a chargehand and potential foreman he had become a strike leader. Yet again, as with Mr Weston, there had been a further disillusioning turn to the story. Both in collective action in industry and when he tried self-employment, he had found that workmates were not to be relied upon. Through his experiences he had lost his faith not only in the industrial order but in religion too. He felt he had become 'twisted' (getting his semi-skilled job at last only through dishonesty) and more uncouth, with lower personal standards of morality and behaviour. He claimed further that the identity of the whole area where he lived had similarly been permanently spoiled by the nature of the working relationships and unemployment there. He now seemed like an animal retiring warily and truculently to lick his wounds after an unsuccessful fight. Yet he still felt he needed work, a job so that he could hold his head up.

Other less-skilled workers in the north-east tended to share Mr McBain's view of what was happening to the whole area. Yet individually they did not all show the same evidence of political learning or a deep change of identity, for their experiences of unemployment had not been as harsh and prolonged. Mr Lucas seemed most like Mr McBain in his experience and situation, but he was inclined to interpret his situation less politically and more superstitiously as relating to the tragedy of his wife's death. Mr Paton remained bouncy, although like Mr McBain and Mr Weston he felt caught in a situation where he could not adequately exploit his energies. He worried about the restrictions on *self*-exploitation which were imposed by his lack of skills and the union rules designed to protect workers from exploitation by employers; and he thought wistfully of self-employment, for which however he felt he lacked the necessary individual drive and application. Mr Miller remained optimistic, trusting in his 'luck' to turn, retaining a kind of belief in a superior providence. Mr Nottingly seemed cowed. Mr Ryan seemed untroubled and was unconvincing when he spoke of his continued willingness to work.

We recall here that among the less-skilled men two of their reactions to unemployment had been the collectively 'dishonest' act of fiddling and the individually 'innovatory' method of getting rewards - theft. Both expressed a lack of faith that the existing system would adequately recognize their worth.

Like the first experiences of these older workers, the entry of the teenagers into work had hardly been calculated to arouse their enthusiasm or to enlist their trust in any notion of work as a responsible relationship or a sphere for ambition. Leaving school without skills they seem to have met employers who offered wages only a little better than the dole and who would sack a boy when he reached the age for a wage rise. Out of work they had been isolated in the day, alone in their homes often with only electronic equipment for company. Their treatment by the Youth Employment Service had been depressing (and seemed less excusable than the accounts we heard of the employment exchanges, in the way these teenagers were sent in droves for jobs they had little chance of getting). Now the State was making some effort to show more responsibility through the scheme for providing work in community service, but the work itself offered rather meagre intrinsic satisfactions and no permanent security or training in skills. Indeed, significantly, the 'work' was not unlike the fiddling of the older workers, small jobs in the cracks of the economy, performed for those with little money and low status. We can only speculate about what had been the effect of their experiences. But already we thought we could see the development of attitudes similar to those among the older men, and perhaps our answer lies in the teenagers' laconic watchfulness and guarded replies on the subject of work.

In marked contrast the chronically sick Mr Coxon stood out as someone with an overwhelming eagerness to work, whose personal need to work seemed on a plane far removed from any kind of wider political commitment. He had survived a succession of jobs where, by the accounts given by both himself and his wife, his willingness to work had been nakedly exploited (we did not print these at length). Over the last ten years he had been kept in poverty by the State. Yet his will to work remained undiminished. We get a sense that work had been the major theatre of his life, as we listen to him describing the triumphs of learning to drive forty years ago, his skill in outwitting the ingenuity of the tester, his stress on being 'well liked'. Work had given him a role, an audience, friendships, a place in a hierarchy, the approval of superiors. Mr Coxon's insecurity and eagerness to be accepted in work seemed to stretch back to his childhood, to his own father's unemployment, and to the material deprivation which may have left him permanently physically weak and without the basic skill of reading. Yet there was more to his eagerness to be well liked. We can only speculate on the way Mr Coxon's attachment to his job and his eagerness for the acceptance and approval he won there contrasted so sharply with a childhood which had been emotionally miserly as well as materially bleak. Had work given him in adult life what his childhood lacked?

Mr Calvert and Miss Hebb had permitted themselves to be carried along by the pull of the educational stream from grammar school to university. But their tentative trust and expectations had been rudely destroyed by adverse experiences of professional training and the working relationships in the careers into which they realized too late they had been swept. Mr Calvert's response had been to intensify his avocation for writing and to seek outside work an individually creative solution to his problems of finding an identity. At the same time teaching in a College of Technology still seemed to him to offer a way of using his training while regaining some kind of contact with the ordinary working class from whom he felt cut off and whom, to some extent, he now sentimentalized. But this was now the only opening he could see into work, and it was by no means certain that the right job would be available.

Miss Hebb now lacked trust and optimism, and she felt she was lacking in ambition (although as long as she felt like this she must retain some vestiges of ambition). She could not quite reconcile herself to working for so little pay on community projects such as the children's playground or to working collectively through claimants' union action. She still thought of a little business, and was not happy to live by exploiting the social security system and doing only irregular work.

Mr Dover, like Miss Hebb, had found difficulty in forming any commitment in work, and both were now inclined to feel that this represented a failure of upbringing (although this connection is a suspiciously glib and popular one). Mr Dover felt he was changing over the years. The young Mr Dover watching the West Indians working hard in the mornings and then idling away the afternoons had been shocked and reproving in a way that the older Mr Dover, looking back, now found naive and amusing. While he had been strong and fit he avoided responsibilities in his working life and in marriage. Indeed his work history affords the clearest example of how heavy manual work, with its irregularity and lack of responsibility on either side, may permit a Thoreau-like freedom of life style and freedom of work which is not open to those who commit themselves to a full work career. Mr Dover's life had been neatly balanced between work and an alternative society. But since his disabling accident he had a growing realization of how precariously his freedom to escape into the alternative society had depended upon his health and the availability of casual work. Almost against his will he was developing needs, a love of creature comforts which the alternative society did not provide. He was also developing a desire to live more 'responsibly', to do a more socially useful job. However, unfortunately he was finding the route to such a new commitment was barred by the problem of getting educational and professional credentials. He was now prepared to live what he felt was a parasitic existence, exploiting the social security system and performing small inadequately paid but useful jobs. But he was nevertheless finding it difficult to retain a sense of identity without some larger role in society.

Finally we come to the disabled workers who were being provided with work, some of it subsidized, in the sheltered workshop. The situation they described was like a microcosm of some of the problems of work and work policy which Britain's ageing economy is currently suffering under increased competition from foreign markets. For example, shortage of work meant that jealousies arose over the sharing out of what was available, and there were fears that only the more-skilled and capable workers might be retained if the recession worsened. Although the situation in the factory embodied a partial assumption by the State of responsibility for the disabled workless, the difficulties of finding enough work in the face of competition from outside the factory meant that some of the disabled were under-employed at work below their capabilities and they might even be unemployed for short spells *within* the factory. Sheltered work did not entirely solve the problems of adjustment to disability: the disabled were still ambivalent about whether they would be capable enough and prepared to work in outside industry; and their attitudes towards the management were not uncritical (indeed it was part of the policy of the workshop to retain the machinery of bargaining and keep an atmosphere as like outside industry as possible). It would be an exaggeration to say that the disabled were uninterested in how much money they received from their work. Nevertheless, the keynote of the interviews was that the disabled were grateful for their work. They were pleased even to come into an environment where they might do boring work or not work at all. The factory gave them status, companionship, a stake in society, and even marriage.

Ultimately when work was stripped of all its other satisfactions, working offered the fulfilment of a sense of duty to society.

THE SOCIAL CONTRACT IN WORK AND THE INTEGRATION OF THE INDIVIDUAL INTO SOCIETY

In asking what lessons the workless had learned about the social contract we have pushed our study to the limits of what the interviews can tell us. The present stances of individuals in relation to work in society do not form a clear and coherent pattern – certainly not as clear as the kinds of experiences which we earlier suggested they had been offered. The personalities of the workless, their upbringing, education and friendships, may all have influenced what they learned. We have hinted at how we sometimes encountered in our interviews emotional links between work and other areas of life deeper than we could probe. Nevertheless there are some important overall trends which may be picked out, which indicate how individual experiences may be relevant for much larger groups in society.

The workless were seeking an activity which they would consider valuable and satisfying and which would also bring them adequate rewards and recognition of their worth, a recognition which our society usually expresses in money but not always. The workless might see the possibility of finding such an activity within the range of jobs offered in the conventional economy, or they might not; they might trust employers to recognize their worth or they might not; if they did not trust employers they might seek a solution in self-employment or in collective bargaining and conflict; they might make overt connections between the industrial, political and religious orders, or they might not; if they made such connections they might see possibilities for change or they might not; and pessimism about the possibilities of change might lead to intransigence, to retreat into alternative activities including crime, or to frustration, detachment or apathy.

The overall trend is that the skilled and more secure remained less deeply affected by their shorter, less arduous experiences of unemployment. The hardships of irregular work and the weight of unemployment fell disproportionately on the less skilled, those who lived in the north-east, and the chronically sick and disabled: it was they who seemed more likely to experience permanent and profound changes of outlook and identity. But in addition the more highly educated – who had had their expectations of work aroused to a higher pitch and then been disappointed before they had developed any very strong financial stake in society – might also suffer quite severe shocks leading to disenchantment and a loss of confidence in the system and themselves.

What remains striking, however, is the persistence of the will to work, to find some kind of socially useful activity. Some of the workless seem to have been more ready to learn adverse lessons from work, and they were helped to do so by their upbringing,

their relatives, and by trade and claimants' unionist friends.
Yet others brought to work aspirations, ambitions, and a desire
for acceptance which remained unshaken and unquenched by the
most adverse experiences: they drew no conclusions about the
unfairness of work and the social order. And, indeed, whether
or not individuals drew political lessons about society from their
experiences, they were likely to retain important ideals of what
work could and should be like.

Of course we have to remember that this was an interview
situation where individuals wished to appear at their best. And
our interviews were largely reconstructions of people's lives
where some of the coherence comes from the way individuals were
trying to make sense of the past, a process which involves selection
and distortion. Nevertheless we were impressed by the way that
these work careers appeared sometimes to have been long-term
strategies to find work nearer to an ideal or to change unsatis-
factory jobs. The more perceptive accounts reveal workers looking
for particular kinds of work satisfactions along with their wages,
compromising by taking more or less satisfactory jobs, trying to
mould to the work, yet at the same time aware of being adversely
moulded by it themselves. In different situations relationships
with employers and workmates blossomed or withered, as they
came nearer or strayed further from the ideal.

One apparently basic tension which some individuals were unable
to resolve was between their own individual desire to work hard
and the restrictions which they felt were imposed on their efforts,
by the nature of the work, by employers and by the collective
action of their workmates. Work for such men became a sort of
double-bind situation. They lost their jobs because they were too
committed to an ideal of what work should be like, and they might
remain unemployed longer for that same reason. We might perhaps
expect to find among the workless a higher proportion of these
individuals who are more idealistic, less prepared to compromise,
and therefore more marginal to work.

A continuing emotional investment in such an ideal of work is
a major reason why it is not easy to say how any individual will
react to the loss of work simply by looking at the arduousness,
tediousness or irresponsibility of the work just left or lost. We
must also take account of what that individual hopes to attain
and believes to be possible in work.

However, the persistence of an ideal of work and a continued
wish to find work did not mean that all these individuals defined
'work' in the same way. Although the workless still needed and
wanted work, it was not always the kind of work the economy
affords, not the social relationship between employers and workmates which now exists, and not work in the current political
condition of society.

THE NEED FOR WORK

In this book we set out to look for evidence which would illuminate the public debate about the unemployed. Much about the security of work - the adequacy of working conditions, and responsibility in working relationships between employers, the State and the worker; what we have called the social contract in work - tends to be obscured or 'taken for granted' in everyday life. The effect of the peak of unemployment in 1971/2 was momentarily to shake our complacency. And in this study we have tried to convey ourselves and the reader through the mental curtain which separates work from unemployment. The interviews were intended to reveal how people like ourselves feel when they are workless, and what happens when people like ourselves react to different inferior work situations and to unemployment, some of them trying to make choices and to break out of the constraints of their situations, others acquiescing in their fate.

Work as it exists today embodies a greater or lesser degree of service and responsibility for different individuals. But there is a pattern to these experiences. For the less skilled, those who live in remoter regions, women, the elderly, sick or disabled workers, and the young, work and social security offer a much less responsible and fulfilling relationship with society and may express disparaging assessments of their worth as human beings. Whatever the overall level of unemployment, high or low, its burden falls more heavily upon these groups. And they are not adequately compensated for the social costs of their unemployment.

Our interviews suggest to us that, contrary to the crudely economic view, the individuals we saw had little choice over their work careers. The overriding impression is of the workers' powerlessness both in and out of work. And here we note an ambiguity in the public debate. Public criticism of the workless implies that they have a duty to be 'realistic' and accept the jobs and wages offered by the economy, yet the jobs offered were often poor and below the capacities of the workless. We are apt to think that people who accept too readily the constraints of their situation are unambitious, unadventurous and lacking in pride: realism is by another name defeatism.

The workless individuals whom we saw were at first refusing to accept personal devaluation, and were trying to choose against the limits of their situation. But their perceived choices were reduced the more they accepted the values of present-day society. Those who tried to make choices all met with barriers. For some with few skills there was even very little choice over whether or not to take up work which was adequately paid *and* covered by insurance. Even the drop-outs hardly felt free. Thus the behaviour of the workless can largely be understood as a quite rational and reasonable response to the lack of power and the very different contracts which were offered them in work and social security.

Our social security system is therefore wrong to treat the workless as though they are entirely responsible for their work histories, for the level of their contributions, and for their failure to find work. And the system is the more unjust when state help with job-finding remains so patchy and the minimum benefits are inadequate.

Our study also has implications for work policies which attempt, through the provision of work, to repair the workless individual's sense of responsibility and commitment to society. The sort of work that the workless want implies a range of criticisms not only of much work today, but of society itself. And if our society wishes to rescue or enlist whole-hearted commitment in working and in a wider social integration, then it will not be enough to provide work without changing the nature of work and working relationships.

We have no right to be surprised or annoyed if some of the workless are less trusting, less diligent, more aggressive or more apathetic. Nor should we be censorious if individuals to whom employers and the State have shown little responsibility should in turn break regulations about working while they are unemployed, or even try to avoid the commitments of regular secure work and the payment of tax and insurance. By criticizing the workless for behaving with a narrowly economic motivation, our society seems to be trying to have its cake and eat it.

We had wondered whether unemployment might be a sort of release and opportunity for some whose work we would consider to be harsh and unrewarding either in itself or financially. We found that so strong are the pressures and informal sanctions supporting work, that some of the workless cling to the desire to work to a much greater degree than our society has a right to expect, in view of what they had experienced through work and unemployment. Indeed in our small study we found no really convincing evidence of the emergence of any viable alternatives to work. For those we interviewed, talk about the 'opportunity' or 'leisure' afforded by unemployment seems decidedly premature.

It is a sad comment on the education system and the opportunities afforded in social relationships and leisure, that some of the workless should still need so badly even that inferior work which had given them so little, either in itself or in social responsibility on the part of the employer and the State; although mass unemployment and the inadequacy of social security benefits were hardly invitations to the workless to feel optimistic or to try to break new ground.

But should we not also be encouraged by the persistence, against the odds, of workless individuals' needs for work and their ideals of what work might be? For when the workless are content only with cash, work will have ceased to be part of the social contract, and the prospects of solving Britain's difficulties will be that much bleaker.

Part Five:
UNEMPLOYMENT IN A DIVIDED BRITAIN:
THE NEED FOR A SOCIAL CONTRACT
THROUGH WORK

12 Blaming the Workless: the Unequal Burden of Unemployment

Our concluding discussion begins by focusing closely on the paradox we called public 'schizophrenia', the tendency to deny that there is a problem of unemployment and to blame and denigrate the workless. The persistence of such hostility towards individuals at a time of mass unemployment raises questions about the character of the workless and the adequacy of various state support services, of the kind we explored in our interviews. We bring this discussion up to date with further evidence, in order to produce an estimate of the true scale of unemployment and the real need for work.

Later we will broaden out the discussion to show how attitudes in the public debate are in line with the historical traditions of classical economics and the ideology of the 'free market' which have dominated British policy. And we will explore the further paradox that such views, although they were apparently discredited by their failure to cure mass unemployment during the Depression, should again have come to the fore with the reappearance of mass unemployment in the 1970s.

In the final chapter we will assess the limits of vision of classical economic 'free market' policies, in relation to the development of Britain's economic and social crisis, and seen in the context of historical developments in international trade. And we argue that if Britain's economic fortunes are to be restored, there will be the need to establish a social contract in society through work.

THE 'NEW UNEMPLOYMENT' AND 'SCROUNGERPHOBIA'

Rather than arousing political protest, the reappearance of mass unemployment and the huge increase in the total cost of benefits[1] paid to the workless have led to complacency about levels of income support and to fears that state generosity is undermining the will to work. There are persistent rumours that many workers can automatically get a higher income from social security benefits. And there are perennial accusations that social security officials are too lax in their dealings with the lower-paid and able-bodied unemployed who, it is claimed by some politicians and newspapers, could find work if they wanted to, but who choose to draw benefits and perhaps to 'fiddle' by doing a job on the side.

The phenomenon already noted by George Orwell in the 1930s has developed almost a regular pattern during Britain's latest economic crisis. In 1962/3, 1968, 1971/2, 1975/6, and during the present Conservative government, upturns or steep rises in unemployment seem to have triggered off outbreaks of 'scrounger-phobia'. [2] The Conservatives have maintained a consistent policy in line with a suspicious public opinion. And while this has some-times been opposed by Labour, when in office they have been forced to acquiesce in scrounger-bashing.

Thus under Labour in the 1960s, following the rises in insur-ance benefits and the beginning of rising unemployment, Richard Crossman asserted there was a 'new unemployment'[3] and became involved in a controversy about work-shyness. Since the early 1970s, Sir Keith Joseph has helped to publicize a 'corrected esti-mate', produced by certain economists, which has shown only a small fraction of the numbers on the official unemployment register, by dint of removing the short-term unemployed, young people, older workers, women, long-term 'unemployables', and allegedly work-shy and fraudulent claimants. [4] Under the Heath government there was so much suspicion that a special committee (the Fisher Committee) reported on alleged social security abuse, and the Labour spokesman of the day, Reg Prentice, complained about the damage done to individuals in need when 'the myth about wide-spread abuse is perpetuated by some of the most reactionary newspapers in the country and is used by the Tories for party reasons'. [5] But when in 1976 there was a particularly nasty phase of scroungerphobia[6] led by a Conservative M.P., Ian Sproat, this was not resisted by a Labour government; and Parliament saw a noted left-winger, Mr Stan Orme, announcing a clamp-down on the unemployed and other benefit claimants,[7] albeit with stress on the need to improve the take-up of benefits by genuine claimants.

During the late 1970s, suspicions that Labour were being soft on the unemployed are said to have cost them seats. [8] The Con-servatives went into the 1979 election, pledged to restore the 'will to work'[9] by cutting taxes, and Mr Prentice, now a Conservative Minister, propounded a new ideology of greater sacrifice to be made by those dependent on state benefits to enable higher re-wards to be paid to 'the successful'. [10] November 1980 saw simul-taneously the largest rise in unemployment and the first cuts in unemployment benefits since the Depression. When unemployment reached 10 per cent, heading for two and a half million, Mrs Thatcher was still arguing that this was not the same as the Dep-ression. She and Lord Gowrie, the Under Secretary for Employ-ment, repeated the suggestions that the unemployed should be prepared to move 'where jobs are available... they have only to look in the situations vacant columns to realise where many of them are'. [11] In 1980 the Conservatives instituted the Rayner review of services for the unemployed, to cut manpower, fraud and over-payment, and still another drive against scroungers was announ-ced. [12] Mrs Thatcher was reported to be 'jubilant' that the review alleged that one out of twelve benefit claims were fraudulent. [13]

It was not until unemployment rose above two million in the autumn of 1980 that the general public began to feel that unem-ployment rather than inflation was the more important political issue. [14] Even so, it is not clear that they have modified their

views of the bulk of the workless as individuals: they have remained convinced that the workless were among the groups doing
best in times of inflation,[15] and held a grossly exaggerated view
of the proportion of national income they were absorbing.[16] By
European standards the British are remarkably more inclined to
believe that the poor are 'lazy'.[17]

We have already explored, through our interviews, how this
hostile climate of public opinion pressed upon the workless, and
how misguided its assumptions were. In the remainder of this
chapter we will take up on a more general plane the questions
posed in the public debate. We begin with an outline of Britain's
developing problem of unemployment, and we move on to see who
bears the burden, and how adequate are the support services of
various kinds which are provided by the State.

THE DEINDUSTRIALIZATION OF BRITAIN AND THE PUBLIC
EXPENDITURE CUTS

Britain has been hit exceptionally hard by the change in the
balance of world trade which has occurred since the Second World
War and by the oil crises of the 1970s. The effects upon British
manufacturing industry have been so catastrophic that they have
been described as 'deindustrialization', with the loss of almost two
million jobs in little over a decade (see Figure 1). There has been
a halving of our share of world trade during the past twenty
years, and a large increase in the 'penetration' of our home markets by foreign goods such as cars and electrical equipment.[18]
At first there was a rise in non-manufacturing jobs in the service
sector, including the social services such as health and education
(see Figure 1). However, since 1976 there have been cuts in public expenditure, and since 1979 the growth in non-manufacturing
jobs has been reversed. Over the winter of 1980/1 the steepening
loss of jobs was a combination of the decline of both the manufacturing and the non-manufacturing sectors.

Many of the job losses have been in the older industries upon
which Britain's prosperity was built, in coal-mining, ship-building,
steel, engineering and textiles. But there have been losses in
newer industries too. The shallow roots of Britain's post-war
industrial growth are revealed by the failure of some New Towns
to reach viability. Industrial black-spots have emerged or re-
emerged where major plants, such as the Linwood car factory, have
been closed, either because parent companies are cutting back
production to their bases or because they are moving production
to new factories overseas. In some inner city areas there has been
a gradual economic and social change; less-skilled workers have
remained trapped in poorer housing, while the better new jobs
have retreated to the outskirts of the city, attracting the more
mobile and more highly skilled.

A place like Liverpool,[19] for example, which was formerly a
centre of the cotton and slave trade, has suffered badly from the

Figure 1

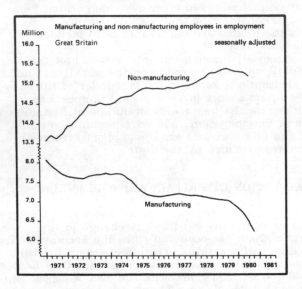

Source: Department of Employment, *Employment Gazette*,
March 1981, p. S6.

decline of textiles and because it is now on the wrong side of the
country for new trade with the European Common Market. Even
so, groups in inner Liverpool or on outlying estates like Speke
are suffering still greater levels of unemployment than the high
average for the region as a whole. The influence of such manufacturing and trade decline spreads more widely with the running-
down of housing, shops, civic buildings and amenities – and along
with them, local pride. Only the financial institutions like banks
and insurance companies seem to be doing well and building smart
new offices for themselves.

Any newer factories have not filled the gap left by the decline
of the older industrial areas. Instead, the ease of transport and
the location of financial institutions in the City have made the
'coffin' between London and Birmingham a more continuously
buoyant area of industrial activity, with a large amount of overtime being worked even when unemployment has risen quite high.[20]

Indications of Britain's industrial decline have flooded in since
1979. Output has fallen more steeply than during the Depression,[21]
and new machinery has been auctioned off to go abroad, despite
the fact that the average age of British plant is thirty-five years,
twice that of our major industrial competitors. Private investment
has fallen faster than anywhere else in Europe,[22] and industry
has been living off what little fat it retains by using up stock.

Housing has been virtually at a standstill. Britain is being 'slimmed down'.

As we write, opinions differ as to whether there are signs of an upturn in the economy. With the City shares hitting record prices, predictions for the economy vary from an upturn which will be sharp or slow, to a bumpy ride along the level or a continuous decline.[23] But prospects for jobs are undoubtedly poor. Any economic upturn will take time, and it will be met by firms using spare capacity or investing in more machinery to increase productivity with a smaller work-force.

THE REAPPEARANCE OF MASS UNEMPLOYMENT

After the Second World War there was a period when for a decade unemployment fell to the unprecedentedly low level of below 2 per cent. But in the mid-1960s, unemployment began to rise, reaching one million for the first time since before the war in 1971. From there on the rise is illustrated in Figure 2, the steepness during the autumn of 1980 being three times the previous record rise. By April 1981 the total passed two and a half million, or one in ten of the workforce.

Figure 2

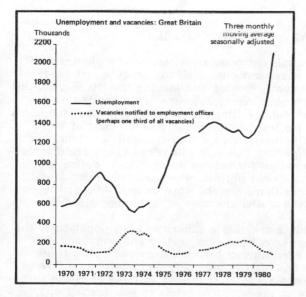

Source: Department of Employment, *Employment Gazette*, March 1981, p. S5.

Britain's rising unemployment has resulted from the failure to create enough new jobs, to meet a rise in the total workforce during the period when industry has been shedding workers. As in other industrial countries during the post-war period, large numbers of married women have been returning to work; and more recently, the post-war baby boom and the subsequent 'bulge' of more children has emerged as a rise in the numbers of young people now looking for work. Because of restricted economic growth during this period, Britain has had a very poor record of creating jobs.

Any new jobs have tended to come in the service sector but, despite the rise in non-manufacturing jobs (see Figure 1), the potential work force has outstripped the available work.

However, even such growth may be precarious. Opinions differ about the impact of the micro-chip,[24] which will hit us in the second half of the decade. Optimistic scenarios from previous technological changes such as computerization predict a rise in jobs and opportunities for much greater flexibility and control over work. However, alternative predictions see a catastrophic decline in jobs, with the micro-chip sweeping away many of the intermediate clerical and service jobs which have so far compensated for the fall in manufacturing work. There are forecasts that unemployment will reach three million by 1982, but if there is a 'collapse of work', unemployment will be five million or more later in the decade.

THE UNEQUAL SHARING OF UNEMPLOYMENT

To visualize the unemployed population, we need a picture not unlike a vast game of musical chairs (if the image is not too trivial). People are constantly joining and leaving the job search, but on the whole their number rises. Jobs are being created or disappearing, but the total is falling. A circulating mass of too many people are chasing too few jobs. But many of the best of these jobs tend to remain securely occupied or difficult to attain, and people's chances of getting the jobs will vary. There are discriminatory social and political influences which help to define who must, who may, who should not and who must not work. And among the job seekers there are the more or less skilled, the more or less eager, and those who are more or less stigmatized by employers.

Because the workless are only a minority of the population, the direct costs of unemployment are not widely shared at any one moment. However, even during high unemployment very large numbers move onto and off the unemployment register, a flow of about four million people a year (although in times of rising unemployment the flow of the workless tends to get dammed up). Over time, then, the costs of unemployment do become shared over a larger number of people; but how widely are they shared and by what sort of people? In fact the degree of inequality remains great. If unemployment was to be shared out equally, a man who left school at sixteen would experience unemployment seven or eight times a year in a working life, or once every six years.[25] However, many people are never unemployed, while 3 per cent of the unemployed bear as much as 70 per cent of the total number of weeks of registered unemployment.

Rising unemployment has shown a pattern discouragingly reminiscent of the Depression, with the same areas and even the same towns emerging as black spots. On the whole, unemployment tends to be higher the further the region lies from London.[26] Unemployment rates have risen during the 1970s, even in the southeast which had previously been insulated, and the thriving west midlands suffered even more (although it now seems to be picking up again). However, while these more recent rises tend to claim public attention, Northern Ireland and other regions further from London have consistently shown much higher rates, two or three times those nearer the capital. Moreover as general unemployment rises, long-term unemployment rises more quickly, as a consequence of the damming up of the workforce, so that the earlier and consistently higher levels of unemployment in the depressed regions mean that a greater proportion of the long-term unemployed are to be found there.[27] As we write, half way through 1981, there are one million people who have been unemployed for over six months, and three-quarters of a million who have been unemployed for over a year.[28]

The changing pattern of industrial and service jobs has implications for the sharing of unemployment between men and women, for by and large workers have not switched from manufacturing to services. A more or less constant workforce of men has experienced increasing redundancy in manufacturing; whereas rising numbers of women have outstripped rising numbers of jobs in the service sector. Thus women have made few inroads on male preserves, and for married women with children returning to work, the jobs have often been part-time. In fact, women's true employment status tends to be concealed in the official statistics of registered unemployment, for although women's wages are vital in single-parent families and as a second wage in families with older children,[29] there are strong pressures on mothers not to work and to define themselves as 'housewives' rather than 'unemployed'. Despite changes in the regulations, a proportion of married women still do not qualify for full benefit, and they tend not to register as unemployed.[30] Nevertheless, there has been a convergence between the levels of women's and men's registered unemployment, although women tend to be registered as shorterterm because of the pressures discouraging them from registering. Women's part-time jobs in services are vulnerable to government spending cuts, and later in the decade the micro-chip may tend to make unnecessary those intermediate clerical and administrative jobs which have become, for the moment, women's preserve.[31] Moreover, as male unemployment rises, men could begin to move into women's jobs, and women are poorly organized through unions to resist competition or job loss.

Among the flow of people who become unemployed, the better-paid and more-skilled workers tend to become unemployed less frequently[32] and continue to find jobs reasonably quickly: even during high unemployment there has remained a balance between job-seekers and vacancies in a few crafts such as tool-setting. But the lower-paid and unskilled have had much more insecure work, becoming unemployed repeatedly,[33] and taking longer and longer to find work as unemployment rises. As a result they are a large proportion of the stock of the long-term unemployed, and over 150 general labourers are registered for every known job vacancy.

Once a worker begins to be unemployed, the chances of repeated and longer-term unemployment grow. Any work remaining tends to be lower in skill, pay and security, the rule being 'last in - first out' when the next sackings come, but it also becomes more difficult to get new work. For being unemployed is not like being in a long queue where everyone gets a turn eventually: employers tend to prefer people who are just changing jobs or who have only recently become unemployed, and the longer-term unemployed become stigmatized, so that in effect they get pushed continually to the back of the queue.[34] Thus, in any future improvement in the number of jobs, the longer-term unemployed will be the last to be taken back into work.

Older workers suffer particularly in this way. They are no more likely to lose their jobs than others[35] (especially after legislation has marginally increased the security of work contracts).[36] But once older workers become unemployed, employers tend to discriminate against them, feeling that they are 'too old at 45'. There has been a trend for older workers to retire earlier and work less after reaching pensionable age; and this is not necessarily from choice, since pensions remain comparatively low in Britain and many older people are living in poverty.[37]

The enforcement of protective legislation on behalf of other workers, like the disabled, becomes even more difficult during high unemployment, when employers have a larger pool of able-bodied workers upon which to draw. The long-term sick who can find a sympathetic doctor will tend to move off the unemployment register (and may be encouraged to do so), to draw sickness benefits paid at a higher rate, although they may still want work of some kind.

The young are now suffering the highest unemployment rates,[38] because they are part of the flow of new workers at a time when recruitment to work is drying up and job opportunities are disappearing. Youth unemployment normally fluctuates a great deal over the year, with many of those who leave school in July subsequently finding work before the end of the year. But registered unemployment has been rising two or three times more quickly among the young,[39] and long-term unemployment has been increasing.[40] (The real unemployment totals will be higher because many young people live with working parents and may not always register for means-tested benefits during short spells of unemployment).[41] Youth unemployment is regionally concentrated and in some areas only a third of young people leaving school may have a job to go to, the only work for the majority being with the Manpower Services Commission schemes (which thus reduce the registered figures of unemployment).

Young school leavers are the least educationally qualified, the least technically skilled and the least experienced in work, so that with legislation on higher pay for the young they have become less attractive to employers. But in any case, unskilled, more menial jobs in distribution and services are disappearing and the system of craft apprenticeships is collapsing.[42] Again, in times of high unemployment employers may be discriminating more against young people (especially young men with ear-rings, or those with brightly coloured hair) and may give preference to older workers and married women whom they regard as steadier.

Members of ethnic minorities also suffer a disproportionate share of unemployment.[43] They tend to be less skilled, employed in more insecure work, in declining industries and small firms, so they are more likely to be thrown out of work. They are more likely than white workers to be dismissed from their jobs, and there is widespread discrimination by employers in hiring. Workers from ethnic minorities are more likely to suffer down-grading when they regain work, and to be dissatisfied in their new jobs. For some younger blacks in particular, the combination of a lack of educational and skill credentials, living in decaying areas where there is no employment, and racial discrimination, makes their prospects of work extremely poor.

If we combine this picture of which groups bear the burden of unemployment with what was said earlier about the continued regional inequalities and crisis areas of unemployment, it can be seen why, even in times of comparatively lower unemployment, there may be a very severe mismatching between the amount and location of work and the training and skills of the workless. And with each successive oscillation of the economy, this visible mismatching has become larger,[44] with greater numbers remaining out of work even during the periods when there has been a demand for workers in the more buoyant parts of the economy.

THE INADEQUACY OF INCOME MAINTENANCE

Income maintanance for the workless is provided in several ways. The system of supplementary benefits (paid on a means-test to those of the workless with insufficient resources) stems in a direct line from the 'dole' of the inter-war period and the old Poor Law, under which the unemployed were supported only grudgingly if they could demonstrate their willingness to work. Spurred on by ordinary people's hatred of the dole, the wartime Beveridge proposals were intended, by expanding the scope of insurance, to lift the vast bulk of the workless off the means-test for good. But the new insurance schemes can now be seen to have failed to resolve basic value dilemmas, for they still closely mirror the inequalities and insecurities of the market forces which determine a worker's career. [45]

Insurance benefits are still related to the number and regularity of contributions paid while in work; and with the introduction of earnings-related supplements in the mid-1960s, the size of insurance benefits was still more closely related to the level and continuity of past earnings. In addition, supplements continue for six months and basic insurance payments for twelve months only. Those who run out of insurance benefits, or whose insurance is too low to meet their needs, become eligible for means-tested benefits. However, in means-tested benefits there are lower permitted earnings for the individual and for other adult dependants, so that there is a ceiling against which not only the workless but their wives hit their heads. [46] Also the long-term unemployed have never been allowed to draw the increased allowances paid to other long-term claimants, and compared with other claimants the workless tend to receive fewer lump sum grants.

The persistent rumours of the workless being better off on social security do not stand up to examination, with incomes in practice less than half those of the employed (often much less), except for a tiny minority who have previously been low-paid and who have allowances for an above average number of dependant children. Ironically it is precisely this group who are suffering the most obvious financial strain, and those with higher levels of benefit resulting from family commitments tend to show more urgency to find work. [47]

Thus workers who, for whatever reason, were more marginal and lower-paid in work are worst protected when they become unemployed, and the time limit implies that failure to find work is the individual's own fault, becoming more blameworthy as unemployment is prolonged. Further, since they were first introduced, flat rate insurance benefits have been eroded so that more and more of the workless have become dependent on the means test. [48] Although the situation was slightly restored in the mid-1960s, only a small minority of the workless have ever received the earnings-related supplements. [49] Less than half of the workless now draw insurance benefits and a proportion of these are topped up with means-tested benefits so that they are subjected to the means test. Thus as a protection against means-test poverty, unemployment insurance schemes must now be counted a failure. [50]

The severity of the deprivation of the unemployed with families living on supplementary benefits has been documented over a period of time in a number of studies apart from our own. [51] The long-term unemployed and those who suffer from repeated unemployment are most vulnerable, because of the lack of any resources to cushion the impact of any small financial crisis. Such poverty is not temporary but persists over time, so that a high proportion of those who have been unemployed in the past are later found still to be poor because of repeated unemployment, sickness, or the fact that they have found only marginal work after their spell on supplementary benefits.

222

Similar strictures must be applied to lump sum redundancy payments. Britain is almost unique in having a scheme for redundant workers which entirely disregards the need for retraining, and instead pays in proportion to the worker's length of service and size of past earnings, no matter how much or little disturbance is suffered through unemployment and having to change jobs or move house. In fact only a small minority of the workless receive such payments and the average sum paid is low. [52] Ironically those who take the money, volunteering for redundancy, tend to be the longest serving, but oldest and least mobile workers, who will have great difficulty finding a new job and whose money will run out before retiring age.

THE CONTROL OF WORK BEHAVIOUR AND SOCIAL SECURITY ABUSE

At the time of our interviews, the employment exchanges, run by the Department of Employment, provided information on jobs and some occupational guidance services, and paid out insurance benefits to the workless, who must register once a week to show that they are available and willing to accept suitable work. [53] Fears that unemployment might prove financially preferable to work have led to various safeguards being incorporated in the system. There is disqualification or the payment of only reduced benefit if it is judged by officials that the individual has lost a job through misconduct, has left voluntarily, or has refused to apply for a job which the officials think is suitable. For a skilled person this would not initially be a job in a different skill or at a very much lower wage, although the unskilled would have less defence against such pressures. Those who do not qualify for insurance benefits may apply for means-tested benefits at an office with different staff, although here again there are regulations about reduction or withdrawal of benefit in cases of what is judged to be poor work behaviour.

To keep a check on fraud there are special investigators, more in connection with means tests than for insurance benefits. Investigators may follow up anonymous letters from the public, keep watch on claimants, and question neighbours, employers and landlords.

In addition, in the employment service, special Unemployment Review Officers interview those who have been unemployed for a longer period of time. The Department of Health and Social Security also runs a number of training courses and residential rehabilitation and re-establishment centres, which are supposed to accommodate volunteers, but whose inmates are reported to be there under pressure of withdrawal of benefit, suffering regimes which have been likened to Colditz. [54] Finally, those who persistently refuse to maintain themselves and their families may be prosecuted and imprisoned.

At the time of our study, evidence from official statistics and investigations gave very little support for accusations of fraud[55] or the abuse of social security by the work-shy,[56] so that public hostility has never been based on substantial evidence. Levels of known abuse are probably very low, for example, relative to petty theft, or to tax evasion in the so-called 'black economy';[57] yet there is much less hostility and suspicion of tax evasion and less investigative activity to detect fraud and reclaim the massive amounts of unpaid tax.[58] By its nature social security abuse, as compared with tax evasion, tends to involve much smaller sums and is more likely to be unwitting (through lack of knowledge of the regulations).[59]

The adverse outcome of the pressures of suspicion and hostility on the workless is revealed by the way that they are found to be classified by the employment services at levels of skill inferior to those they actually possess, and they tend to take jobs at skill levels which are lower still.[60] In short, the pressures of public hostility and the employment services tend to de-skill workers.

Since our study, job-finding has been split off from the payment of benefits, with the creation of separate Job Centres which concentrate on work for those changing jobs, as well as the unemployed. However, it has been argued that the Job Centres cater mainly for the employers' preference for the currently employed or very recently employed workers. In some ways, pressure on the longer-term unemployed to take work has been reduced - as well it might be in times of very high unemployment when jobs are scarce and employers can be highly selective. However, the potentially important process of review and placement of the longer-term unemployed becomes a separate, more stigmatized and more difficult task, carried out by officials who have less close contacts with the place where employers register vacant jobs.

Meanwhile because of public suspicion attaching to benefit claims and services, officials are likely to find the work unpleasant, and the low status of the claimants has tended to be associated with poor training for officials and poor working conditions. There are distasteful confrontations in the offices and officials develop semi-legal or illegal practices which ration benefits and make the claiming of benefit more difficult. As a result there is widespread unmet need.[61]

SOCIAL SECURITY PAYMENTS AND WORK MOTIVATION

Despite the inadequacy of benefit and the strength of built-in controls, as we have seen there has been sustained discussion among the public, politicians and economists about the erosion of the will to work. However, specialist opinion seems to be agreed that the effect (of income maintenance), if any, must have been small and mainly concentrated in the early period after the mid-1960s rise in benefits.[62] Benefit levels can thus in no way be held responsible for any substantial part of the massive recent rises in unemployment. Similarly, studies of redundancy payments have continued to confirm that they have very little effect, and indeed there is a major difficulty in assessing the influence of benefits as opposed to the increasing scarcity of jobs.

Larger effects on work incentives may have come from the unintended consequences of the P.A.Y.E. system, where someone losing a job receives a lump sum tax rebate which varies according to wages and the time of year when unemployment begins.[63] It has been principally the operation of these tax rebates which may bring higher-paid workers' living standards above their previous wage levels. The Conservative government proposes from 1983 to tax insurance benefits to prevent this happening. Meanwhile in anticipation, earnings-related benefits are being phased out by early 1982, and insurance benefits have been cut in real value for the first time since the Depression, and there are fears that when taxation comes in, the recent cuts in insurance benefits will not be restored.[64] The impact of these changes will be a further flow of the unemployed into the means-test trap.[65]

A more serious problem of work incentives comes from the interaction of tax, social security, and means-tested benefits and rebates, which creates the 'poverty trap': a situation where the workless who try to re-enter work may stand to gain very little increase in income. This situation has drastically deteriorated with the failure of the 1981 Budget to raise tax thresholds in line with inflation.[66]

A lack of enthusiasm for work on the part of the workless is thus not a consequence of too generous benefits but a judgement on the prospects of gaining good, well-paid employment, a fact confirmed when some of those said by officials to have poor prospects and to be lacking in enthusiasm were subsequently offered and took work. But as we saw from our interviews, the fact of being out of work is stigmatizing, so that employers are less willing to employ someone who has been out of work for a·longer period. And being out of work reduces motivation: the longer-term unemployed develop a 'spoiled identity' and become less employable as time passes. A recent official study concluded, 'There comes a point when people can no longer sustain their motivation in the face of continued rejection, heightened awareness of their own shortcomings, disillusionment with the job-finding services, belief that all the available options have been covered, and a knowledge that jobs are scarce anyway. In short, people become locked into a vicious circle: lack of success in job-finding reduces their motivation and this subsequently reduces even further the chances of finding work.'[67]

RECENT DEVELOPMENTS AND PROPOSALS FOR CHANGES IN SERVICES FOR THE WORKLESS

The advent of a Conservative government committed to restore the will to work and to cut inefficiency in public administration has brought to completion certain earlier proposals for changes in the system of supplementary benefits, and the Rayner Committee[68] has reviewed the employment services in general and made proposals for wide-ranging changes.

In supplementary benefits, following a review,[69] there has been no raising of the amount of cash available for allowances, but some sharing out of benefits to give more to young children (but the same to older children). However, a tighter specification of the regulations (which will have legal status), and the prospect of publication of the hitherto secret codes, have meant a cutback in flexibility and officials' discretion to meet need through varying allowances or by making lump sum payments: official discretion is now in the direction of *not* providing benefits. Under new regulations, school leavers cannot claim benefits for the school holidays, a move which is reported to have led to widespread early leaving at Easter by pupils who will now miss taking their exams.[70] Redundant older workers with redundancy pay and insurance policies in excess of £2,000 will no longer qualify for supplementary benefit (a change which is in marked contrast to the raising of the already much higher limit of tax exemptions or the 'golden handshakes' of the better-off redundant executive). At the same time official advertisement of the availability of benefits has been discouraged, fraud procedures are being tightened, and officials are being encouraged to withdraw benefit in instances where evidence might not stand up on appeal or where claimants might get too sympathetic a hearing.[71]

The Rayner Committee has produced an estimate that 8 per cent of claims are fraudulent, but this has been based often on inference of payments rather than evidence, and on only two areas of the country. The figures have been rejected by officials, who are already worried about the problems of their image as 'the S.S.' and by any further extension of the special fraud squad whose activities they mistrust.[72]

The Rayner Committee was also critical of even the residual job-placement function which the Job Centres now retain.[73] They advocated instead an end to compulsory registration at the Job Centres, which would further cut contacts between the workless and possible counselling and employment services. Meanwhile, various suggestions were made about tightening up the test of availability for work (especially for the able-bodied, and for married women with children) with less allowance to be made for individual preferences and the state of the job market, and shorter review intervals. More staff would be transferred to become Unemployment Review Officers. Although it was admitted that the counselling function of U.R.O.s tends to be only token, reshuffling the unemployed rather than creating new jobs, it was argued that their role of reinforcing good work behaviour and discouraging fraud should be strengthened.

THE INADEQUACY OF ALTERNATIVE MANPOWER POLICIES[74]

The decline of profit-making work and private industrial training opportunities has been met by the expansion of alternative manpower policies for increasing the skills and mobility of the workless. Labour has pursued these schemes with more enthusiasm, while the Conservatives have tended to mistrust them as palliatives or as harmful to private initiatives, so that they have instituted cuts in the budget of the Manpower Services Commission (M.S.C.).[75] But under neither Party have the schemes ever approached an adequate alternative to work.

Private schemes for training and apprenticeships have suffered during the present depression,[76] but in attempting to provide state-funded alternatives the Manpower Services Commission has identified a major problem: the more workless people that are wanting to be trained or retrained, the less chance there is that they will get jobs.[77] Faced with this dilemma, the M.S.C. has opted to concentrate on training for present limited industrial needs where there is a higher chance of placement, rather than attempting to predict shortages and to provide a more widespread and comprehensive training service in anticipation of a brighter industrial future. As a result there remains a major shortage of training schemes for redundant craftsmen, and there are fears that any upturn in the economy will quickly bring shortages of skilled workers.[78] Even so, the small number of government-trained workers have sometimes met with hostility from skilled workers and management, because of the way that brief training challenges established routes into 'skilled' work, and threatens to dilute worker monopolies and erode pay differentials.[79]

Schemes to promote the freer geographical movement of workers have been frustrated by the problems which the workless experience in moving house. For owner occupiers must face higher prices in areas where there is a more buoyant job market, while council tenants have had to wait their turn among existing queues of people who have residence or other priorities. The shrinking pool of council housing, due to sales and government cuts, made these pressures worse, although there is now a new scheme to ease transfers. However, the major problem is that in times of high unemployment and with the future of many jobs uncertain, the workless tend to stay put.[80] Many of those who have moved return home, preferring to be unemployed in their home area among friends rather than risk a growing chance of unemployment elsewhere.

Early retirement schemes, or the less costly and more efficient job release schemes where the elderly are given early retirement on condition that a younger worker is taken on, have proved insufficiently attractive to older workers because of the prospects of poverty in retirement.[81]

Priority is now being given to expanding schemes for the younger workless, from motives compounded of genuine concern and fears that work is a habit caught early or not at all, with a mistrust of the opportunities for mischief that idleness provides. Expansion of work experience, work induction and job creation schemes, are intended to provide opportunities for approaching half a million young people. However, again, the schemes are running into serious problems. Under various names (which seem to change as the schemes get discredited) job creation has suffered from the requirement that it must not encroach on industry and the profit-making sector of the economy.[82] Although some of the jobs have had a social content (cleaning up beaches, digging gardens for the elderly),[83] such work has been difficult to defend in times when there have been public expenditure cuts of much higher priority services for the disabled and the elderly. Moreover, the work has attracted hostility because it has provided 'jobs for the lads' (participants were often male) 'but not for the dads'.[84] Although job creation has survived it remains a minor part of the programme for the senior among the young unemployed and more emphasis is being given to useful services akin to voluntary work.

Most of the manpower schemes for the young unemployed are now under the Youth Opportunities Programme (Y.O.P.), a majority being so-called work experience and the remainder work induction. However, for the young unemployed with few or no educational qualifications or work skills, it can hardly be expected that short work induction courses can make a very significant contribution to their employability.

In times of high unemployment, the alternative work experience schemes have also met problems.[85] As the schemes expand, their rate of placing participants in work drops drastically, so that some young people are reported to be unemployed after two or three spells on Y.O.P.s.[86] The schemes act as a shuffling and filtering mechanism for employers, selecting out the more willing young people, from whom the employer can then further select. Expansion may also reduce still further the quality of what are already inferior jobs; for work experience has tended to be in small firms or labour intensive service and distributive industries, where there is minimal skill, high labour turnover and low pay.[87] Most seriously, the trade unions are beginning to complain more strongly that young people are being taken on under Y.O.P. schemes when older workers leave, rather than the employer taking on a full-time adult worker.[88] Employers themselves, who are unlikely to exaggerate, have confessed that at least one third of work experience is fraudulent. Future expansion of the scheme will therefore be more jealously watched by the unions.

Although young people themselves seem to find the scheme useful, disillusion must set in as placements provide less training content with less chance of work at the end. There is the possibility that the overall effect of schemes for specific groups of the workless, like young people, is to stigmatize them in the eyes of employers, suggesting that they are inferior workers and only to be taken on with the incentive of subsidies.[89]

Towards the end of the 1970s a more sinister note has crept into the discussion of jobs for the workless on manpower schemes and in the voluntary sector. It sometimes seems that there may be only a small step to suggestions that as a condition of drawing benefit the workless may be required to do the 'voluntary' work which will be needed to fill the gaps resulting from cuts in public expenditure. From a position where voluntary work was frowned upon, recent schemes now positively encourage it. Allowances for Y.O.P. participants have already been eroded and there are now threats of a unified allowance which will be below present means-tested benefits. There have been Conservative proposals to use the threat of withdrawal of benefit as a sanction to make people do community work. [90] Now there seems widespread support for proposals that the young should be taken out of the labour market into some comprehensive scheme of 'community service'. [91] A military service 'option' has been advocated, [92] although the Manpower Service Commission has objected that this is not consistent with Y.O.P.'s criteria.

To summarise, in spite of their increased scale, the M.S.C. schemes are reminiscent of government activity in the employment services. That is, the useful schemes seem to be geared towards a limited number of the easiest to employ, and they work in the employers' interest in selecting from the pool of the workless. Otherwise they are palliative, with little skill content or future: they de-skill. And now there may be emerging a greater element of coercion.

THE INADEQUACY AND STIGMA OF THE INFORMAL ECONOMY
AS A SOURCE OF WORK-LIKE ACTIVITY

Failing paid work or adequate alternative government schemes, there also seems little likelihood in the reasonably near future that the workless will find adequate alternative 'work-like' activity in the informal economy or in family life at home. Continued hostility towards the workless, and the perception of their role as peripheral to the economy, run counter to any idea that as unemployment rises there may be an imperceptible merging of unemployment with the leisure of the employed to create a new freer and more informal way of work.

It has been suggested, [93] for example, that various factors will cause activity to switch from the formal (wage) economy into the informal (casual paid and part-time) economy and the domestic (hitherto unpaid) sphere. The greater availability of cheaper and better tools and craft or domestic equipment may make do-it-yourself activities of various kinds more feasible, at the same time as increased wages of craftsmen make the hiring of labour more expensive. So people will more often decorate their own homes, make furniture, service cars and so on. At the same time, changing attitudes towards domestic tasks and child-care may mean that there can be more participation of men in the home and women in work. It is argued that the whole balance of work, leisure and

229

domesticity could shift, and in this shift there may be a blurring of present divisions between the activities of the workless and the workers.

In addition there is a partial overlap between the 'informal' and the 'black' economies because while payments in the formal economy tend to be visible and taxed, those in the informal economy tend to be invisible and are frequently not declared for tax, they are 'black'. (The overlap is only partial because the formal economy has a very large area of grey, if not actually black, activity which can hardly be called productive work.) And here again it might be questioned whether there may be some overlap between the activities of workers and the workless.

There was in fact some evidence on changes and overlaps between unemployment, the informal economy and domestic activities from our interviews. We noted how 'fiddling' and the 'black economy' may be valuable work for the workless themselves, [94] and a source of cheap, flexible, and informal labour for some firms and other members of society. [95]

However, any merging of the activities of the employed and the unemployed remains only very marginal, and society sets very different moral standards for the two groups. The employed craft worker who 'moonlights' and gets paid in 'dirty pound notes' with no traceable receipts is in the black economy, as is the unemployed worker who does the same; but these activities attract very disparate official surveillance and legal sanctions. Do-it-yourself activities at home, in which both the employed and the unemployed engage, tend to attract more social disapproval for the unemployed, to the extent that at some periods in various countries such activities have been strongly officially frowned upon for the workless, and even legally banned. The workless are also likely to be criticized by officials if they are seen to be caring for small children when they register as available for work in the unemployment benefit office; yet child-care is, of course, approved for the employed shift or part-time worker or housewife.

The work done by the workless who 'fiddle' is mostly exploitative. Denied full-time work, the workless are living off the scraps and left-overs of work that society is not prepared to pay anyone adequately to do. Other kinds of developments, in paid home work and domestic production, also tend to be low-paid, a deliberate cost-cutting exercise by firms who want to tap a more exploitable workforce for which they will not need to be committed to provide secure work, or to pay the necessary social security taxes. And our interviews have indicated that enforced participation in unpaid domestic work can be, for women as well as men, a highly frustrating and even threatening experience which may lead to tensions and violence. [96] Thus any switching of activity between work, the informal economy and the domestic sphere will depend on a whole series of formal political and economic decisions and will also be guided, controlled and limited by more informal processes and sanctions. Accordingly we should beware of any predictions that an easy, natural, voluntary shift of activities from work into the informal economy and domestic sphere will automatically solve the problem of unemployment.

THE TRUE SCALE OF UNEMPLOYMENT AND THE NEED FOR WORK

We can now return to the major question which was raised in the public debate: what is the true scale of the unemployment problem and the need for work? Claims that unemployment is 'not like the Depression' are based on the fact that at its worst unemployment in the 1930s was around 20 per cent of a smaller workforce. But in fact unemployment peaked fairly sharply in the Depression, whereas forecasts now seem to agree that we have entered a spell where registered unemployment will rise above three million from 1982 and will be prolonged. Whatever percentage of the workforce this is, there are over three million people, a large proportion of whom will suffer long-term unemployment. Already the long-term unemployed who have been out of work for over twelve months outnumber those in the 1930s.

Attempts to discount a proportion of the registered unemployed are either misrepresentations or show a naivety about the economic and social processes which underlie what is happening. Most unemployment during the present period of industrial decline is involuntary, and is neither caused nor cushioned by adequate social security benefits. Proposals to remove women, the old, and young people from the statistics of unemployment merely serve to reinforce the range of discriminatory official and informal processes, and employer and worker practices, which are already tending to define these groups as not part of the main workforce, and to exclude them from work.

Evidence that the scale of unemployment is really much larger than the registered figures came after the initial controversy in the early 1970s, when surveys revealed that as many as 30 per cent more people said they were seeking work than appeared on the official register. It can also be observed that as jobs are lost from the economy, the number of people registered as unemployed does not increase at the same rate; that is, some drop out because they retire or are otherwise discouraged. [97]

If we try to estimate how many people need and would take up work, we must understand above all that work motivation is social as well as economic. The major influences which determine who works are the amount and quality of work available, and the quality of supportive services in education and training that society provides. And such support would need to include active policies for removing discriminatory barriers in work. Given such policies, we would need to add to the registered unemployed not merely the unregistered who are seeking work, but those who could and would work under the right conditions. The number of willing and capable workers depends upon our ability to organize work in such a way that people's energies are enlisted to solve the problems which Britain faces.

231

NOTES

1 Between June 1979 and June 1980 the cost of benefits rose
   from £138,704 to £220,641 (excluding the costs of administration).
2 A. Deacon, *Social and Economic Administration*, no. 12, 1978;
   and in B. Showler and A. Sinfield (eds.), *The Workless State*,
   Martin Robertson, 1981, pp. 81-5.
3 Broadcast, 8 September 1968.
4 'Sir Keith and the phantom dole queue', *Sunday Times*, 26
   October 1975. For the latest low estimates, see R. Miller,
   Economic Affairs, October 1980; and P. Mintford, *Lloyds
   Bank Review*, Spring 1981.
5 *Hansard*, vol. 816, col. 89/90, quoted by A. Deacon in B.
   Showler and A. Sinfield, op. cit.
6 P. Golding and S. Middleton, 'Why is the press so obsessed
   with welfare scroungers?', *New Society*, 26 October 1978.
7 'Big new war on dole cheats', *News of the World*, 25 July 1976.
8 *Sunday Times*, 21 November 1976.
9 *Conservative Manifesto*, 1979.
10 'If you believe economic salvation can only be achieved by
   rewarding success and the national income is not increasing,
   then you have no alternative but to make the unsuccessful
   poorer.' Quoted by David Donnison in *New Society*, 22 January 1981 (original speech, May 1979).
11 *Guardian*, 28 January 1981; *Guardian*, 25 July 1980; and *New
   Society*, 28 August 1980.
12 P. Moore, 'Scroungermania again at the DHSS', *New Society*,
   22 January 1981.
13 *Guardian*, 4 March 1981.
14 In a Gallup Poll as late as June 1980, only 23 per cent said
   unemployment was the most important issue.
15 In a Marplan Poll, 83 per cent thought the unemployed were
   doing well out of inflation, *Sun*, 17 January 1977.
16 A. Deacon in B. Showler and A. Sinfield, op. cit., p. 88.
17 In an opinion poll carried out in E.E.C. countries, 27 per
   cent of the British said poverty was due to laziness, compared
   with an average of 14 per cent in other countries.
18 In 1955 the U.K. accounted for 20 per cent of the world trade
   in manufactured goods. By 1976 the share was less than 9
   per cent. Imported manufactured goods rose from 8 per cent
   in 1961 to 13 per cent in 1971, but to 21 per cent by 1976. In
   1979 alone they rose by 15 per cent over the previous year.
   See S. Aaronovitch, *The Road from Thatcherism*, Lawrence
   and Wishart, 1981, p. 8; K. Hawkins, *Unemployment*, Penguin,
   1979, pp. 82-7; and F. Cairncross, 'Where have all the jobs
   gone?', *Guardian*, 6 April 1981.
19 F. F. Ridley, *Unemployment* (*Political Quarterly* special issue),
   vol. 52, no. 1, Spring 1981.
20 On new factories and industry, see P. Hall, *New Society*, 26
   March 1981. Until very recently over a third of workers in

manufacture did overtime, the highest proportion of any country in Europe and equivalent to 400,000 jobs, *New Society*, 26 February 1981. For union moves to cut overtime, see *New Society*, 2 April 1981.

21 According to Phillips and Drew, between 1979 and 1981 manufacturing dropped by 15 per cent, compared with a fall of 11 per cent between 1929 and 1931.

22 Investment per head in Britain, already very low (one third of U.S. and half or below of West Germany, Japan and France) fell by 10 per cent in 1980, and is estimated to fall a further 15 per cent in 1981. S. Aaronovitch, op. cit., p. 8 and p. 22.

23 The I.T.E.M. group forecasts a decline until 1983 to 3½ million unemployed. The Cambridge Economic Policy Group (whose forecasts have been the most consistently accurate hitherto) forecasts a continuous decline as far as the prediction runs, to 1985, with 3.6 million unemployed by 1983 and 4.3 million by 1985. *Guardian*, 28 April 1981, and C.E.P.G., *Economic Policy in the UK*, Gower Hampshire, 1981. For a range of forecasts, see *MSC Manpower Review*, M.S.C., 1981, pp. 18–19.

24 See, for example, *MSC Manpower Review*, M.S.C., 1980; and A. Sinfield, *What Unemployment Means*, Martin Robertson, 1981, Ch. 6. Also P. Hall, op. cit.; and S. Williams, *Politics is for People*, Penguin, 1981.

25 See D. Metcalf, 'Unemployment: history, incidence and prospects', *Policy and Politics*, 8:1, pp. 21–37; also, D. Metcalf and S. Nickell, 'The plain man's guide to the out of work', *Royal Commission on the Distribution of Income and Wealth*, Report no. 6, H.M.S.O., 1978. See also *MSC Review of Services for the Unemployed*, 1981, p. 8; and P. Kelner, 'Maggie's Missing Million', *New Statesman*, 27 March 1981.

26 The *Employment Gazette*, March 1981, gave regional unemployment (for February 1981) as: south-east, 7 per cent; Greater London, 6.7 per cent; East Anglia, 8.4 per cent; south-west, 9.3 per cent; east midlands, 9.2 per cent; north-west, 12.3 per cent; north, 13.6 per cent; Wales, 13.5 per cent; Scotland, 12.7 per cent (now helped in parts by oil); Northern Ireland, 17.3 per cent.

27 On the 'flow' and 'stock' of the workless, see W. W. Daniel, *New Society*, 19 March 1981; also *MSC Manpower Review*, M.S.C., 1981, pp. 8–10. The *Employment Gazette*, op. cit., gave figures for the duration of unemployment for January 1981 as: up to 26 weeks, 1,430,300; 26 to 52 weeks, 460,000; over 52 weeks, 430,000. Long-term unemployment is probably much understated because any slight intermission (for example through a claim for sickness benefit) means that the spell has ended and further unemployment is counted as short-term.

28 A. Sinfield, op. cit., pp. 89–90 (and Ch. 3 for a discussion of all the other groups covered in this section). On the piling up of long-term unemployment in the regions, see North

Tyneside C.D.P., *In and Out of Work*, Home Office, 1978; also, M. Hill, 'Unemployment: an isolated experience or a recurrent event' in *Royal Commission on the Distribution of Income and Wealth*, op. cit.

29 C. Pond and M. McNay, *Low Pay and Family Poverty*, Study Commission on the Family, 1980.

30 *General Household Survey*, Annual Reports. About half the married women who say they are 'looking for work' are not registered, and a quarter of single women. See also P. Kelner, op. cit.

31 See, for example, the T.U.C. report, quoted in *New Society*, 5 February 1981; and the report submitted to the House of Lords select committee on remedies for unemployment, by the Equal Opportunities Commission, in 1980. See especially, I. Breugel, 'Women as a reserve army of labour', *Feminist Review*, no. 3, 1979.

32 D. E. published figures, op. cit., for December 1980, give unemployment by skill level: managers and professional, 8.6 per cent; clerical, 13.1 per cent; other non-manual, 5.9 per cent; craft, 13.9 per cent; general labourers, 32.7 per cent; other manual, 25.7 per cent. See also, B. Showler and A. Sinfield, op. cit., p. 127.

33 M. Hill, op. cit. The D.H.S.S. Cohort study, *Employment Gazette*, August 1980, showed that over half the men becoming unemployed in 1978 had been unemployed in the previous year.

34 M. Colledge and R. Bartholemew, *Study of the Long-term Unemployed*, summary in *Employment Gazette*, January 1980. See also, T. F. Cripps and R. Tarling, *Economics Journal*, vol. 84, no. 334.

35 W. W. Daniel, *A National Survey of the Unemployed*, P.E.P., 1974.

36 *Employment Protection Act*, 1975.

37 See P. Townsend, *Poverty in the United Kingdom*, Penguin, 1979, Ch. 19.

38 The proportions of the unemployed (not rates) by age are given by the D.E., op. cit., for January 1981: below 18, 8.2 per cent; 18-19, 10.1 per cent; 20-24, 20 per cent; 26-34, 22.2 per cent; 35-44, 13.0 per cent; 45-54, 11.8 per cent; 55-59, 6.9 per cent; 60 plus, 7.9 per cent. Looked at another way, the eight-year group of young workers provided almost two-fifths of the workless, while the thirty-year group of middle age workers contributed not much more. The numbers were: under 25, 888,100; 25-54, 1,090,000; 55 plus, 342,400.

39 *Employment Gazette*, March 1981; *MSC Manpower Review*, op. cit.; O.E.C.D. annual survey in *Times Educational Supplement*, 2 January 1980.

40 A. Sawdon, *Youth Unemployment*, Youthaid, 1980.

41 See Cohort study, op. cit.; also, *Community Relations Council Report*, 1974, Table 12, which shows 50 per cent of young blacks not registered.

42 K. Hawkins, op. cit., pp. 108-10.
43 D. Smith, *Unemployment and Racial Minorities*, P.S.I., 1981 (summary, *New Society*, 26 February 1981). Showler estimated that ethnic minorities suffered 40 per cent more unemployment, quoted B. Showler and A. Sinfield, op. cit.
44 *Department of Employment Gazette*, no. 84, October 1976.
45 For a more detailed discussion of the hierarchy of work and work insecurity, see P. Townsend, op. cit., Chs. 12, 17 and 18. On contributions, see R. Lister and G. Fimister, *Social Security: The Case Against Contribution Tests*, C.P.A.G., 1981.
46 The 1971 Census gave 47 per cent of all wives but only 31 per cent of the wives of the unemployed as working; the 1978 G.H.S. gave 58 per cent of all wives but only 33 per cent of the wives of the unemployed as working (too large a difference to be explained merely by the distribution of work opportunities where the workless live).
47 *Social Assistance, A Review of the Supplementary Benefits Scheme in Great Britain*, D.H.S.S., 1978, gives a ratio of short-term benefit plus rent allowance for a married couple, compared with average male earnings, as 50 per cent. For insurance benefits, the ratio to average earnings between 1971 and 1976 never exceeded 67 per cent, N.I.E.S.R., *National Institute Economic Review*, February 1977. But the question is not the ratio, but what people actually receive: A. B. Atkinson and J. S. Fleming, 'Unemployment, Social Security and Incentives', *Midland Bank Review*, Autumn 1978. The Cohort study, op. cit., found only 1 per cent better off on benefit than in work. See also note 62 below.
48 For charts of the changing values of benefit in relation to average male net income, see *Poverty*, C.P.A.G., no. 46, August 1980, pp. 38-41.
49 *Social Assistance*, op. cit:
50 See A. Sinfield, op. cit., p. 108ff.
51 Cohort study, op. cit.; D. Smith, op. cit., 1980; W. W. Daniel, op. cit., 1974; M. J. Hill et al., *Men Out of Work*, C.U.P., 1973; M. Clark, 'The unemployed on supplementary benefit', *Journal of Social Policy*, vol. 7, no. 4, October 1978; M. Colledge and R. Bartholemew, op. cit.; P. Townsend, op. cit., Chs. 16 and 17.
52 See *Employment Gazette*, August 1980; Cohort study, op. cit., 1980; W. W. Daniel, op. cit., 1974. Less than one in ten gets £500 or more. The bulk of the one in 25 who get £2,000 or more are near retiring age.
53 For a good account of procedures at the time of our interviews, many of which remain, see M. J. Hill, *Policies for the unemployed: help or coercion*, Poverty Pamphlet 15, C.P.A.G., 1974. We discuss changes below.
54 'Jobless Centres run like Colditz', *Sunday Times*, 7 September 1980.
55 In 1977-8 detected fraud in the payment of unemployment

benefit was less than £440,000, or less than 1 per cent of all payments. For all social security payments the figure was £2.8 million, or 0.1 per cent. *Public Accounts Committee Report* (1976/7), H.C. 532.

56 Disqualification (for voluntary leaving) has dropped below 8 per cent since 1971, and for misconduct has varied between 6 and 3 per cent, and for refusal of 'suitable work', below 1 per cent. Prosectuions for refusal to maintain have always been below 100 per year.

57 Estimates vary between the high £3½ billion tax loss (said to have been worked out by Sir William Pile 'on the back of an envelope'), *29th Report from the Committee of Public Accounts*, H.C. 778, and about one third of that amount, estimated by the Institute of Fiscal Studies, *Guardian*, 4 March 1981; and *New Society*, 26 March 1981. In 1979 82 per cent of a group of selected cases of self-employed workers and companies were found to be understating their income for tax purposes. Petty theft runs at at least £1 million per day.

58 Prosecution rates in 1972-3, for example, were 25 per cent for social security fraud and only 1.3 per cent for tax evasion. In 1978 it was estimated that around £370 million in unpaid taxes would not be collectable, *Poverty Fact Sheet*, C.P.A.G., February 1980. Estimates of switching staff onto social security fraud are that £50 million might be saved. See also, the Rossminster tax evasion exposure, *Sunday Times*, 15 March 1981, and the Vestey exposure, *Sunday Times*, 1980.

59 For a small study of 'fiddling', see A. Ballantyne, *Guardian*, 18 November 1980.

60 See Cohort study, op. cit.; W. W. Daniel, op. cit., 1974; M. J. Hill, op. cit.

61 Unclaimed benefits were estimated at £½ billion, *Family Finances*, Study Commission on the Family, 1980.

62 Showler, in B. Showler and A. Sinfield, op. cit., pp. 42-5; A. B. Atkinson and J. S. Fleming, op. cit; *Social Assistance*, op. cit.; W. W. Daniel, op. cit., 1974; Cohort study, op. cit.; M. Colledge and R. Bartholemew, op. cit.; W. W. Daniel and E. Stilgoe, *Where are they now?*, P.E.P., 1977; K. Hawkins, op. cit., pp. 33-8.

63 A. B. Atkinson and J. S. Fleming, op. cit.

64 M. Dean, *Guardian*, 18 March 1981; T. Lynes, *New Society*, 6 April 1981; also *Guardian*, 12 May 1981.

65 R. Lister, *Moving Back to the Means Test*, Poverty Pamphlet 47, C.P.A.G., 1980.

66 It has been estimated that the failure to upgrade thresholds has worsened the poverty trap by 40 per cent. *Why Work?*, Conservative Political Centre, 1981. See also D. Piachaud in C. Sandford et al., *Taxation and Social Policy*, Heinemann, 1981.

67 M. Colledge and R. Bartholemew, op. cit. For a review of various studies of the long-term unemployed, see R. Harrison et. al., *The Effects of Prolonged Unemployment*, D.E., 1976,

summarized in *Department of Employment Gazette*, no. 84,
April 1976; also, M. Jahoda, *New Society*, 6 September 1979.
68 *Payment of Benefits to Unemployed People*, H.M.S.O., 1981.
69 A detailed account of the changes is given in *New Society*,
20 November, 27 November and 4 December 1980.
70 *Sunday Times*, 12 April 1981; also *Guardian*, 28 April 1981.
71 *Guardian*, 24 January 1981.
72 'These figures seem to be based on special drives through
the Specialist Claims Control, who our members regard as
producing rather dubious data.' Society of Civil and Public
Servants, *Guardian*, 21 March 1981. See also, *Guardian*, 24
January 1981. The figures refer to s.b. claimants, not
insurance.
73 For evaluations of Job Centres, see *Department of Employment Gazette*, 15 March 1978; *Guardian*, 5 November 1979 (a
suggestion that less pressure has led to higher unemployment
levels); and D. Cromwell, 'How Job Centres do their job',
New Society, 15 March 1979; also, W. W. Daniel, 'In Defence
of Job Centres', *New Society*, 16 April 1981.
74 For discussions of various manpower programmes see, M. J.
Hill in B. Showler and A. Sinfield (eds.), op. cit., Ch. 4;
and K. Hawkins, op. cit., Ch. 5. In fact, the Manpower
Services Commission deserves some praise for acting as a
pressure group against government policies.
75 £290 million and 5,500 jobs.
76 See reports, *Sunday Times*, 26 April 1981; *Guardian*, 21 April
1981, referring to M.S.C. estimates that apprenticeships
could be 25 per cent down.
77 *MSC Manpower Review*, 1980, pp. 20-1.
78 See K. Hawkins, op. cit., pp. 53-6, 108-11; and W. W. Daniel,
op. cit., 1974.
79 *MSC Manpower Review*, op. cit.; B. Showler and A. Sinfield,
op. cit., p. 102; and K. Hawkins, op. cit., p. 108.
80 C.D.P., op. cit.; see also K. Hawkins, op. cit. On our suggestion from the interviews that there might be family patterns and relationships with differential effects on likelihood
of wanting and being able to migrate, see E. Bott, *Family and
Social Network*, Tavistock, 1957.
81 *Employment Gazette*, November 1980, discusses these schemes.
82 For an early assessment, see B. Showler, 'Job Creation or
Job Evasion', Wasted Labour Conference, 11 November 1978.
83 Work experience seems to have some of the same kinds of jobs.
See *The Times*, 19 March 1981, for a report of eight teenage
girls, on an M.S.C. scheme, counting dustbins in Chester-
field.
84 *Sunday Times*, 7 December 1975.
85 C. St J. Brooks, 'No opportunity for youth', *New Society*,
15 January 1981.
86 *Jobless: a study of unemployed young people in Tyneside*,
Youthaid, 1981; see also report, *Guardian*, 24 March 1981. An
M.S.C. survey gives placement rates as 36 to 38 per cent,
Sunday Times, 17 May 1981.

87 *Quality or Collapse*, Youthaid, 1981.
88 See reports in *Sunday Times*, 2 March 1981; *Guardian*, 21
    April 1981; and *Sunday Times*, 16 March 1981 ('Union anger
    over bosses who cheat on teenage jobs'). Cases mentioned
    were a teenager stacking tins on supermarket shelves all day
    and two farmers swopping sons to employ them under Y.O.P.
89 B. Reubens, in I. V. Sawhill and B. E. Anderson (eds.),
    Youth Employment and Public Policy, reviews various schemes
    in Europe and the United States.
90 Birmingham Conservative Council proposed it in 1978, *Guard-
    ian*, 21 November 1978; and Lord Gowrie in 1980, *New Society*,
    24 July 1980.
91 *Guardian*, 8 March 1981; C.B.I., *The Will to Win*, 1981;
    Guardian, 14 May 1981.
92 *Guardian*, 26 March 1981. A poll of *Daily Telegraph* readers
    showed 60 per cent in favour of National Service as a means
    of solving the unemployment problem (Spring 1981).
93 J. Gershuny, 'The informal economy: its role in post-
    industrial society', *Futures*, February 1979; J. Gershuny and
    R. E. Pahl, 'Britain in the decade of the three economies',
    New Society, 3 January 1980; S. Henry, *The Informal Econ-
    omy*, Macmillan, 1978.
94 The relationship between the clamp-down on fiddling and the
    frustration of individuals who might otherwise start small
    businesses is discussed in *Guardian*, 27 March 1981.
95 Small businessmen protested that too much clamping down on
    the 'black economy' would rob them of a valuable source of
    cheap labour, *Guardian*, 5 March 1981.
96 See, for resilience in roles, A. Oakley, 'Are husbands good
    housewives?', *New Society*, 1972; on violence, D. Marsden,
    'Sociological perspectives on family violence' in J. Martin
    (ed.), *Violence and the Family*, Wiley, 1978.
97 A. Sinfield, op. cit., pp. 11–12; and *Employment Gazette*,
    November 1980. The T.U.C. periodically states that the real
    figure for unemployment should be a million higher, *Plan for
    Growth*, T.U.C., 1981; report in *The Times*, 26 November
    1980. See especially P. Kelner, op. cit., and *MSC Manpower
    Review*, M.S.C., 1981, p. 8.

13 Abandoning Full Employment: the Resistible Rise of Free Market Policies

If real unemployment and the need for work are so great, why have there been such persistent attempts to deny that there is a problem? In this chapter we show that these public prejudices are elevated to the status of a theory in classical economics, which has been the dominant orthodoxy underlying policy in Britain. But then there arises a further paradox to be explained. Classical 'free market' policies were commonly thought to have been discredited in the 1930s because of their failure to solve the problems of mass unemployment. Yet it is precisely with the reappearance of the highest levels of unemployment since the war that classical economic policies have again assumed a dominant political role.

We can better understand policy arguments if we describe them in terms of several historical traditions: classical economics, Marxism and state administrative intervention. The dominance of these traditions in shaping policy has shifted with the changing balance of political power, and as various attempts have been made to cope with the emerging problems of the economy. Yet there have been underlying continuities which we will be able to trace during the present century, particularly the recent post-war period.

THE IDEOLOGY OF CLASSICAL ECONOMICS AND THE 'FREE MARKET'[1]

The classical economics of present-day policies preserves intact an ideology which was developed during the heyday of Britain's industrial growth, and which appealed particularly to businessmen who wanted to be left alone by the State to pursue their own private profit. At the core of classical economics is a simple view of human nature and society, where economically-motivated individuals pursue their own interest in a free market which operates as a self-balancing system, that is, without state intervention. Governments should intervene only to protect individual freedoms to buy and sell goods, labour and services. Otherwise, state intervention is harmful, serving only to divert economic activity into channels which are less profitable and hence, ultimately, less valuable to society as a whole and to mankind in general.

Classical economics maintains that the mass involuntary unemployment of individuals who have any value as workers cannot exist in a truly free market society. There will be some so-called 'frictional' unemployment caused by workers changing jobs, but this is necessary to give employers and workers choice and to give the whole system flexibility. Otherwise, the trade cycle will be self-balancing, because as unemployment grows the cost of employing workers will become less, with the result that eventually more workers can be taken on and unemployment falls. The processes of saving and investment are also argued to be self-balancing, via the machinery of automatically varying interest rates. On this theory, prolonged large-scale unemployment can arise only if workers combine in trade unions to push up the price of their labour so that employers cannot afford to take workers on. The role of government thus becomes to restrict the power of the unions and so prevent wages rising above what the market can afford. By the same token, the role of government should also be to prevent investors and employers from combining to fix prices.

It can now be seen that the attitudes expressed in the public debate about social security for the workless are in line with classical economic thinking on work motivation and on individuals' responsibility for their own work record in the free market. For centuries Britain has shown mistrust of the able-bodied unemployed and a marked reluctance to provide them with an adequate income, lest their condition should be more comfortable than the lowest-paid worker and the will to work should be eroded.

TRADITIONS OF CRITICISM OF CLASSICAL ECONOMICS

There are several long traditions of criticism of classical economics, in literature, political economy and sociology. Sociologists since Marx and Durkheim have objected to the narrowness of the classical economic view of human nature and society. There have been accusations that free market policies have not been applied even-handedly but that they are deployed as an ideology to reduce workers' power to oppose the operation of dominant financial interests. Rather then exemplifying and protecting liberty, so-called 'free market' societies may infringe human freedoms, through the fostering of growing inequalities and the erosion of any feelings of common purpose. It has been argued that a society founded on the principle of the unfettered pursuit of economic self-interest cannot hold together, but must eventually destroy itself through social conflict.

In Marxism there is a highly pessimistic prediction that unemployment will grow until eventually capitalist society is overthrown by revolution. Mass unemployment is seen as the deliberate creation, by the employers, of a 'reserve army' of the unemployed in order to undermine the bargaining power of the workers and so keep wages down. Technological innovation, too, will be used to drive down workers' living standards by creating further unemployment. The State, as merely an arm of the employers' power, will not intervene in this process unless forced to do so by mass political action on the part of the workers.

240

Clearly as a policy-guide for non-communist countries, Marxism has nothing to offer governments. And as a theory it has had to face the problem of why living standards have risen, and why there was until the riots so little mass protest during times of high unemployment. Nevertheless, when unemployment rises, developments of Marxist theory are invoked as increasingly relevant explanations of what is happening. We will be returning to these questions of living standards and political protest later in the discussion. Meanwhile, however, we will describe the non-Marxist direction taken by British politics.

STATE ADMINISTRATIVE INTERVENTION: KEYNES AND ECONOMIC POLICY

British politics after the Second World War saw the development of a middle ground between classical economics and Marxism. There came the belief that any undesirable and inegalitarian outcomes of the unfettered operations of the free market can and must be ameliorated by an administrative extension of state activity in a mixed economy where there will still be a role for private industry.

It was Keynes who opened up the possibility of a major role for government in reducing unemployment, by suggesting that there was a need for government spending to counteract deficiencies of investment and the lack of demand for goods during recessions. He argued that investment was not self-balancing, so that there could be a continuing lack of demand for workers, with resulting mass involuntary unemployment. Government investment would 'multiply' demand because the workers released from unemployment would spend their wages creating further demand for goods.

In view of the frequent invocation of Keynes's name today as a backing for calls for government spending, it must be remembered that Keynes's policies did not represent as radical a departure from classical economic thinking as his would-be disciples sometimes imply. [2] Before the war Keynes argued that existing unemployment levels of up to 20 per cent could be brought down by government policy. However, he believed that 10 per cent of unemployment was due to rigidity and mismatching in the labour market, so that government spending when unemployment was below that level would not reduce unemployment but would merely lead to inflation. This was because the unions would be able to force up their wages, in a situation where the demand for labour exceeded supply, without any extra production.

Later, Keynes came to believe that industrial reorganization during the war had removed some of this rigidity in the economy, but that the 'full employment level of unemployment' would still be 5 per cent. He died in 1946, and so had nothing to say on Britain's post-war economic successes of full employment or the later crisis.

BEVERIDGE'S POLICY FOR WORK IN THE SOCIAL SERVICE STATE[3]

It was left to Beveridge to provide a statement of the social value of a full employment policy achieved by state intervention. In his earlier 'organisationist' policies he had accepted classical economic theory and sought, via Labour Exchanges, merely to ease the flow of workers who were dammed up in declining industries with obsolescent skills. And in some of his views he was highly punitive, advocating the setting up of penal colonies for workshy industrial defaulters. After the experience of the Depression, however, he made a synthesis of Keynesian economic theory with a social vision where government administrative action in industry and adequate social insurance would banish the fear of unemployment, in what he preferred to call not the Welfare but the Social Service State.

The solution was not to be found merely in adequate unemployment benefits, and Beveridge warned against the danger that governments and the public might be corrupted into thinking that the unemployment problem had been solved by cash payments alone. Above all there must be work, full employment, for 'a person who cannot sell his labour is in effect told that he is no use', and, 'The first condition of human happiness is the opportunity to serve.'[4] The evils of unemployment blighted more than the unemployed themselves: 'Unemployment makes men live in fear and from that fear springs hate. So long as chronic mass unemployment seems possible, each man appears as the enemy of his fellows in a scramble for jobs. So long as there is a scramble for jobs it is idle to deplore the inevitable growth of jealous restrictions or demarcations, of organised or voluntary limitation of output, or of resistance to technical advance.'[5] He wrote that, 'It might be that cattle must be driven by fear. Men can and should be led by hope.' To remove the fear of unemployment there must be full employment (which he put at 3 per cent), defined as: 'having always more vacant jobs than unemployed men (sic), not slightly fewer jobs. It means the jobs are at fair wages, of such a kind and so located that the unemployed men can reasonably be expected to take them; it means, by consequence, that the normal lag between leaving one's job and finding another will be very short.'[6] These proposals for full employment would: 'make the labour market always a seller's rather than a buyer's market' and 'remove not only unemployment but the fear of unemployment (which) would affect the work of many existing institutions. It would change and is meant to change fundamentally the conditions of living and working in Britain, to make Britain again a land of opportunity for all.'

Beveridge stood as a Liberal in the 1945 election, failing to gain a seat, but he was in no doubt that 'Full employment cannot be won and held without a great extension of the responsibilities and powers of the State.' There remained the central question of whether workers' cooperation could be won 'under conditions of enterprise conducted for private profit'. This, however, Beveridge preferred to leave to the future.

THE POST-WAR POLITICAL CONSENSUS ON FULL EMPLOYMENT AND MILD INTERVENTION [7]

Adrian Sinfield has pointed out how Beveridge's position on work was never really debated, although his recommendations on insurance were implemented in part (he wanted no time limit on payment of benefit). The vision of a service society was more fully realised during the expansion of the Welfare State in other areas of policy such as health. In contrast there was little discussion of the quality of work, its rewards, or how far it provided real security, autonomy and fulfilment for the mass of the working population. The reason was that, somewhat to everyone's surprise, there was a spell of unprecedentedly low unemployment.

Indeed for twenty years it looked as though the mixed economy would work. Industrial and social reorganization during the war had brought full employment, a greater sense of national unity and some reforms of social security. For a while the continuation of wartime controls gave governments the powers and authority to intervene in the economy. Unemployment remained below 2 per cent and inflation fell to zero, and it was believed that economic growth was being held back by labour shortages: women were encouraged to work, elderly people were discouraged from retiring, and the disabled found employment. It has been suggested that as late as 1963 a Conservative Chancellor of the Exchequer, Selwyn Lloyd, fell from office because he failed to reflate the economy to control rising unemployment.

There had developed a political consensus during the 1950s about the necessity of full employment and government planning, which became known as 'Butskellism'. Political and social ideology emphasized the gently regulated development of the mixed economy as a prime mover in bringing about a rise in general standards of living and greater equality without the necessity of major political action. The shared role of the State and private interests in the provision of various social services seemed to be permanently assured. It was said that there was an 'end of ideology', that the people were 'all middle class now'.

Then from the late 1950s and throughout the 1960s Britain began to experience the effects of changing trends in world trade and the oil crisis, and the cosy consensus on intervention was split apart by a conjunction of economic and social phenomena which posed severe questions for each of the perspectives which we have outlined above.

BRITAIN'S PROBLEMS OF LOW GROWTH, INFLATION AND UNEMPLOYMENT

From the early 1960s attempts (which had usually been made just before election time) [8] to stimulate the economy by limited fiscal measures began to fail. Instead of giving a boost to Britain's industrial investment and output, reflation began to fuel consumer booms of spending on imported goods, which resulted in a succession of balance of payments crises, with runs on the pound, the threat (as it was seen) of devaluation and a return of deflationary policies. This was the notorious 'stop-go' cycle. [9]

Government fiscal intervention did not seem to be curing unemployment either, for the numbers of people registered as unemployed during successive booms rose, even when there was overtime working and widely-publicised reports of shortage of some key workers. Nor did rising unemployment cure inflation. Britain developed a combination of industrial stagnation and inflation which became known as 'stagflation': indeed at one point soon after the oil crisis inflation threatened to become 'hyper-inflation'. A further turn of the screw has come with a massive rise in unemployment at the same time as continuing inflation and falling industrial production.

There have been other puzzling features in Britain's developing crisis. With rising unemployment, instead of falling, the wage demands of various groups of manual and professional workers have risen, with the result that the wages of the most powerful have kept ahead of price inflation throughout the decade. Nor did rising unemployment bring any great protest or even (as we saw in the last chapter) much sympathy for the workless. The different traditions of political economy, outlined above, would lead to very diverse analyses of these problems, identifying different causes and pointing to contrasting policy solutions. In the event, Britain's reaction to the growing crisis has been to oscillate between increasingly timid forms of Keynesian intervention and an ever more determined attempt to promote the free market policies of classical economics.

ABANDONING KEYNES AND FULL EMPLOYMENT: THE DEATH OF THE 'SOCIAL CONTRACT'

Over the post-war period there has never been anything like the extension of state control over financial investment and industrial reorganization which was certainly contemplated by Beveridge in his most radical mood, and which (as we saw above) seems to have been required even by milder Keynesian theory, in order to ensure full employment. Although nationalized, the Bank of England has continued to act as an arm of the City rather than government. Attempts at planning under the National Economic Development Council in the 1960s were disappointing. The pattern of the first phase of nationalization, where ailing rather than successful industries and services were taken over by the State, has been largely maintained. [10] The National Enterprise Board has never played more than a peripheral role in promoting, let along controlling, successful industry, and its scope is being reduced. Present worker subsidies tend to go to ailing or dying industries to support part-time employment, rather than to promote successful exporting companies. [11] Subsidies for small firms have come

extremely late, but in any case small firms are a very minor part
of Britain's economy, and they will need large customers if they
are to thrive.

In industrial relations there has been scarcely any move towards
permanent security of work, worker participation or the democrat-
ization of work relationships. Of particular interest in view of the
theme of this book, was the ill-fated 'social contract' or 'social
compact', between Labour and the trade unions.[12] With the fall of
the Heath government over a failure to impose pay restraint,
Labour attempted to expand a previous voluntary arrangement
with the unions into a system of voluntary pay restraint. In
return, under the 'social contract', the government was to pursue
socially responsible economic policies in relation to employment and
public expenditure. However, this was just after the beginning of
the oil crisis, and the attempt at a social contract followed the ill-
fated 'Barber boom' which had brought down unemployment, but
only at the expense of the threat of hyper-inflation and a massive
balance of payments crisis. The social contract collapsed. As the
price of an I.M.F. loan, Labour returned to deflationary policies,
with the largest proportional public expenditure cuts that have
yet been made.[13] The Government later fell from office over the
attempt to set a wage norm for public sector workers which was
below inflation and which resulted in the 'winter of discontent' of
public sector workers' strikes. And this was but the last of a long
line of attempted pay policies which had failed to disturb the
unions' basic stance, that the normal mode of fixing wages should
be 'free collective bargaining'.

The collapse of the social contract after the Barber boom proved
to be the end of faith in even the limited Keynesian intervention -
through tinkering with tax, credit and exchange controls - which
had been practised since the war. The arrival of North Sea oil has
meant that there has been less fear of a balance of payments
crisis in the late 1970s. However, the conclusion has been drawn
that governments cannot spend without causing inflation. And
1979 saw the election of a Conservative government which has so
far resolutely refused to contemplate government spending whatever the level reached by unemployment.[14]

THE RISE OF FREE MARKET IDEOLOGY AND MONETARISM

The spasmodic retreat from Keynes has alternated with an ever
more determined advocacy of a free market ideology, which indeed
never really had been totally banished from thinking in official
and private financial circles. The decade has ended with the
espousal by the Conservative leadership of a modern variant of
classical economics, monetarism.

In fact it was a Labour government which began the move towards free market policies in the mid-1960s, with its tax on
employment and a new redundancy scheme. Attempts were made
to suggest that lump sum redundancy payments constituted a

recognition of the workers' rights and prospects in their jobs, a sort of 'job-ownership' or 'property'.[15] But they conferred no permanent ownership of jobs in the form of control over employment decisions, working conditions, work security, or the right to alternative work and retraining. Indeed, the policy was really to assist the so-called 'shake-out' or 'redeployment' of 'surplus labour'. And in this it was successful because individual workers tend to 'take the money and run' rather than fight redundancy collectively through the unions. The net effect is to give more power to management, and to emphasize business rationality. Redundancy payments thus increase rather than decrease general job insecurity; and this increase is by no means offset by the still limited security of contract which was achieved in the 1970s.

A full-blown and explicit classical economic ideology returned to Parliament with Mr Heath's Conservative government at the beginning of the 1970s.[16] There were tax cuts for the better-off (given as 'incentives' on the assumption that high tax rates were crippling investment and frustrating management) and a policy of refusing to spend government money to save industrial 'lame ducks'. Entry to the European Common Market was intended to provide larger markets and a bracing cold douche of competition for industry. And a determined attack was made on trade union power through the law.[17] These policies collapsed when unemployment passed the million mark: there was a sit-in by redundant Scottish ship-workers; Rolls Royce was on the brink of bankruptcy; and a series of bitter industrial disputes exposed the difficulties of controlling the highly decentralized union structure by law (since this time more indirect means, such as cutting social security payments to strikers' families, have been favoured). However the temporary retreat into Keynesian intervention, with the Barber Boom, was strongly criticised by Sir Keith Joseph as 'inflationeering'.[18] And when Mr Heath mistimed and lost the election in 1974, advocates of the free market ideology were to win power in the Conservative Party, a power which was finally consolidated with the victory in 1979 of a Conservative government committed to monetarism.

In view of the novel nature of many of the problems faced by Britain, and the oscillations of policy over the last few years which have meant that no policy has been tried very thoroughly for very long, adherence to any kind of theoretical position must be to some extent an act of faith. It therefore seems all the more remarkable that adherents of monetarism should be so convinced that monetarism and classical economics are not 'ideological', not just another theory, but the truth.[19] Lord Gowrie has broadcast on the B.B.C.'s early morning religious programme, and Mrs Thatcher has preached in church, that wealth creation is morally good; and Mrs Thatcher regards inflation as a 'moral issue',[20] and work as a duty and a virtue. Could there be a clearer expression of the continuing links between free market ideology and the Protestant work ethic?[21]

246

AN OUTLINE OF MONETARISM, THE 'FISCAL CRISIS' AND THE RATIONALE OF PUBLIC EXPENDITURE CUTS

Seen historically, monetarism is a variant of classical economics which focuses its attack on Keynesian intervention and government spending. As we saw, Keynes himself was worried about structural rigidities in the labour market, which would mean that below a certain level of unemployment spending would create inflation. Monetarism takes such rigidities as a fixed and given 'natural' level (different for each economy), and argues that the economy will be self-balancing around this level if the government does not intervene. [22] In particular they focus on the 'money supply': if governments hold this constant it is argued, then there cannot be inflation (this is the modern equivalent of the return to the gold standard which took place in the Depression years). If the unions continue to press for higher wages, the fixed supply of money will be monopolized by the more powerful only at the expense of the loss of some workers' jobs. So on monetarist theory it is governments, not unions, which create and can prevent inflation. It is the free operation of the market, and not government spending, which will create more wealth. And it is union power and irresponsibility, not governments, which create unemployment.

Monetarist arguments for cutting public expenditure have meshed with another growing debate, about the so-called 'fiscal crisis' of the State. [23] It is argued that the capacity of citizens to consume services outstrips the ability of the State to raise revenue through taxation, a problem which is exacerbated when, as in Britain, the so-called 'wealth-creating' manufacturing sector is shrinking. As a result, it is argued, more and more taxation becomes loaded onto individuals with a consequent stifling of their incentive to earn, save and invest, and there is a growing resistance by citizens to state taxation for spending on state services. (A more sophisticated economic argument asserts that the growth of state spending crowds out industry, by starving it of the resources which are necessary from private investment to sustain growth.)

Thus the arguments of monetarism and the fiscal crisis pointed together towards cuts in public expenditure, to free industry from supposedly harmful constraints and to bring down inflation. It was argued by the Conservative government that further public spending on services must await the regeneration of Britain's industrial base, and in the meantime any contraction of services must be made up by voluntary work and an expansion of private payment.

In line with the monetarist free market ideology (and mindful of the failure of previous pay policies), workers in the private and public sector were allowed to engage in free collective bargaining. The constraints in the private sector were to be high interest rates which would squeeze the money supply, reduce profit margins, and make it difficult to borrow to pay wages. There was a built-in incentive to management to shed workers, and to workers to cut manning levels and engage in productivity deals which would permit technological innovation and more flexible working. The constraint in the public sector was intended to be the cash limits which have been put on spending in the various services and nationalized industries. If workers tried to bargain outside these constraints, and did not respond to appeals for 'responsible' pay settlements and wage restraint in the interest of keeping down inflation and unemployment, then they would face the direct threat that they or their fellow-workers were likely to become unemployed.

THE RESISTIBLE RISE OF CLASSICAL ECONOMICS

We can now begin to understand the paradoxes of Britain's present crisis. Governments from both Parties have initiated and sustained policies which they knew would lead to rising unemployment, yet they have stayed in office as unemployment reached levels which would have been considered politically suicidal in the immediate post-war period. Instead of protests, unemployment has brought attempts to pretend there was no problem and to blame the workless for their own condition. And the decade has ended with the resurgence of monetarist classical economics - thought to have been discredited by its failure to cope with mass unemployment in the Depression - which raises public prejudices against the workless to the status of a theory, and which asserts that full employment is neither possible nor desirable.

Seen in retrospect the period of full employment after the war seems almost accidental, and may not even be attributable to any great extent to the timid Keynesian management of the day. Since the going has got rough and the national 'cake' has failed to grow quickly enough for everyone to get what they think is a fair share, there have developed squabbles about who is responsible and how the cake is to be shared out. 'Scroungerphobia' and the tendency to scapegoat the unions[24] may be seen as part of the 'moral panic'[25] engendered when a tension-ridden society has experienced an inexplicable threat to social order.

But of the range of possible policies, why should classical economics have had such an appeal? One explanation must be that it is in line with a very deeply engrained and individualistic work ethic which sees idleness as morally blameworthy. But there are also political and structural reasons. Because of the lack of adequate debate of work policy during the vital post-war period, and the consensus about economic growth as a solvent of social tensions during the 1950s, Labour had really no alternative coherently worked-out economic and social policy for full employment. Indeed when monetarism assumed dominance at the end of the decade, the leadership of the Party was seen to be in the grip of advice from economists of a basically classical persuasion.[26] The monthly publication of the rising statistics of unemployment became a ritual for Labour to mouth slogans from the folk-memory of the Depression; and Conservative monetarists could rightly argue that they were following policies which Labour had initiated.

The goal of full employment slid from view, as it became 'redeployment', or 'shake-out', and later the 'slimming down' of industry. From the late 1960s inflation was erected as the main target of public policy and, in tackling inflation, free market policies seem to have had a more powerful appeal for the electorate. 'Freedom' has a brighter ring than the austerity of control and planning. Moreover, free market policies have offered tax-cutting for the better-off and 'free collective bargaining' for the workers. And the so-called 'fiscal crisis' was there at least to the extent that taxation had increased and tax thresholds had fallen until they caught a larger fraction of the population in the tax net. [27]

The goal of full employment could be displaced more easily because, as we saw in the last chapter, its costs fall so unequally on a minority of the population. The majority (among whom are the opinion-formers of the mass media and M.P.s) tend to be isolated from the risk of unemployment, and even if they do become unemployed they are protected from suffering its worst impact because the inequalities of better security and rewards in work are matched by more generous and less punitive social security provisions.

We are seeing here the process of political and economic 'incorporation'[20] of a proportion of the working population to support policies which penalize the workless. Over the decade average wage increases have kept ahead of price inflation. [29] Meanwhile the 'reserve' army of the unemployed has tended to be different in character, composed of various kinds of non-unionized and more marginal workers. The social and organizational separation of workers from the workless was for a while maintained by the fact that unemployed workers lost their union membership.

Predictions for organized political action against unemployment are difficult. If unemployment grows it will challenge the very basis of incorporation[30] (and indeed there are signs that present Conservative policies have lost them the support of the skilled manual workers' votes which were said to have won them the last election). [31] Some unions now offer their unemployed members cheap membership, and they are beginning to organize services. [32] But future developments will depend on the further rise of unemployment, and, ironically, this means falling resources for the unions to organize protest. In any case, organized union action tends to get poor or adverse press coverage. Significantly, so far, organized political protests (as opposed to sporadic outbreaks of violence such as at Brixton) have remained muted. Mass marches have been in Liverpool and Glasgow, far from the south-east where there is still much less impact from widespread and long-term unemployment.

Meanwhile the spate of youth riots produced a characteristically mixed set of responses. Mrs Thatcher insisted that they had nothing to do with unemployment and government policies on spending, and clearly favoured tougher action. But the 'wet' Mr Prior advocated improved youth employment programmes, with however the possibility that entitlement to alternative supplementary benefit might then be withdrawn for the whole age group. So yet again there was evidence of sympathy for, but also a backlash against, the workless.

The lack of an alternative economic strategy and the absence of mass political protest have made room for the rise of the free market policies of classical economics, and monetarists have always claimed that the purging of British industry of workers' bad practices will take a while to achieve. But two years of monetarist government have seen a huge rise in unemployment and a catastrophic fall in production. While official claims are made that the economy may be about to pick up, a further deterioration is expected in unemployment. Time may be running out for monetarism now that the electorate has finally swung round to seeing unemployment rather than inflation as the most important political issue.[33]

NOTES

1   Discussions of economics in this and the next chapter, follow Showler, in B. Showler and A. Sinfield (eds.), *The Workless State*, Martin Robertson, 1981; see also, K. Hawkins, *Unemployment*, Penguin, 1979, Ch. 4.
2   See, D. Moggridge (ed.), *J. M. Keynes, Collected Writings*, vol. 27, Macmillan, 1980; see also A. Deacon in B. Showler and A. Sinfield, op. cit.
3   A. Sinfield, *What Unemployment Means*, Martin Robertson, 1981, builds on Beveridge to make a compelling case for full employment.
4   W. H. Beveridge, *Full Employment in a Free Society*, Allen & Unwin, 1944.
5   W. H. Beveridge, *Unemployment: a Problem of Industry*, Longmans, 1930.
6   W. H. Beveridge, op. cit., 1944. The remaining Beveridge quotations are also from this source.
7   For a lively and much more detailed discussion of the politics of unemployment since the war, see A. Deacon in B. Showler and A. Sinfield, op. cit.
8   M. Barrett Brown, 'The causes of unemployment', *The Spokesman*, no. 22, 1972.
9   K. Hawkins, op. cit., has a good account of Britain's problems of productivity and the balance of payments constraint; see also W. W. Daniel, *A National Survey of the Unemployed*, P.E.P., 1974.
10 Although reluctant, the investment has so far been massive and has swallowed up much of the North Sea oil revenues: £1 billion to British Steel Corporation, £900 million to British Leyland, £834 million to the National Coal Board and £800

million to British Rail. See Cambridge Economic Policy Group, *Economic Policy in the UK*, Gower Hampshire, 1981; F. Cripps and T. Ward, *Guardian*, 28 April 1981.

11 See K. Hawkins, op. cit., for a discussion of the problems of worker subsidies.

12 See H. Clegg, *The Changing System of Industrial Relations in Britain*, Macmillan, 1980; also J. F. Goodman, 'Great Britain: Towards the Social Contract' in S. Barkin (ed.), *Worker Militancy and Its Consequences, 1965-1975*, Praeger, 1976.

13 For a detailed discussion of the cuts, see A. Walker, P. Ormerod and L. Whitty, *Abandoning Social Priorities*, Poverty Pamphlet 44, C.P.A.G., 1979, Chs. 1 and 2, and the follow-up, 'Surveying the Cuts', *Poverty*, no. 47, December 1980.

14 See K. Hawkins, op. cit.; also F. Blackaby (ed.), *Britain's Economic Policy 1960-1974*, C.U.P., 1978, for an account of the increase in levels of unemployment which 'triggered' reflation.

15 See appendix by R. H. Fryer in R. Martin and R. H. Fryer, *Redundancy and Paternalist Capitalism*, Allen & Unwin, 1973 (since that time capitalism looks decidedly less 'paternalistic'). Also R. H. Fryer, 'Redundancy and the Rest of Work', Social Administration Association Conference Paper, 1978. On 'shake-out', see Harold Wilson, *Hansard*, col. 628, 20 July 1966.

16 In February 1971, Mr Enoch Powell, an early advocate of the free market, said, 'Every time the State steps in with tax-payers' money to maintain a company, industry or service that cannot maintain itself, it is striking a blow at the well-being of the worker...Profit and competition are the worker's best friend, because they are the only sure guarantee that he will not be producing lower value when he could be producing higher value.'

17 *The Industrial Relations Act*, 1971.

18 *New Society*, 28 September 1974.

19 Mrs Thatcher on 'Weekend World', I.T.V., said '(monetarism) is not a theory. It is borne out by everything that's happened in this country in the last twenty years.' *Guardian*, 2 February 1981. See also, *Sunday Times*, 8 February 1981: 'I am not concerned with economic theory... I am concerned with what is happening in practice.' Sir Geoffrey Howe referred to monetarist theory as not theory but 'fact', *Guardian*, 16 March 1981.

20 'It is, in my view, a moral issue, not just an economic one.' *Guardian*, 5 March 1981. On this occasion she also spoke of work not just being a necessity but a duty and a virtue.

21 F. F. Ridley, op. cit., has an interesting comment on Mrs Thatcher's lack of connection with traditional Conservative Party leadership roots.

22 Sir Geoffrey Howe now claims this rate is 5 per cent, 'far higher than previously thought', *Guardian*, 26 March 1981. Showler in B. Showler and A. Sinfield, op. cit., suggested that there was a consensus between monetarists and Keyne-

sians at 2 to 3 per cent as the 'full employment rate of unemployment'.

23 J. O'Connor, *The Fiscal Crisis of the State*, St. Martin's Press, 1973. The thesis was clearly influencing Labour thinking as far back as the mid-1960s: see H. Wilson, op. cit., and A. Deacon in B. Showler and A. Sinfield, op. cit.

24 See I. Crewe, *A New Conservative Electorate?* for evidence on anti-union feeling.

25 S. Cohen, *Folk Devils and Moral Panics*, Penguin, 1975.

26 A. Deacon in B. Showler and A. Sinfield, op. cit., suggests that Callaghan's key speech rejecting public spending was written by his son-in-law, Peter Jay, an economist.

27 In 1939 there were only four million tax payers out of a working population of 20 million. Since then incomes have risen, but also tax policies, and inflation and the failure to adjust tax thresholds (until 1977 and then from 1981) have increased the proportion of tax payers and the burden on the individual. F. Cairncross, *Guardian*, 16 February 1981.

28 F. Parkin, *Class Inequality and Political Order*, McGibbon and Kee, 1971; see also, F. Hirsch and J. Goldthorpe, *The Political Economy of Inflation*, Martin Robertson, 1978.

29 Although averages conceal large inequalities: see Ch. 14. See Low Pay Unit publications; see also W. W. Daniel, *New Society*, 19 March 1981, on why the unemployed do not protest (for most the experience is too short).

30 For an example of the kind of swing which might take place, see our interviews. Two sets of attitudes, akin to incorporation and exclusion, are outlined in D. Lockwood, 'Affluence and the British Class Structure', *Sociological Review*, vol. II, no. 2, 1963.

31 P. Jenkins, *Guardian*, 18 March 1981.

32 *Services for the Unemployed*, T.U.C. Discussion document, T.U.C., November 1980.

33 A. Walker gives results of a Gallup poll which shows that increasing proportions of people wish more money to be spent on social services, even if it means putting up taxes. *Poverty*, no. 47, December 1980, p. 20. However, Labour is not necessarily picking up votes from the unemployed: see P. Kelner, 'Maggie's Missing Million', *New Statesman*, 27 March 1981.

14 The Need for a Social Contract through Work

Since the collapse of timid Keynesian intervention, the Labour Party has been thrown into confusion and has threatened to split apart. But equally, two years of monetarism, bringing a record rise in unemployment and fall in production, have opened visible rifts among Conservatives[1] and among their supporters in British industrial management. Now, although there have been some renewed calls for 'reflation', the word means very different things to different groups (to the T.U.C., fiscal measures and investment in the public sector;[2] to the C.B.I., investment in industry but more savage public expenditure and government service cuts).[3] At least it seems to be agreed that the old form of Keynesian intervention has been discredited and stronger measures of some kind will be needed. But what measures?

The different traditions of political economic analysis identify different culprits and propose very contrasting solutions. As a result, British political life now reveals an enormous range of policies, stretching all the way from free market to 'wet' (state interventionist) Conservatism, via a pragmatic 'mixed economy' alliance of the Liberals and new Social Democrats, to advocacy by the Left of a much more thorough-going state control of the economy, with more nationalization of key firms and major financial institutions, and the use of tariff barriers or devaluation to protect British industry.

There seems little point in attempting a detailed description and analysis of the whole range of possible policies[4] (especially when the range of middle-ground positions seems to be deliberately left open and unformulated, to maintain maximum electoral appeal with a minimum of commitment to policies which might be discredited). Rather, we will concentrate first on the major obstacles to solving Britain's problems, the continuing failure of policies for investment and pay restraint. We will then discuss the controversies which have arisen over monetarist free market policies and economic theories. And, finally, we will attempt to provide an outline analysis of Britain's crisis which will draw together the various political and economic changes and theories which we have described in this concluding section.

Such an analysis must look at Britain's crisis in a historical and international context. For it is sometimes claimed that Britain's problems are only part of a wider general pattern of rising unemployment and inflation suffered by many other countries: the implication is that we may not have been able to solve our problems, but neither have other countries been able to solve theirs. But it cannot be stressed too strongly that this is not true. Britain has suffered higher rates of unemployment and inflation, with a steeper loss of production and private investment, and with poorer prospects of recovery, than any comparable advanced industrial country in the world.[5] Moreover, our unemployment is borne by a narrower section of the population, who are relatively more stigmatized. Any comprehensive analysis, therefore, must attempt to discover not only the problems which Britain shares with other countries, but why our economy and social relationships are now so much worse.

THE CONTINUED FAILURE OF INVESTMENT

Ever more determined attempts to pursue a free market policy have so far served merely to expose much more clearly the lack of competitiveness of British manufactured goods, and the problems of stimulating private investment in British industry while the return on capital investment remains low.

When tax cuts were made in the early 1970s, there was the development of what Mr Heath was moved to call the 'unacceptable face of capitalism',[6] with property speculation, the growth of tax evasion and tax havens, and attention paid by investors to industry only for the purpose of making money through take-over bids and asset stripping. Late entry to the Common Market on very disadvantageous terms was a drain on Britain's resources,[7] and has served further to reveal how uncompetitive British products are:[8] they have not been up to date with what consumers have wanted, quality and delivery have been poor and prices high. The recent removal of exchange controls has led to a massive outflow of investment, some of it into the industry of our major competitors in Japan, Europe and America.[9] Ironically a proportion of this investment comes from British workers' pension and insurance funds.

A major clash of interests has been revealed between British manufacturing industry and the City's role as a centre maintaining international financial interests and a world reserve currency. We noted earlier how attempts to stimulate economic growth always had to be nipped in the bud because they promoted a run on sterling and a balance of payments crisis, with what was regarded by the Treasury as the threat of the devaluation of sterling. Keeping up the value of sterling, however, has tended to make our exports more uncompetitive and imports cheaper to the detriment of British export industries. After the 1976 I.M.F. loan, the recommendation was for devaluation and an export-led boom. However, since 1976 the value of the pound has risen, at first following the deliberate intervention of the Bank of England,[10] and subsequently because of the confidence inspired in financial circles by North Sea oil and the government's policies of high interest rates. As a result it is estimated that sterling has appreciated by 30 to 40 per cent, creating enormous problems for the sale of our manufactured goods overseas.[11] At the same time there has been growing criticism of the way our financial institutions seem not to be sufficiently geared towards helping industry and exports, compared with finance among our competitors.[12]

The continuing failure to invest enough in Britain becomes more critical with the advent of the micro-chip. Japan and America are five years ahead of Britain in the application of this new technology, and whether one believes the optimistic or the pessimistic scenario for the future, at least in the short-term the effects of greater competition from leading countries could have a very adverse effect on countries which are lagging in investment.

THE CONTINUED FAILURE OF PAY RESTRAINT

The failure of the 'social contract' discussed in the last chapter was only one among a series of attempts to achieve more moderation in pay claims. Assessment of the impact of these various policies is extremely complex, but there are no claims that such intermittent attempts to control pay have had any clear and lasting success.[13] Not only the trade unions but powerful groups of professional workers, such as doctors (who are pay leaders) and airline pilots, have not been prepared voluntarily to take rises in income below inflation levels, and when necessary have used strikes to good effect.

Paradoxically, the more stress which has been laid by governments and the mass media upon the need for wage restraint to bring down inflation and unemployment, the more dissatisfied the various groups of trade union and professional workers seem to have grown. At one point Labour had to set up a pay comparability review in the attempt to even up the levels of pay between some public service workers and the more powerful (or more militant) trade unions and professions.

Even during times of imposed wage restraint, the trade unions have engaged in 'productivity' deals (sometimes phoney) which have increased the incomes of those in work, but at the expense of a net loss of jobs. Meanwhile, there has been a reluctance by the employed either to reduce their working hours or to engage in work-sharing with a view to giving the unemployed work, if this would mean a reduction of income.[14] Workers' behaviour has had the appearance not of a co-ordinated resistance to government policies but of a highly fragmented pursuit of self-interest by the more powerful at the expense of the weak.

Meanwhile, for administrators and managers with larger companies, rising taxation and attempts to impose wage restraint have been countered by a massive extension of fringe benefits and tax deductable perks, such as cheap home loans, company cars, clothing, private medical and insurance schemes, fees for private education and so on. (Indeed, seen historically, this has been a continuation of the trend for companies to promote occupational benefits, for a proportion only of their employees and for which tax deductions are claimed.) The monetarists have not so far made any major attacks on this structure of tax reliefs, for although there was discussion of the massive drain on public resources from tax reliefs on home ownership, private ownership is a basic tenet of free market ideology. So the government drew back from the political implications of cutting tax reliefs and concentrated instead on the sale of council houses, increasing council rents, and cutting council house building. A small start was made in 1981 by cutting perks on company cars, but meanwhile tax relief on private medical insurance was extended.

The new monetarist industrial strategy for pay-bargaining has also had only a partial impact in the industrial sector where there have been what are officially hailed as more 'responsible'[15] lower wage settlements in industries where profitability is low. A tougher line has been taken by employers on worker militancy, with the sacking of shop stewards, and the negotiation or imposition of new manning levels and flexible working.[16] And the same changes seem to be taking place in some of the more beleaguered areas of the public sector. However, bank workers are attacking the huge windfall profits made by the banks through high interest rates. And in the public sector the more powerful miners and the water and energy workers have gained pay rises which are double the cash limits, by threatening to strike.

Now it is the turn of industrialists to complain that public sector pay rises are too high. Meanwhile, however, the response of leading corporations to the tax cuts (which were supposedly made partly to switch more income into the pockets of management and thereby improve their performance) has been to award its top management pay rises of up to 100 per cent, with an average of 40 per cent.

ARGUMENTS ABOUT MONETARISM[17]

How well will monetarist policies cope with Britain's economic, political and social crisis? Just as politicians have become more prone to argue about economic theory, the effect of the rise of monetarism has been to create political arguments between economists about the rival merits of the free market and state intervention. In fact, probably only a minority of economists are monetarists,[18] but the remainder by no means unite behind a single alternative policy. As we have seen, Keynesian economics itself allows for inflation caused by the push of wages when there are rigidities in the labour market. Economists who are not strict monetarists might also nonetheless allow for some influence from the money supply among a range of other factors; although some see the money supply as completely irrelevant, a consequnce of economic activity rather than a cause.

Indeed there seems to be no clear agreement among economists about the truth of some of the basic tenets of monetarism,[19] such as the role of the money supply, the speed at which policy acts, the effect of tax cuts on behaviour (which can be argued equally to decrease or to increase effort), the conflict between public spending and private investment, and the self-balancing nature of the free market economy. There is a great deal of vagueness and room for argument about the 'transmission' mechanisms[20] (whereby the very simple basic policy of restricting the money supply is supposed to alter behaviour and expectations of individuals and to bring about changes in finance and industry); for example, the conditions for more or less saving or investment, and for 'slimming down' industry, and improving industrial relations. Before monetarist policies were implemented, their predictions were not verified (nor were they apparently verifiable) by any of the computer models of the economy available to the Treasury or monetarist theorists.

With this degree of conflict among academic economists, the notion that economics is a non-ideological science becomes difficult to sustain, and certainly there is no case for claiming that any one set of policies is bound to succeed. We have already noted how political espousals of monetarism had close ideological links with religion. For economists also, it seems that theory may serve the function of myth or dogma.[21]

In view of the heat of controversy even among academic economists, there seem to be great dangers in the way that politicians have suddenly become economic experts, and in particular in the way that simple nostrums drawn from grocery or housekeeping, of the kind propounded by Mr Micawber, have been used to lecture the public on what are really highly complicated economic, social and political processes.

It might be generally agreed that monetarists are correct as to the failure of the timid form of Keynesian intervention which has been practised hitherto. But this seems no reason to accept as given the various economic,[22] political and social constraints of society, which is what the monetarist (and timid Keynesian) assumption of a 'natural' rate of unemployment amounts to. Such a supine acceptance of unemployment, which assumes that workers' labour is of little value and that they cannot be put back to productive work, has enormous economic costs. Each person thrown out of work cost the Exchequer in 1980 at least £2,500; and a family with two children where the wage earner had been earning £6,000 actually cost more than that to keep idle (estimates ranging between £6,006 and £6,207).[23] The cumulative loss of national output had, by 1980, exceeded £20,000 million, which would have generated tax revenue greater than the projected income from North Sea oil in the mid-1980s.[24] It is difficult to find an everyday housekeeping image to convey the potential benefits of a more thorough-going Keynesian intervention undertaken along with industrial and social reorganization, where spending on investment will actually create extra resources, and where the amount of money recouped by putting the workless to work would immediately be a very large fraction of what it costs at present to keep them idle, apart from the value of what they might produce.

The implementation of the key monetarist policy of controlling the money supply has run into various problems apart from political opposition, so that (hedging their bets) monetarists may claim that the theory has not been given a true 'experimental' test. There are various possible indicators of money supply which tend to move in contradictory directions. And rather than control money more directly (which might have led to wild fluctuations in interest rates) the government imposed high interest rates. Even so, the financial community of the City has found various ways of circumventing attempted restrictions.

There are also extensive difficulties entailed in the other main part of the monetarist programme, cutting public expenditure. Suspicions of the deeply ideological basis of present enthusiasm for the notion of the 'fiscal crisis' and the policy of public expenditure cuts are reinforced by the way in which the neo-classical 'liberal' economists have been attacking the so-called 'burden' of the Welfare State[25] (on the grounds that all services are best treated as consumer goods) since long before the 'fiscal crisis' was said to be at all pressing.

The argument used to justify cutting public expenditure has been that it is draining resources away from private industry. However the two sectors are not competing for the same workers, and the continued massive outflow of capital from Britain for investment abroad makes this argument difficult to sustain. With the real problem apparently lying in the low return on investment in British industry, public expenditure may merely be mopping up resources which would otherwise find a less productive use, or even go to help our foreign industrial competitors. A comparison with other countries reveals that Britain is not (as the myth fostered by government, and acquiesced in by the public, would have it) the most heavily taxed country in the world: Britain is about half way down the league of industrial nations;[26] and comparisons with more successful competitors in the E.E.C. reveal that they have larger public expenditures.[27]

The myth of an industrial 'wealth-creating' sector of industry with a parasitic public service sector has been assiduously propagated by monetarists on ideological grounds and eagerly taken up by a beleaguered industry. But this myth is socially and economically naive or disingenuous. There is an argument (parallel with that for work) that apart from the more direct services provided for workers, the social services can perform a vital function of social integration;[28] without them there would be less of a sense of giving to the community, less of the spirit of altruism and common purpose upon which peaceful survival will depend in a time of crisis. Yet the public expenditure cuts have begun to dismantle the Welfare State,[29] and they have so far been highly inegalitarian in effect. They are almost completely unplanned, and must inevitably hurt most those who can least afford to pay for alternative private services.

In the economic sphere also, far from being in direct competition, the public and private sectors are interdependent, so that cuts in public expenditure affect other parts of the economy including private industry. Nationalized industries and public services are suppliers and customers of the private sector, particularly the construction industry which is where public expenditure cuts have bitten most deeply. As Keynes pointed out, the cuts and loss of jobs lead to a general shrinking of the money available for spending on goods and services, and hence to a general lack of demand, which creates a still greater loss of jobs in all sectors. The latest cuts combined disastrously with a fall in demand as a result of the Middle East oil crisis. So whatever its newly elaborated rationale, a policy of cutting expenditure is akin to old-fashioned deflation, with the consequence of rising unemployment which used to be the traditional weapon for breaking the political power of the unions.

But monetarist theory makes deflation potentially more disastrous. Because of the practice of including in public expenditure the 'transfer payments' of benefits for the unemployed, as unemployment rises so does the apparent size of public expenditure. So by a dreadful irony, rising unemployment caused by the so-called 'fiscal crisis' will exacerbate that crisis, and so lead via monetarism to a prescription of the need for further cuts in public expenditure. Even monetarists are divided about strict monetary targets during times of recession and rising unemployment. [30] The reverse effect of Keynes's multiplier, further accelerated by monetarism, has been said to be rather like pulling a brick with a piece of elastic: at first nothing much happens but then suddenly it hits you in the eye.

The effects of cutting the money supply and public expenditure are indiscriminate, and monetarist policy has been criticized by industrialists and trade unionists for not singling out investment for special protection, although they want investment in different sectors. By a further turn of the monetarist screw the high interest rates, maintained to keep down the money supply, may actually push up the need to borrow, increasing pressure on industry and public expenditure while preventing investment. Attempting to squeeze industrial management and unions into a more productive relationship by cutting the money supply may thus help to make even efficient firms go to the wall, at a time when goods are made much more difficult to sell abroad by the high exchange rate, which is in turn a consequence of monetarist policies and international financial confidence in Britain's oil and economic policies. Usually, productivity rises during economic expansion and falls during contraction, so firms may experience what has been called the 'school dinner' or 'British Rail' syndrome, [31] where running an enterprise below capacity, because of reduced custom during the recession, brings an increase in unit costs which puts up prices, which further drives away custom, and so on.

A proportion of firms will manage to 'slim down' (the latest euphemism for making workers unemployed), but it may prove easier for multi-national companies to shut down production in Britain and move abroad. Apart from the scale of unemployment in a 'slimmed down' Britain, a major question is whether there will survive a large enough industrial base to take advantage of any future upturn in trading prospects. In an authoritative review of the theoretical foundations and effects of monetarist policies, an all-party Select Committee[32] could not agree that a monetarist 'experiment' had really been tried, but they did estimate that the cost of attempting to bring down inflation by monetarist policies would be too great, resulting in a permanent loss of production. They concluded that it was misguided so single-mindedly to pursue one goal, the bringing down of inflation, by one policy, squeezing the money supply, to the exclusion of other social goals such as keeping down unemployment. Nevertheless the criticism was rejected by the government. Almost alone among European countries, Britain still shows no sign of government spending to try to boost jobs.

THE ROOTS OF BRITAIN'S CRISIS OF 'NATIONAL IRRESPONSIBILITY'

The real failures of monetarism (and other purely economic policies) lie not so much in the details of economic technique as in the narrowness of the political analysis of Britain's economic situation, and in defects of moral vision. On the face of it, Britain has a crisis of 'national irresponsibility'. The workless are blamed for unemployment, but the failure of the unions to moderate their wage claims has also been seen by various governments, the mass media and public opinion as highly irresponsible, if not the main cause of Britain's present difficulties. And any comprehensive discussion must also focus on the less publicly-condemned but equally important refusal of Britain's financial interests to invest in British industry 'in the national interest'.

The monetarist response has been a single economic technique, with a denial that its origins, application or outcomes are ideological. What is required is a much broader political, social and moral vision, which encompasses the questions of why Britain's industrial performance, once so good, now seems so disastrously vulnerable to foreign competition.

(i) Britain's Mercantile History

Seen in an international and historical perspective, Britain's colonial past has had a profound and lasting effect on the relationship between manufacturing industry and the financial institutions of the City.

Britain's easy industrial lead and early involvement in overseas markets meant that instead of developing a set of financial institutions geared to building up a firm home manufacturing base with appropriate technical training and educational institutions (as major industrial competitors like Germany and Japan were forced to do), Britain's finance became more geared to overseas trade and investment.[33]

While Britain had the Empire, the combination of finance and industry worked well. Along with our manufactured goods, we exported a 'free market' ideology which prevented the build-up of any substantial competition, and tended to kill incipient or indigenous local industries. Meanwhile the City of London, its financial institutions and sterling assumed a world role. It has even been argued that British industrialism was only temporarily in the ascendency, and that since the nineteenth century industry has returned to take second place in our longer tradition of mercantilism.[34]

(ii) The Rationalization of International Finance and Industry

Competition for manufactured goods has got tougher since Britain lost the Empire, spent a great deal on two world wars, and began to be overtaken by newer-style industrial nations. (Although the oil crisis came as a further turn of the screw, it may be seen as almost incidental to other general trends, related to the volume of world production of armaments and so on.) During the rationalization of international industry and finance, Britain has been forced to adapt. But because of historical developments, there has been an increasing clash between, on the one hand, our international financial interests and, on the other, the need to preserve and consolidate the base of British manufacturing industry, which has hitherto provided the bulk of the jobs and resources for the development of service industries and the social services.

Since the Second World War business has been reorganized on an international scale through combination into larger multi-national corporations.[35] Such corporations have the advantage that they can look for the lowest-paid and most pliable workers, who are least able or inclined to resist the application of the new technologies which create profits for the owners of capital but throw people out of work.[36] The corporations can also arrange to produce goods in countries where tax conditions are most favourable, or they can fix the price of any goods or products which they transfer across national boundaries in such a way that their profits emerge in countries where tax conditions are most favourable.

The consequence of these international developments is that private manufacturing investment and production in any particular country tend to become increasingly a question of business rationality rather than national interest. Continuing industrial production depends on the degree to which financial institutions and industry are tied down to operating within national boundaries, or how great an incentive can be provided by government investment and tax concessions.

In this new situation, Britain is unusually badly placed to pin down any industrial investment. The traditional role of sterling means that Britain's financial institutions are already geared to an international free market: it was Britain which pioneered tax havens in ex-British colonies where profits and income can be recovered outside the British tax net. With an exceptionally large number of big corporations, many of them operating multi-nationally, Britain itself has now become a tax haven for corporations which are based in other countries.[37]

Lack of profitability or resistance to innovation in a particular country, for whatever reason, will lead to investment and industry going elsewhere. And in Britain there have been such obstacles.[38] In part, the lack of success of British industry may be attributed to the continuing social gulf between management and workers, the second-class status of industry and technology, and the discounting of business, management and marketing skills. British products have tended to be poor. But of course there have been deeper problems of industrial relations.[39]

(iii) The Problem of Securing Workers' Cooperation[40]

Britain's history of early industrial development has had a profound influence on workers' institutions and behaviour. Workers are highly unionized (or alternatively, professionalized), and when the general principle of union power to strike is challenged they are capable of acting in coordination to fend off attack. But the union structure grew up with the experience of exploitation and it is fragmented, so that in other ways the unions do not act collectively at all. Wage bargaining is highly decentralized and uncoordinated, with different unions within one firm or industry, local bargaining and a variety of negotiating dates. This so-called 'free collective bargaining' is, in effect, an individualistic and atomistic process.

The system has resulted in a highly differentiated structure of working and wages, where job boundaries and pay inequalities are traditional, and reinforced by the relative power of different unions or professional associations, rather than based on rational criteria of skill, education or social utility. Moreover, the division of jobs means that particular groups of workers have power way beyond their actual economic or social usefulness to bring production or service delivery to a halt.

The clash of the international rationalization of finance and industry, meeting such a fragmented, precariously balanced but potentially powerful structure of workers' institutions, has been highly divisive. Had the collapse of British manufacturing been more general and more sudden, it seems possible that a more co-ordinated workers' movement might have emerged to resist the changes, and to attempt to control the international operations of finance in such a way as to serve the interests of Britain as a whole. There would then have had to be a major confrontation of the kind predicted by Marx, for which, of course, there is no scenario for Britain. But, as we have seen, the tradition of hostility to the workless, the partial 'incorporation' of more powerful workers, and their social separation from the 'reserve army' of the unemployed, have all contributed to defuse militancy and prevent mass protest against unemployment.

Instead, the collapse of British industry has been sporadic, varying over time, by industry and region. In these circumstances, any resistance by workers to attempts to peg or cut back their living standards has had the appearance of selfish guerrilla or rearguard actions, fought as and when the occasion has arisen. On the whole, as we saw, these union and professional activities have been successful – but only for those who have retained their jobs.

In spite of appeals for pay restraint, there has been no guaranteed mechanism for sharing communal resources more evenly (nor the will to share with the unemployed). On the contrary, in industry any profits foresworn might go largely into the pockets of investors, or even overseas to help our competitors. In the public sector, there has arisen the dilemma of the 'public good' to frustrate any kind of social contract: it might be agreed that there could be some general good in overall wage restraint, but individual unions which step out of line will gain relative to the rest.

Failing the development of any common ethic or machinery to control pay demands, in the unions' view it has remained the government's responsibility to devise measures to cure inflation and unemployment. [41] But meanwhile, it is up to each individual union negotiator to do the best possible to secure for members their maximum share of available profits from industry or of public spending. In industry, the 'slimmed down' workforce has pushed to receive the rewards of greater productivity; and in times like the late 1970s when what has been called the 'social wage' (various allowances, benefits and so on, from the State) has been falling, [42] to maintain the same living standards workers' pay claims have moved ahead of price inflation. A more sophisticated Keynesian argument deployed by the unions has been that in a time of expenditure cuts, pressure for higher wages keeps up spending power which keeps up demand and jobs, although this argument is disingenuous in so far as it ignores the higher unemployment which results from productivity deals and indirectly via public expenditure cuts.

All these arguments add up to a situation where the failure of economic growth, rising inflation and unemployment, and cuts in public expenditure and services in the interests of economy, all have the effect of pushing up the wage claims of those unions which have any power to monopolize their jobs and prevent production or service delivery. And attempts to impose wage restraints on this fragmented and unequal structure will interfere with traditional, power-defended differentials, in such a way that there will be greater questioning of the whole basis of pay inequalities, rather than a move towards common agreement.

(iv) The Origins of Inflation [43]

Inflation and unemployment may be seen as the integral consequences of this unresolved clash between international industry and local, powerful British unions. At first, during the post-war period, Britain was a relatively unproductive but also low-wage economy. The early advantage enjoyed by Britain meant that high employment could be maintained along with increased output and productivity.

The failure of economic growth and the increasing power of the unions brought some pressure on wages. But at first when wages rose faster than productivity, the slack was not all made up by structural reorganization and fresh investment, so that in effect the government was financing part of inflation by printing more money. At first this tended to assuage wage demands but only at the expense of inflation, which imposed wage cuts which the employed would not have been prepared to accept directly. Such inflation penalized the small saver, who could not take advantage of the more profitable larger-scale transactions which were open to financial interests. In that sense then, inflation and rises in workers' wages were being at least partly financed by people like the elderly whose savings were being eroded. And to the extent that this was happening, inflation could indeed be said to be 'immoral', and the government has moved to prevent this from happening, at least to the extent of some index-linking of pensions and savings.

(v) The Origins of Unemployment

When the unions realized what was happening, negotiators began to build into their pay claims the expectation of wage cuts via inflation, with the result that when inflation turned up towards hyper-inflation, wage bids threatened to become astronomical. Once governments attempted to tackle inflation by clamping down on public spending, this became an increased threat that wages would not rise.

Pressure on wages, coupled with industry's push for profits and rationalization, meant that if wages and productivity were to rise simultaneously, jobs must be shed. The alternative open to multi-nationals was to move abroad to more favourable climates. The unions could maintain their living standards through productivity deals, but not through work-sharing (which in any case employers did not favour because it put up unit costs). The result was a loss of jobs through redundancy or through productivity deals which entailed what was euphemistically called 'natural wastage' or 'early retirement'.

Unemployment thus arises from a three-way squeeze: the push of investors, owners and management for profits; the fight of unions and professions for higher pay; and the determination of governments to clamp down on inflation. The greater the determination of any of these, the higher unemployment will be. The more extensive and powerful the organization of the unions and professions to fight this process, the narrower will be the fraction of the population of non-unionized and marginal workers who are squeezed out of work, and the heavier the costs they will have to bear.

264

It is because unemployment originates in this three-way squeeze that the public and academic debates have been so wrong-headed when they focus on the social characteristics and motivation of the workless, as if these were fixed and the cause of people's unemployment. The fractions of the population which are squeezed or kept out of work will have very different characteristics, depending on the power, opportunities, training and education of various groups in society, or the discrimination and discouragement they experience. But the workless are the victims; they suffer rather than cause unemployment.

(vi) The Origins of the 'Fiscal Crisis' and 'Thatcherism'

The 'fiscal crisis', and the rise of the most determined form of classical economic ideology called monetarism or 'Thatcherism', may also be seen as an integral part of this squeeze. [44] With profitability under pressure (at least from the 1960s) [45] it has become increasingly difficult for the State to tax industry in Britain, or even to find out what profits are being made where and to latch onto any share of elusive multi-national financial transactions. [46] As a result, a larger and larger share of taxation has been loaded onto individuals, who have in turn been the more easily persuaded that they were over-taxed. [47] In their turn they have fought a rearguard action by diverting some of their activities into the black economy, thereby further reducing tax revenues.

But we must add to this picture, for it presents business, financial, and professional elites as beleaguered and in retreat, whereas in fact they have mounted an extremely effective counterattack, not merely against state intervention but within it, by using or colonizing state interventionist strategies and machinery.

Work itself is now becoming a privilege, but before mass unemployment there had already begun the development of greater inequalities within work. During the period of the growth of the Welfare State, the rationalization of industry into larger units and the rise of the professions and semi-professions have meant the expansion of occupational privilege. Better jobs have come to mean, apart from better pay, more security, better working conditions, and differential access to a range of 'perks', occupational privileges and welfare services, such as private pensions, golden handshakes, cheap loans, free private medical insurance, education fees, company cars, cheap clothing and so on. [48] In larger firms and professions there are ladders of jobs with graded rewards and fringe benefits, where promotion tends to be available only to internal applicants. To the extent that they have chosen to fight on grounds of improving jobs for their members (and to enforce legislation about working conditions in the areas where their members work), the trade unions, too, have contributed to the greater differentiation of working conditions and privileges. Some observers have likened the situation to a 'dual labour market' where a fraction of the population become included (or, as we said above, economically and politically 'incorporated') but the rest are

excluded. However, in the highly fragmented state of British
work the situation is probably better described as a pronounced
hierarchy.[49]

The relevance of these developments for the fiscal crisis is both
direct, in terms of the amount of taxable income which remains
available or visible to the State, and political. For companies and
professions have developed the system of perks and occupational
welfare partly to improve the motivation and keep the allegiance
of key staff, but also as a means of doing this in the cheapest
way, by avoiding the payment of tax. Fringe benefits and perks
may be largely offset against profits by their providers, and they
are tax-free or virtually so to their receivers. There is, in
addition, a system of tax concessions for better-off individuals,
particularly concessions on property ownership, insurance,
inherited wealth and investment income. And this too siphons off
taxable income and further erodes the base upon which the State
can raise tax.

But it also means the consolidation or the new development of
powerful groups who have a vested interest in the continuation
or increase of inequalities, through the erosion of progressive
tax rates and the expansion of a system (for privileged workers
and the better-off only) which is an alternative to the Welfare
State. Meanwhile, the Welfare State must attempt with increasing
difficulty to provide services for all, including the poor and most
needy who have few or no resources from work. Among such
newer interest groups are the private insurance companies and
pensions funds, who control large amounts of the private investment which is now flowing abroad or into non-industrial ventures.
The new welfare state professions and semi-professions, in education and health, must also be included, as must government
administrators, the civil servants. Moreover, to the extent that
they have won privileges for their members only or have participated in the concessions won by other powerful interest groups,
trade union members, too, are deeply implicated in the development and maintenance of the hierarchy of occupational, economic
and social inequality.

Because of these powerful interests, governments of various
political persuasions have acquiesced in, connived at, or actively
fostered, developments which have taken place at the expense of
starving the Welfare State of resources. The 'fiscal crisis' is
therefore a manifestation of elected governments having neither
the political power nor the will to raise through taxation the resources which would be adequate for the provision of effective
communal services and necessary to achieve any real redistribution
of income and wealth.

Although the development of the alternative 'welfare state'[50] of
fiscal concessions and occupational welfare is largely hidden or
unremarked in the press, it is by no means accidental. Among the
more powerful and the more affluent, it is widely believed that
state intervention has narrowed income differentials too far, and
that the Welfare State is extending its services to the point where

they are unnecessary or indeed damagingly over-generous.

The adoption, first of free market ideology, and then of that most determined form of monetarism which is called 'Thatcherism' - with its talk of 'wealth creation', 'incentives', the 'need' for higher salaries for managers and tax cuts for top earners and investors, and the 'burden' of the Welfare State; while the bulk of the population are asked for 'responsible' income restraint, the unemployed are subjected to 'scroungerphobia' and the poor are told they must share in the 'sacrifices' which must be made by 'the country' - may thus be seen as an integral part of a wider stratagem for returning to greater inequality in society.[51]

BUSINESS RATIONALIZATION AS THE CAUSE OF THE 'CRISIS OF IRRESPONSIBILITY'

If this analysis is correct (and of course it is offered here not as a finished proof so much as the overall picture which best seems to explain the paradoxes of the last few chapters), then the behaviour of the various contributors to Britain's 'crisis of irresponsibility' appears in a very different light. We do not need any kind of conspiracy theory to understand the failure of invest-ment. The financial community of the City is behaving in a way which is nationally irresponsible, but which is perfectly econom-ically rational in the international free market.

Unfortunately, international economic rationality no longer operates in the interests of Britain's industry or the general pop-ulation. There may be little incentive for investment in British industry unless and until the living standards and industrial power of British workers have been reduced to levels comparable with the Third World countries which are now becoming our major competitors.

The increasing power of the trade unions (but also of the pro-fessions) does contribute fairly directly to rising unemployment, and if it does not cause inflation, helps to keep up the level. In that sense trade union and professional pay claims are irrespon-sible. But seen in the context of threatened living standards and the lack of any ethic of sharing or common goals, this behaviour, too, is perfectly economically rational.

THE MORAL CONTRADICTIONS OF CLASSICAL ECONOMIC 'FREE MARKET' IDEOLOGY

A conspiracy theory of some sort, based on Britain's international financial interests, does however seem to be necessary to explain how on earth, in its present condition, Britain has come to pursue a free market policy in investment which is so wrong-headed and inimical to the interests of the bulk of the population. Obviously there are powerful groups which benefit from a free market in capital, but there are few guarantees that the bulk of the population or even British industry will share in those benefits. Some means must be found to defend Britain's industrial base from the ravages of international competition. On the other hand, Britain's mercantile tradition means that the problems of control are greater and we have much more to lose than most other countries from any return to outright protectionism in international trade. A siege economy, even backed by North Sea oil, would bring massive disruption to daily life, but in any case if we are to retain any substantial position in international trade, Britain's industry cannot be protected forever behind tariff walls against the cold winds of competition blowing outside. [52]

One thing is clear however. In the past days of the British Empire it may have served our interests very well to adopt a free market ideology through which our goods could dominate the world's markets. But now that goods from other countries are 'penetrating' Britain's home markets, to advocate a return to nineteenth-century free market policies is to lie back with every appearance of inviting and enjoying economic rape. [53]

Wage restraint and peaceful industrial cooperation will be necessary to solve Britain's crisis, and here again the adoption of free market ideologies is crassly misguided, especially when the error is compounded by deploying the ideology so unequally between different fractions of the population. But, as we have just shown, monetarism is an integral part of a much larger and continuing strategy, fought by various elites against government intervention with the express purpose of bringing about increased inequality. With no appeal to a communal ethic, monetarist policies therefore seem doomed to promote a series of industrial and social conflicts which will lead to growing inequalities between the more and the less powerful or privileged, and which will only be contained by the use of force. And in their apparent eagerness to break the power of the unions even at the expense of the destruction of a large part of British industry, the monetarists seem themselves to be a symbol of how Britain's declining fortunes have brought self-destructive social divisions.

Nor are free market ideologies adequate for the regeneration of the non-industrial sector, from which must come the bulk of the new jobs and the services which will be necessary to meet expanding social needs. Monetarists have fostered the highly divisive myth of a separate 'wealth-creating' sector upon which the social services are parasitic. Apart from the grossly inegalitarian effects of the public expenditure cuts, there is a basic contradiction in promoting the value of individualistic economic rationality while at the same time advocating that social needs should be met through voluntary, unpaid and altruistic caring by something called the 'community'. [54]

Classical economic ideology is also, of all policies, the least appropriate to meet rising unemployment in the drastically 'slimmed down' Britain which will be the result of the pursuit of monetarist policies. For monetarists have been in the forefront of those who have tried to minimize the scale of the problem. They have denigrated the workless, and denied their abilities and need for work.

The deepest moral contradiction of all is that classical economic policies have gained ascendency precisely because of their superficial appeal to selfish economic individualism. But in a society where the fundamental problem is that behaviour is too economically self-seeking, advocating an expansion of selfish economic freedoms is like prescribing more of the poison that is killing the patient.

THE NEED FOR A SOCIAL CONTRACT THROUGH WORK

Workless follows on a long tradition of criticism of classical economic theory on the grounds that the appeal to individual economic self-interest is divisive and destructive. If Britain's economic fortunes are to be restored, there will be the need for difficult industrial reorganization and greater cooperation from members of society at all levels. We have tried to show how the problems of inequalities in work security and rewards, poor industrial relations, and inflation and unemployment are so inextricably linked that they demand a common solution.

The costs of Britain's failure to develop an adequate work policy are an enormous economic loss, but we have argued that the loss is also social, and the costs of unemployment are very unequally borne. As Britain's economic fortunes decline, we are witnessing how a variety of weaker and more marginal groups are squeezed out of work, and how there is increased quarrelling about the causes of Britain's crisis and scapegoating of the workless themselves. More and more of the workless are remaining without jobs for longer and longer periods, and for lack of an adequate work policy whole generations of the workless and regions of the country are being written off and lost.

We have argued the need for a social contract, a greater sense of participation and of shared goals, to be achieved through work. Rather than gearing work to the limited 'needs of the economy', the guide to economic and social policy must be a much broader conception of social motivation to work and people's need for work; for a sense of achievement, creativity, a realization of capacities, control over activity, a sense of autonomy and, above all, a sense of service to some wider group. Such policies would include the pursuit of the goal of full employment or at the very least a more equitable sharing of work, improvements in the quality of work, and the removal of barriers to people working.

Beveridge, forty years ago, but no major figure in public policy since, has argued the social case for full employment. In the period after the war its desirability was assumed; yet its real meaning and the conditions for securing it were never fully argued. As a result, when the economic going got rough, the goal of full employment was too easily abandoned.

It has taken the reappearance of mass unemployment to bring

the issue of the right to work back into the public debate. And, following the long tradition of discussion of work policy, we find ourselves returning to the basic unresolved problem of what kind and degree of collective control over economic and social institutions will be needed to defend Britain from the ravages of the international free market, and to enlist the cooperation and energy of all the people in the solution of Britain's economic and social crisis. Recently the government has tried to move further away from controls, in the direction pointed by the ideology of the free market. But as unemployment grows we must at last begin to face up to the question: how much freedom will remain in a society where the workless are numbered in millions?

NOTES

1 *Daily Telegraph*, 11 March 1981.
2 T.U.C., 'Plan for Growth', see *Sunday Times*, 29 March 1981.
3 *The Will to Win*, CBI, 1981.
4 But see, S. Aaronovitch, *The Road from Thatcherism*, Lawrence and Wishart, 1981; C.S.E., London Working Group, *The Alternative Economic Strategy*, C.S.E., 1981 (and review of both by F. Blackaby, *New Society*, 2 April 1981); S. Williams, *Politics is for People*, Penguin, 1981 (and review by B. Wootton, *New Society*, 16 April 1981); S. Holland, *The Socialist Alternative*, Quartet, 1975; T. Benn, *Arguments for Socialism*, Penguin, 1980; C.E.P.G., *Economic Policy in the UK*, Gower Hampshire, 1981; A. Sinfield, *What Unemployment Means*, Martin Robertson, 1981; B. Showler and A. Sinfield (eds.), *The Workless State*, Martin Robertson, 1981; K. Hawkins, *Unemployment*, Penguin, 1979; S. Mukherjee, *There's Work to be Done*, H.M.S.O., 1974.
5 See S. Aaronovitch, op. cit.: inflation has been, from 1966-78, 7.6 per cent in O.E.C.D. countries and 11.8 per cent in the U.K.; in 1980, it was 12.6 per cent in O.E.C.D. countries but 19 per cent in the U.K. The Department of Employment, *Employment Gazette*, March 1981, gives unemployment rates as: U.K., 9.5 per cent (excludes some groups); Canada, 7.3 per cent; Denmark, 8.3 per cent; Germany, 4.7 per cent; Japan, 2.2 per cent; Sweden, 2.0 per cent; U.S.A., 7.3 per cent. C. Smee, 'Unemployment and Poverty: some comparisons with Canada and the U.S.', shows that unemployment is more concentrated in Britain, with people taking twice as long to get a job as in the U.S., where the chance of unemployment is spread three times as widely across the population (Paper to S.S.R.C. Workshop on Employment and Unemployment, June 1980). For an overall discussion, see B. Showler and A. Sinfield, op. cit., Chs. 6 and 7.
6 For a bitter comment, from Mr Heath to industry, on the failure of investment, see S. Aaronovitch, op. cit., p. 33.
7 An article in *Cambridge Journal of Economics*, December 1979,

estimates that in 1978, the U.K. ran a deficit on *manufacturing* trade with the E.E.C. of £2,000 million, and on all *visible* trade in 1979 of £2,750 millions.

8   See K. Hawkins, op. cit., pp. 77-81.

9   R. Minns, *New Society*, 25 December 1980, discusses overseas investment in 1979 of £600 million (*Investment Abroad and Jobs at Home*, CBI): 140 out of 159 investments gave no boost to exports and 4 actually harmed them. Newspapers now regularly carry advertisements for 'long term capital growth' investment in Japanese and other Far Eastern countries; see, for example, *Sunday Times*, 8 February 1981 and 28 February 1981. An estimate that £5 billion might go abroad in 1981 was given in *Guardian*, 21 April 1981. 'The Money Programme', B.B.C., Spring 1981, quoted figures of £3,000 million going overseas and half that amount of foreign capital coming in. The external assets of the U.K. now exceed the entire G.N.P. See also M. Smith, 'Tide of UK cash laps on foreign shore', *Guardian*, 14 May 1981.

10   See A. Mitchell in *Unemployment*, (*Political Quarterly* special issue), vol. 52, no. 1, Spring 1981.

11   D. Gould et al., *Monetarism or Prosperity*, Macmillan, 1981; see also A. Mitchell, op. cit.; *New Society*, 9 April 1981.

12   For a summary of a special day conference run by the *Sunday Times*, see *Sunday Times*, 1 February 1981. The City is very favourable towards Mrs Thatcher and high interest rates: see *Guardian* survey of City opinion on the 1981 Budget, 2 March 1981. See also F. Cairncross, 'Has the City failed industry', *Guardian*, 18 May 1981, who attributes the major problem to the structure of tax concessions.

13   H. Clegg, *The Changing System of Industrial Relations in Britain*, Macmillan, 1980, chapter on incomes policies.

14   See *Department of Employment Gazette*, April 1978, for a discussion of work-sharing; also K. Hawkins, op. cit.; and J. Hughes, 'Now's the time for a 35 hour week', *Full Employment Charter*, Bulletin no. 1 of the Full Employment Campaign, 1977.

15   *Department of Employment Gazette*, February 1981: wage rises were 9 per cent for the three months up to the end of January 1981, compared with 16 per cent for the months to October, 1980.

16   Hours lost through strikes at British Leyland, where shop-stewards' militancy was attacked by management, were cut to one quarter between 1979 and 1980; see *New Society*, 29 January 1981. See also Mr P. Lowry, chairman of A.C.A.S., in *Guardian*, 8 May 1981.

17   This section draws heavily on P. Ormerod, in A. Walker, P. Ormerod and L. Whitty, *Abandoning Social Priorities*, Poverty Pamphlet 44, C.P.A.G., 1979; and Showler in B. Showler and A. Sinfield, op. cit.; see also, G. Akerlof, 'The Case against Conservative macro-economics', *Economica*, no. 46.

18   Three hundred and sixty-four economists sent a letter of protest to the government, *Guardian*, 30 August 1980.

19 The arguments have been continuous over the past year, but for correspondence and articles of special interest, see, for example, *Guardian*, 28 February, and 9, 10, 12, 16, 18, 20 and 25 March 1981. Even the City could not decide whether the Budget would be 'inflationary' or 'deflationary', and split almost evenly, *Guardian*, 2 March 1981.

20 F. Blackaby, *Guardian*, 9 March 1981.

21 G. Routh, *The Origin of Economic Ideas*, quoted in B. Showler and A. Sinfield, op. cit.; see also S. Holland, *Guardian*, 8 January 1981.

22 M. Peston, in *Unemployment (Political Quarterly)*, op. cit., quotes various notions of the 'natural level' of unemployment in the Treasury during the 1950s.

23 *Unemployment: the Fight for TUC Alternatives*, T.U.C., 1981. The *Review of Services for the Unemployed*, M.S.C., 1981, p. 8, estimates the annual cost of unemployment at £7,405 million.

24 B. Showler and A. Sinfield, op. cit. In addition there are the costs in mental distress and illness which may result: see J. Popay, 'Unemployment: a threat to public health', quoted in A. Sinfield, op. cit.; also, *Financial Times*, 18 August 1980.

25 See, D. Wedderburn, 'Facts and Theories of the Welfare State' in R. Miliband and J. Saville (eds.), *Socialist Register*, 1965; also, R. M. Titmuss, 'The Social Division of Welfare' in *Essays on the Welfare State*, Allen & Unwin, 1958.

26 Britain is seventh: *Guardian*, 16 February 1981.

27 Table 2, *The European Social Budget 1980-1975-1970*, Belgium, Commission of the European Communities, 1979, pp. 22-3. The U.K. is the lowest, apart from Ireland, in expenditure as a percentage of G.N.P.

28 R. M. Titmuss, *The Gift Relationship*, Allen & Unwin, 1971.

29 M. Dean in *Guardian*, 18 March 1981, estimates that £1.5 billion has been cut so far. *Guardian*, 23 August 1980, reports the *Lancet*'s condemnation of the three million people, many trade unionists, who are now privately medically insured (see also note 13, p. 251). In fact under the Conservatives total public expenditure has gone up 3 per cent compared with Labour's last year in power, but the balance of spending has shifted away from social services: D. Walker, *New Society*, 19 March 1981.

30 *Guardian*, 2 March 1981.

31 A. Mitchell, op. cit.; also F. Blackaby in G. D. N. Worswick (ed.), *The Concept and Measurement of Involuntary Unemployment*, Allen & Unwin, 1976; and K. Hawkins, op. cit., p. 77.

32 *Monetary Policy - a Report from the Treasury and Civil Service Committee to the House of Commons*, H.M.S.O., vol. 1, 1981. The committee estimated that to get 8 per cent permanently off the inflation rate would require a 30 per cent reduction in output and the loss of five million man years of unemployment.

33   'England's role as "Clearing House of the World" preceded its emergence as the "Workshop of the World"; it has outlived it and even during the mid-day of Victorian prosperity, it has predominated over it.' W. D. Rubenstein, 'Wealth, Elites and the Class Structure of Modern Britain', *Past and Present*, no. 76, 1977. See also B. Simon, *Studies in the History of Education, 1780-1870* (and *1870-1920*), Lawrence and Wishart, 1960 (and 1965).

34   M. J. Wiener, *English Culture and the Decline of the Industrial Spirit, 1850-1980*, C.U.P., 1981 (see also, note 12).

35   G. Bannock, *Shell UK Report*, 1981. In 1979, out of 1,550 industrial concerns on the London Stock Exchange, the six largest accounted for over a quarter of the turnover and the top 180 for 80 per cent. A *Labour Research* survey (January 1980) showed that for the 50 largest U.K. firms, one third of their output is now produced overseas, their overseas production is three times more important to them than their exports from the U.K. and it is increasing more rapidly than production in Britain. Britain is second only to the U.S. in capital invested overseas, S. Aaronovitch, op. cit.

36   F. Frobel et al., *The New International Division of Labour*, C.U.P., 1980; see, P. Townsend, Introduction to B. Showler and A. Sinfield, op. cit., who argues that multi-nationals operate at a cost to both the developed and the underdeveloped world.

37   L. Blackstone and D. Franks, *The UK as a Tax Haven*, Economist Intelligence Unit, 1981. See *Guardian*, 30 March 1981, for an estimate that there are 4,000 multi-nationals with bases overseas, operating here tax-free.

38   For an article on the comparatively low return on investment in Britain compared with other countries, see *Sunday Times*, 8 April 1981. British industry comes bottom and the much greater returns on Japanese investment are clear.

39   K. Hawkins, op. cit., pp. 77-81, argues that British labour is relatively cheap, and the real problem is productivity, i.e. investment *and* the use of that investment: 'with the same power at his elbow and doing the same job, a continental car-assembly worker normally produces twice as much as his British counterpart', (quoting from a report by the Central Policy Review Staff, 1975). The cause was attributed to over-manning, slow pace of work, quality faults, high fixed overheads and strikes. Since then, of course, there has been a massive shake-out of car workers in the west midlands - into unemployment. Japanese productivity is double that of Germany in the car industry.

40   See H. Clegg, op. cit.; and K. Hawkins, op. cit., pp. 73-7. We have also drawn on J. Goldthorpe, 'Social Inequality and Social Integration in Modern Britain', *Advancement of Science*, vol. 26, no. 128, December 1969. For a general sociological discussion of the various articles on the lack of social cohesion shown in industrial life, see M. Gilbert, 'Neo-Durkheimian

Analyses of Economic Life and Strife: from Durkheim to the Social Contract', *Sociological Review*, vol. 26, no. 4, November 1978.

41 S. Glynn and S. Shaw, 'Wage Bargaining and Unemployment' in *Unemployment, (Political Quarterly)*, op. cit.

42 See A. Walker et al., op. cit., Ch. 3, 'Public expenditure and the social wage', p. 44. The 'social wage' was cut by 10 per cent between 1976 and 1981.

43 K. Hawkins, op. cit., Ch. 4, combines, unusually, skills in economics and industrial relations to produce an account of the 'squeeze', described in outline in the next two sections, which leads first to inflation and then unemployment.

44 We are particularly indebted to Peter Townsend, and to a seminar paper by Bob Jessop, for helping us to make these connections: see also, P. Townsend, Introduction to B. Showler and A. Sinfield, op. cit., and 'Ending the phoney war against unemployment', *Community Care*, May 1978; and I. Gough, review of J. O'Connor, *Bulletin of the Conference of Socialist Economists*, June 1975.

45 K. Hawkins, op. cit., Ch. 4.

46 It is interesting to see how the banks, too, landed with large 'windfall' profits by the government's high interest rate policies, at first protested loudly against a windfall tax but are now managing to rearrange their affairs so that less of their gains appear in the form of taxable profits. See, for example, R. Minns, *New Society*, 2 April 1981.

47 See F. Cairncross, op. cit.; and A. Walker et al., op. cit. The burden of taxation on industry has fallen from 21 per cent to 16 per cent. On profits of £5,072, industry paid only £388 millions tax, and eleven of Britain's 20 largest companies paid no corporation tax in 1979. J. Kay and M. King, *The British Tax System*, O.U.P., 1980.

48 For the earliest discussion of the development of fiscal and occupational welfare, see R. M. Titmuss's classic essay, 'The social division of welfare', *Essays on the Welfare State*, Allen & Unwin, 1958. For a more recent documentation and discussion of inequality in Britain and the question of who benefits from various 'resource systems' including pay, tax concessions, social security and occupational welfare, see P. Townsend, *Poverty in the United Kingdom*, Penguin, 1979.

49 A. Sinfield describes the complex processes which lead to better and worse job security and conditions in B. Showler and A. Sinfield, op. cit., Ch. 5.

50 F. Field, *Inequality in Britain*, Fontana, 1981, suggests there are no fewer than five 'welfare states', among them £20,000 million of income which escapes tax through mortgage interest and life insurance tax concessions, and the 'perks' which can add up to 36 per cent to top management salaries without attracting tax (which mean, in effect that they do not pay the top tax rate). On our analysis, however, this suggestion seems confusing in looking at a variety of outcomes, rather

than trying to focus on processes which are all essentially comparable ways of subverting collective government intervention to redistribute incomes.

51 It is thus no accident that since the Conservative government wound up the Royal Commission on the Distribution of Income and Wealth, there are official proposals and a start has been made to curtail the collection and distribution of information on economic and social conditions in the population, *New Society*, 5 March 1981, and 9 April 1981, and that funds for independent social research are being cut.

52 Although this is not to deny that there is a need for some degree of tariff protection and, indeed, depending on the kinds of tariff arrangements which are proposed, there may be ways of reducing the likelihood of retaliation and the growth of protection. The problem with devaluation is the inflationary pressures which it might bring.

53 The contradictions in free market policies in a time of industrial decline appear most clearly in the car industry. Chrysler, encouraged to go to Scotland by the Conservatives in 1963, were bailed out by Labour in the 1970s, but always had production problems and bad industrial relations in their Linwood plant. When Chrysler hit trouble in America, they sold out to Peugeot who, in trouble in France, closed the Linwood plant. (The workers asserted that the books were rigged to show poor profits, but did not fight in case they jeopardized their redundancy pay.) Now the Japanese are getting V.I.P. treatment to bring in a plant that will employ few workers and pay little if any tax, but which could destroy British Leyland's domestic and European market. If we don't take it, some other country will. Meanwhile, Ford of Europe's reaction has been to ask for a 40 per cent cut in its British workforce, and to threaten to import cheaper parts from its Spanish factory (a move which Mrs Thatcher has approved in another context). See *Daily Telegraph*, 11 March 1981, 'Can Europe trust the Japanese?'. Also *Sunday Times*, 4 May and 11 May 1981.

54 *Growing Older*, D.H.S.S., says that care *in* the community will increasingly mean care *by* the community.